Black and White
Racial Identity

Recent Titles in
Contributions in Afro-American and African Studies

Visible Now: Blacks in Private Schools
Diana T. Slaughter and Deborah J. Johnson, editors

Feel the Spirit: Studies in Nineteenth-Century Afro-American Music
George R. Keck and Sherrill V. Martin, editors

From a Caste to a Minority: Changing Attitudes of American Sociologists
Toward Afro-Americans, 1896–1945
Vernon J. Williams, Jr.

African-American Principals: School Leadership and Success
Kofi Lomotey

Class and Consciousness: The Black Petty Bourgeoisie in South Africa, 1924
to 1950
Alan Gregor Cobley

Black Novelist as White Racist: The Myth of Black Inferiority in the Novels of
Oscar Micheaux
Joseph A. Young

Capital and the State in Nigeria
John F. E. Ohiorhenuan

Famine in East Africa: Food Production and Food Policies
Ronald E. Seavoy

Archetypes, Imprecators, and Victims of Fate: Origins and Developments of
Satire in Black Drama
Femi Euba

BLACK AND WHITE RACIAL IDENTITY

Theory, Research, and Practice

Edited by
Janet E. Helms

GREENWOOD PRESS
Westport, Connecticut • London

Library of Congress Cataloging-in-Publication Data

Black and white racial identity : theory, research, and practice /
  edited by Janet E. Helms.
    p. cm. — (Contributions in Afro-American and African
studies, ISSN 0069-9624 ; no. 129)
  Includes bibliographical references.
  ISBN 0-313-26352-3 (lib. bdg. : alk. paper)
    1. Afro-Americans — Race identity. 2. Race awareness — United
States. 3. Whites — United States — Race identity. I. Helms,
Janet E.
II. Series.
E185.625.B554   1990
155.8'496073 — dc20   89-17030

British Library Cataloguing in Publication Data is available.

A paperback edition of *Black and White Racial Identity* is
available from the Praeger Publishers imprint of Greenwood
Publishing Group, Inc. (ISBN 0-275-94612-6).

Library of Congress Catalog Card Number: 89-17030
ISBN: 0-313-26352-3
ISSN: 0069-9624

First published in 1990

Greenwood Press, 88 Post Road West, Westport, CT 06881
An imprint of Greenwood Publishing Group, Inc.

Printed in the United States of America

The paper used in this book complies with the
Permanent Paper Standard issued by the National
Information Standards Organization (Z39.48-1984).

10 9 8 7 6 5 4

Copyright Acknowledgments

The author gratefully acknowledges permission to quote from the following:

Janet E. Helms, "Toward a Theoretical Explanation of the Effects of Race on Counseling: A Black and White Model," *The Counseling Psychologist*, Vol. 12, No. 4, (1984), pp. 153–165. Copyright © 1989. Reprinted by permission of Sage Publications, Inc.

Extracts from "The Oprah Winfrey Show," episode entitled "Transracial Adoption," transcript #W214. Authors: Oprah Winfrey, host, Debra DiMaio, executive producer, Jim McPharlin, director. Reprinted with permission.

Robert T. Carter and Janet E. Helms, "The Relationship of Black Value-Orientations to Racial Identity Attitudes," *Measurement and Evaluation in Counseling and Development*, Vol. 19, No. 4, (1987), pp. 185–195.

Dedicated to: Kimberly, Mara, Erin, Little Joe, Barrett

And so the quest continues...

Contents

Illustrations

TABLES

Preface

As psychology in the United States moves toward celebrating its centennial, it seems appropriate to note the relative absence of models designed specifically for the purpose of addressing racial/ethnic development by which to guide the study of behavior. As a substitute for such models, psychologists have deluded themselves into believing that by locating a person in one sociopolitical racial category or another they can indeed predict that person's behavior. While such a belief system might be comforting to its adherents, its result has been a lacuna in the field where issues of race/ethnicity are concerned. Consequently, practitioners and researchers frequently find themselves guessing about how such matters should be managed.

My purposes in writing this book are threefold: (a) to demonstrate that race can be studied from a psychological perspective; (b) to gather in one place much of the relevant literature that has remained scattered in nontraditional social science and behavioral literature for many years; and (c) to inspire others not only to begin to examine the utility of racial identity models for understanding the behavior of Blacks and Whites, but also to begin to consider the usefulness of racially/culturally explicit models for guiding research and practice.

In producing this book, I have received a great deal of encouragement from practitioners and graduate students around the country. Graduate students especially have invested considerable amounts of their own financial and emotional resources, often without the support of their academic communities. Some of their contributions are reflected in the subsequent pages. For the others, especially the newcomers, I hope this book will serve as a resource in your war with the "nonbelievers."

I am indebted to the secretarial pools at the University of Maryland and Southern Illinois University. Without Gordon Rice, who handled the monumental task of typing the manuscript once my computer began its key-by-key suicide, I could not have finished this project. Donelda Cook graciously contributed her collection of racial incidents to my project and Marty Rawlins contributed many thoughts about racial identity conflicts in the real world. Additionally, the Computer Science Center at the University of Maryland provided the funds for most of the analyses presented in these pages. Finally, I would like to thank my family and colleagues who for me are a never-ending source of racial identity questions.

PART I
THEORY AND MEASUREMENT OF RACIAL IDENTITY

1

Introduction: Review of Racial Identity Terminology

JANET E. HELMS

In discussing racial identity development, theorists have used diverse terminology, sometimes to describe the same or similar phenomena and sometimes not. Reconciling this linguistic diversity is beyond the scope, intent, or capability of this book. Rather it might be more useful and parsimonious to explain how various racial identity concepts are used in this work, particularly since in many instances, this usage represents the first time that such constructs have been used to describe the racial identity development of Whites as well as Blacks.

Many people erroneously use a person's racial categorization (e.g., Black versus White) to mean racial identity. However, the term "racial identity" actually refers to a sense of group or collective identity based on one's *perception* that he or she shares a common racial heritage with a particular racial group. Racial designation or category and ethnicity per se are confusing issues in the United States. As McRoy and Zurcher (1983) have pointed out, one needs only to have one-sixteenth black African ancestry or some physical features deemed typical of such ancestry in order to be classified as Black. Nevertheless, for the sake of simplicity, Casas's (1984) definition of race will be used. Quoting Krogman (1945), he defines race accordingly: "a sub-group of peoples possessing a definite combination of physical characters, of genetic origin, the combination of which to varying degrees distinguishes the sub-group from other sub-groups of mankind [sic] (p.49)" (p. 787). As Casas further points out, this biological definition has no behavioral, psychological, or social implications ipso facto. However, what people believe, feel, and

4 Theory and Measurement

think about distinguishable racial groups can have such implications for individuals' intrapersonal as well as interpersonal functioning. Racial identity development theory concerns the psychological implications of racial-group membership; that is, belief systems that evolve in reaction to perceived differential racial-group membership.

Dizard (1970) indicates that the two significant contributors to a perceived collective or group identity are: "[a] a common thread of historical experience and a sense that each member of the collectivity, regardless of how distinct he [or she] may be, somehow shares in this historical experience, and [b] a sense of potency or strength inhering in the group" (p. 196). In partial agreement with Dizard's analysis, racial identity theories generally postulate a common thread of historical experiences; that is, they agree with the first part of Dizard's definition. However, in such theories, whether or not group identification is assumed to result in "a sense of group potency" depends on one's manner of identifying.

In distinguishing ethnicity from race, Casas (1984) defined ethnicity "as a group classification of individuals who share a unique social and cultural heritage (customs, language, religion, and so on) passed on from generation to generation" (p. 787). As he points out, ethnicity is not biologically defined and, therefore, race and ethnicity are not synonymous. Conceivably, members of different racial groups could belong to the same ethnic group; members of different ethnic groups need not belong to different racial groups. In contemporary social science literature, the mental health issues of Blacks typically have been examined without regard to ethnicity, and those of Whites typically have been examined without regard to race. That is, in the former case, one rarely finds analyses of how different categories of Black ethnics differ (e.g., how descendants of free and freed people or slaves in the United States differ from those of Haitians or Cape Verdeans or Black Hispanics and so on). Rather one's ostensible "Africanness" is assumed to account for one's psychosocial development regardless of ethnicity. On the other hand, though one occasionally finds analyses of how White ethnics (e.g., Irish, Polish, etc.) differ from one another (cf. Giordano & Giordano, 1977), with few recent exceptions (e.g., P. Katz, 1976), one rarely finds scholarly consideration of how the condition of being White influences Whites' psychosocial development.

Black and White racial identity theories examine psychological development from the level of racial rather than ethnic similarity. Therefore, although various theorists (cf. Helms, 1987) have proposed group identity theories to account for the psychosocial development of various ethnic groups (usually of color), it should be emphasized that ethnic group theories are *not* the focus of this book. Moreover, some writers use the term "ethnicity" as a euphemism for "race." So as not to distort these authors' language too severely, ethnicity will be used in this manner when an author's perspective seems to be better represented by such usage.

In this instance, racial identity and, by implication, racial identity theory in general refers to a Black or White person's identifying or not identifying with the racial group with which he or she is generally assumed to share *racial* heritage. In other words, racial identity partially refers to the person of black African ancestry's acknowledgment of shared racial-group membership with others of similar race as previously defined or the person of white European ancestry's acknowledgment of shared racial-group membership with others of similar race as previously defined.

Additionally, racial identity refers to the quality or manner of one's identification with the respective racial groups. Therefore, racial identity theories generally describe a variety of modes of identification. More specifically, Black racial identity theories attempt to explain the various ways in which Blacks can identify (or not identify) with other Blacks and/ or adopt or abandon identities resulting from racial victimization; White racial identity theories attempt to explain the various ways in which Whites can identify (or not identify) with other Whites and/or evolve or avoid evolving a nonoppressive White identity.

Additionally, one's quality of adjustment has been hypothesized to result from a combination of "personal identity," "reference group orientation," and "ascribed identity" (cf. Cross, 1987; Erikson, 1963; 1968). Personal identity concerns one's feelings and attitudes about oneself, in other words, generic personality characteristics such as anxiety, self-esteem, and so on. Reference-group orientation refers to the extent to which one uses particular racial groups; for example, Blacks or Whites in this country, to guide one's feelings, thoughts, and behaviors. One's reference-group orientation is reflected in such things as value systems, organizational memberships, ideologies, and so on. Ascribed identity pertains to the individual's deliberate affiliation or commitment to a particular racial group. Typically one can choose to commit to one of four categories if one is Black or White: Blacks primarily, Whites primarily, neither, or both. Hence, a person who considers one race or the other to be the important definer of Self has a mono-racial ascribed identity; a person who feels a connectedness to both racial groups has a bi-racial ascribed identity; and the person who commits to neither group has a marginal ascribed identity.

It seems possible that each of these components varies relatively independently. So, for example, a Black or White person might feel positively about himself or herself, treat the experiences of racial group members as irrelevant to her or his own life circumstances, and feel a commitment to neither racial group. The "assimilating" Black (i.e., the Black person who wants to become a nondistinguishable member of White society), for instance, might feel good about herself or himself (i.e., positive personal identity), consider her or his racial-group membership to be irrelevant to her or his life circumstances (e.g., marginal ascribed identity), while attempting to live according to "White" beliefs about the world (i.e., White reference-group orientation). Similarly, a "melting pot" White (i.e., the person who believes everyone should be defined by the tenets of White socialization experiences) might feel good about herself or himself (i.e., positive personal identity), use Whites as a reference group for defining appropriate behavior (i.e., White reference-group orientation), and feel a commitment only to other Whites (i.e., White ascribed identity).

Nevertheless, the three components—personal identity, reference-group orientation, and ascribed identity—undoubtedly interact with each other. For instance, to the extent that society stereotypes one racial group as "dirty," "shiftless," and "ignorant" and another group as "clean," "industrious," and "intelligent" and can enforce such stereotypes, then it is likely that the individual will find it easier to use the second than the first group as both a reference group and source of ascribed identity. Relatedly, if one identifies with the positively characterized group, then it is likely that one will feel more positively about oneself than if one does not. However, such identifications become problematic to the extent that they require denial or distortions of oneself and/or the racial group(s) from which one descends.

From the discussion so far, it might be apparent that one's racial identity can involve various weightings of the three racial identity components. Racial identity theories attempt to describe the potential patterns of the personal, reference group, and ascribed identities, though not always so explicitly. Such theories also attempt to predict the varied feelings, thoughts, and/or behaviors that correspond to the differential weightings of components. The resulting variations might be called racial identity resolutions. Two different kinds of racial identity models have been used to describe potential resolutions. These can be characterized as "type" or "stage" perspectives.

Type models propose that potential racial identity resolutions can be grouped into one of several or a few categories (e.g., Dizard, 1970; Kovel, 1970). A basic supposition of such theories is that it is by appropriately "diagnosing" the person's category membership that one comes to understand the person's behavior. Seemingly, according to this perspective, one's racial identity category is assumed to be a fairly stable aspect of one's personality. Stage theories (e.g., Cross, 1971; Thomas, 1971) describe racial identity as a developmental process wherein a person potentially, though not necessarily, moves from one level of identity to another. According to stage theorists, one comes to understand a person's present behavioral dispositions by analyzing his or her identity at the present time, though the present identity may or may not have long-term implications for the person's future characteristics. Whether or not one's present level of racial identity development influences one's later development seems to depend on a complex mixture of environmental forces (e.g., economic factors), individual attributes (e.g., general cognitive development), and personal life experiences (e.g., the extent to which racism was a recognized element of the environment in which one grew up).

With regard to other common terminology, as used herein, racial identity and racial consciousness are considered to be interrelated but not synonymous, although such usage differs from that of other theorists (e.g., Caplan, 1970; Terry, 1977). Racial consciousness refers to the awareness that (socialization due to) racial-group membership can influence one's intrapsychic dynamics as well as interpersonal relationships. Thus, one's racial awareness may be subliminal and not readily admitted into consciousness or it may be conscious and not easily repressed. Racial identity pertains to the quality of the awareness or the various forms in which awareness can occur, that is, identity resolutions. Awareness of race may be accompanied by positive, negative, or neutral racial-group evaluations. The major racial identity theories propose that, within racial groups, various kinds of racial identity resolutions can exist, and consequently, racial consciousness per se usually is not considered to be dichotomous, present, or absent, but rather is polytomous.

In a similar vein, "cultural" is often used as a substitute for "racial" or "ethnic." Since one's racial-group designation does not necessarily define one's racial, cultural, or ethnic characteristics if racial identity theory is accurate, the interchangeable usage of these three terms will be avoided as much as possible.

OVERVIEW OF BOOK

In subsequent chapters, theory, research, and practical implications of racial identity development for Blacks and Whites will be presented. Although the historical, theoretical, and empirical development of racial identity theory as it pertains to these two groups has taken converse tacks, a basic premise of this work is that the racial identity constructs, as previously outlined, apply in some manner to both racial groups, though their manner of expression may differ because of the groups' virtually opposite racial experiences in the United States.

Also, it will be noted that counseling psychology has been chosen as the basic discipline by which to orient the subsequent treatment of racial identity development. Whereas other disciplines might have been used equally efficaciously, counseling psychology was chosen because it seems to fit naturally with two additional premises underlying the book: (a) racial identity development is a "normal" developmental process in the United States in the sense that it probably occurs in some form in all individuals, and (b) the understanding of racial identity development offers a framework by which theorists, researchers, practitioners, and laypersons can intervene in their environments to promote healthy identity development for themselves as well as others.

The book is divided into three parts: theory and measurement, correlates of racial identity, and practice. Each of these sections differs in the amount of emphasis given to theory, research, and practice, though each of these categories is represented in some degree in every section.

Part I presents basic racial identity theory (chapters 2 and 4) and measurement issues (chapters 3 and 5) as they pertain to individuals and intergroup functioning. Ideally these chapters will be useful to persons who are seeking a basic introduction to Black and White racial identity theory.

In Part II, some empirical attempts to examine the correlates of racial identity are presented. In particular, Black and White racial identity attitudes are used to explore aspects of the psychodiagnostic model presented in chapter 6. This section is primarily intended for the reader interested in generating research questions and/or evaluating some of those that already have been generated.

Part III includes both speculative and empirical papers whose raison d'être is to examine the influence of racial identity on everyday interactions of some sort. In line with the previously mentioned emphasis on using racial identity theory for understanding common situations as well as the formal helping process, chapters 9, 10, and 11 describe the influence of racial identity attitudes on various kinds of counseling interactions. Chapters 12 and 13 expand the racial identity interactional model, the framework for counseling interventions, to cover social dyadic and group interactions, respectively. Finally, chapter 14 shifts to an educational focus as information concerning interventions for promoting healthy racial identity development is discussed.

2

An Overview of Black
Racial Identity Theory

JANET E. HELMS

Theories and models of Black racial identity began to appear in the counseling psychology and psychotherapy literature around the early 1970s in response to the Civil Rights Movement of the era. Ostensibly, theorists were attempting to present a framework by which practitioners could be more sensitive to the racial issues that were hypothesized to influence the therapy process. In actuality, one can find two major Black racial identity theoretical strands. The first strand might be called the Black client (or person)-as-problem (CAP) perspective; the second might be called the Nigrescence or racial identity development (NRID) perspective. Each of these perspectives seems to have had a different underlying purpose and, consequently, different implications for how Black racial identity was and continues to be conceptualized.

THE CLIENT-AS-PROBLEM PERSPECTIVE (CAP)

The CAP approach represented the first attempts at explaining intra- and inter-racial dynamics. As Black people began to demand recognition and social acceptance during the 1960s, many Whites and assimilated Blacks in society reacted with considerable anxiety and discomfort to this ostensibly sudden disruption of the status quo. Even though the well-publicized Black-initiated public protests made it difficult for Whites as well as Blacks to continue to ignore completely the injustices that characterized Black lives, American society was not accustomed to witnessing Black assertion and leadership on such a massive scale (cf. J.

Williams, 1987). Unfortunately, Whites seemingly equated Black assertion with aggression (cf. Cheek, 1976), militance, and property destruc-
tion or Black racial rioting (cf. Caplan, 1970). Therefore, this new type
of Black visibility contributed to general impressions that Blacks were
no longer predictable and that this unpredictability might manifest itself
in violence and hostility in cross-racial interactions, in society in general
and in counseling and psychotherapy relationships in particular.

In counseling and psychotherapy, much of the literature of the era
played on (primarily) White fears that Blacks would act out their anger
toward White society via passivity, mistrustfulness, and/or overt hostility.
Additionally, since there were no psychological models available for explaining how it was possible for Black people to develop healthy non-
vengeful personalities in spite of the racial discrimination to which they
had been exposed, most of the psychological literature engaged in deficit-
modeling or the enumeration of all the alleged deficiencies but none of
the strengths in "the Black personality" (cf. Acosta, Yamamoto, & Evans,
1982; Gardner, 1971; E. Smith, 1980). Therapy interventions were proposed primarily for the purpose of helping the (usually White) therapist
cope with the Black client's intrapersonal and interpersonal dynamics,
which were presumed to be unique to Black people (Grier & Cobbs,
1968; A. Jones & Seagull, 1977; Pinderhughes, 1973).

It was in such an atmosphere that the CAP models of racial identity
development began to appear (Dizard, 1970; G. G. Jackson & Kirschner,
1973; Siegel, 1970; Vontress, 1971a, 1971b). In general, CAP models
suggested that differences in overt behaviors (primarily racial self-
designation) would allow counselors to decide which Black clients were
likely to be most problematic for which race of counselors.

Vontress' (1971b) typology, which is summarized in Table 2.1, is the
most sophisticated representative of this perspective. He proposed that
there were three types of Black people, "Black," "Colored," and "Negro."
Each type hypothetically demonstrated a different type of racial identity
via their inter- and intra-racial thoughts, feelings, and behaviors. For
instance, it was assumed that clients who referred to themselves as
"Black" would value their African physical characteristics, understand
the suffering inflicted upon their racial group, and would be intolerant
of Whites who attempted to interact with Blacks from a racist stance.
Vontress described Negroes as integrationists who would accommodate
Whites who were not blatantly racist. Coloreds were described as Black
people who perceive and evaluate themselves as Whites do. In establishing counseling relationships, Vontress speculated that Negroes would
actually be most amenable, Coloreds would *appear* to be, and Blacks
would be least so.

What defines perspectives in client-as-problem models is their virtually
exclusive focus on Black identity development as a consequence of so-

Table 2.1

Summary of Nigrescence Models of Racial Identity

Authors	Date	Model Type	Name	Components	Description
Akbar	1979	Typology	1. Alien-Self Disorders		1. Preoccupied with material values, deny race, racism, and oppression in identifying with European culture.
			2. Anti-Self Disorders		2. Identifies with European culture and expresses overt and covert hostility toward anything African.
			3. Self-Destructive Disorders		3. Identifies with neither cultural group, believes in survival at any cost.
J.A. Banks	1981	Stage	1. Ethnic Psychological Captivity		1. Person internalizes society's negative view of his/her ethnic group.
			2. Ethnic Encapsulation		2. Person participates primarily with own ethnic group which is idealized.
			3. Ethnic Identity Clarification		3. Person learns to accept self.
			4. Biethnicity		4. Person possesses healthy sense of ethnic identity and can function in ethnic and White culture.
			5. Multiethnicity		5. Person is self-actualized and can function beyond superficial levels in many cultures.

Table 2.1 (continued)

Authors	Date	Model Type	Name	Components	Description
				6. Globalism and Global Competency	6. Person can use universal ethnic knowledge to function within ethnic groups worldwide.
Cross	1971	Stage	1. Preencounter		1. Identifies with White culture, rejects or denies membership in Black culture.
			2. Encounter		2. Rejects previous indentification with White culture, seeks indentification with Black culture.
			3. Immersion-Emersion		3. Completely identifies with Black culture and denigrates White culture.
			4. Internalization		4. Internalizes Black culture, transcends racism.
			5. Internalization-Commitment		5. Internalizes Black culture, fights general cultural oppression.
Dizzard	1971	Typology	1. Assimilated		1. Except for White prejudice moves comfortably and easily into White culture.
			2. Pathological		2. Exhibits pathology as the predominant response to life's hardships.
			3. Traditional		3. Attempts to preserve a group identity and a sense of dignity.

		Typology	
Gibbs	1974	1. Withdrawal mode	Feelings of apathy, depression, depersonalization lead person to withdraw from conflictual racial situation.
		2. Separation mode	Feelings of anger, hostility, conflicts in relationships expressed as rejection of Whites and White culture.
		3. Assimilation mode	Social anxiety and desire for acceptance lead person to avoid Blacks and/or conceal racial-group membership.
		4. Affirmation mode	Person accepts self, has a positive racial identity, high achievement motivation, and engages in autonomous self-actualizing behavior.
		Stage	
Gay	1984	1. Preencounter	Ethnic identity is subconscious or subliminal or dominated by Euro-American conceptions of ethnicity.
		2. Encounter	An experience or event shatters person's feelings about ethnic group or self and causes person to search for new foundations for an identity.
		3. Post-Encounter	Person experiences and exudes inner security, self-confidence, and pride in one's ethnicity.

Table 2.1 (continued)

Authors	Date	Model Type	Components Name	Description
B. Jackson	1975	Stage	1. Passive/ acceptance	1. Copes by imitating Whites.
			2. Active resistance	2. Rejects White culture, militantly identifies with Black culture.
			3. Redirection	3. Primary focus on Black identity and pride, little attention given to Whites.
			4. Internalization	4. Fulfilled sense of self and cultural identity.
Milliones	1980	Stage	1. Preconscious	1. Individuals who are not engaged in and are antagonistic to conversion to Blackness.
			2. Confrontation	2. Person has begun converting to Black, expresses strong anti-White feelings and attitudes.
			3. Internalization	3. Positive acceptance of Blackness rather than denigration of Whiteness is the theme.
			4. Integration	4. Person internalizes positive Black consciousness and acts to eradicate oppression of humans.
Thomas	1971	Stage	1. Negromachy	1. Poor sense of self-worth, depends on White society for self-definition.

Author	Year	Typology		
			2. Stage 1	2. Anger directed toward Whites.
			3. Stage 2	3. Expresses pain associated with denying and becoming Black self.
			4. Stage 3	4. Immerses self in Black/African culture.
			5. Stage 4	5. Black identity emerges via social action.
			6. Stage 5	6. Transcendence, person no longer uses culture cues to judge others.
Toldson & Pasteur	1975	Stage	1. Separation from Nature.	1. Objectively views Black people's misery.
			2. Submission into Personal Misery.	2. Person feels anger stemming from racism-based misery.
			3. Identification with Oppressed People.	3. Person feels a sympathetic link with all oppressed people.
			4. Extension of Self into the Past.	4. Person becomes aware of inhumanity toward and past glories of African people.
			5. Careful Self Analysis	5. Abandons White definition of self.
			6. Affirmation of Blackness	6. Develops realistic plans for affirming self.
Vontress	1971	Typology	1. Coloreds	1. People of African descent who perceive and evaluate selves according to White standards.

Table 2.1 (continued)

Authors	Date	Model Type	Name	Components	Description
			2. Negroes		2. Uncertain about how they feel about themselves, Blacks, or Whites.
			3. Blacks		3. Person is no longer ashamed of African racial characteristics, resists affronts to human dignity.

cietal pressures and their linking of clients' other-directed negative reactions (e.g., anger, hostility, rage) and behaviors to Black rather than assimilated identities or personality types. Thus, the primary goal of such models seems to have been to diffuse counselor anxiety by making the occurrence of aversive Black behaviors more predictable. Nevertheless, the perspective did recognize that Black identity comes in many forms and it challenged the a priori assumption that cultural assimilation was necessarily the most healthy form of adjustment for the Black person.

NIGRESCENCE OR BLACK RACIAL IDENTITY MODELS (NRID)

Nigrescence can be defined as the developmental process by which a person "becomes Black" where Black is defined in terms of one's manner of thinking about and evaluating oneself and one's reference groups rather than in terms of skin color per se. The NRID models attempted to separate those aspects of Black identity development that occurred primarily in response to racial oppression (e.g., some forms of ascribed identities and reference-group orientations) from those aspects (e.g., personal identity) that occurred as a normal part of the human self-actualization process or the need to be the best Self that one can be (cf. Maslow, 1970). Thus, self-actualization was assumed to be expressed at the most sophisticated level or type of racial identity development whereas less sophisticated resolutions were assumed to represent various kinds of reactions to racial discrimination.

Furthermore, the NRID theorists attempted to define the direction of healthy Black identity development and argued that overidentification with Whiteness and White culture (i.e., assimilated identities) was a psychologically unhealthy resolution of the identity issues resulting from one's need to survive in a racist culture (cf. Akbar, 1979). This perspective ran contrary to the melting pot philosophy of healthy development that had prevailed in American society heretofore for most other racial/ethnic groups (Hale, 1980).

With the exceptions of Akbar's (1979) and Gibbs's (1974) typologies, the Nigrescence racial identity models were stage models in which theorists proposed that individuals could potentially move from least healthy, White-defined stages of identity, to most healthy, self-defined racial transcendence. As shown in Table 2.1, stage theorists differed in their manner of labeling the stages (e.g., "Alien-Self Disorders" versus "Ethnic Psychological Captivity"), somewhat in the amount of differentiation proposed within assimilated, Black, and transcendent identities (e.g., Thomas, 1971, proposes 1 or 2 stages of "White" or assimilated identification whereas B. Jackson, 1975, proposes 1), and in the sequence in which some of the stages were thought to occur.

In attempting to integrate the J. A. Banks (1981), Cross (1971), and Thomas (1971) models, Gay (1984) described the similarities among the models accordingly: "Each, in its own way, accounts for an ideological metamorphosis of ethnic [sic] identity, assumes that the transformation is a liberating process which symbolizes a psychologically healthier state of being, and uses the idea of developmental stages to account for movement of individuals from negativism to positivism in their self ethnic [sic] identities" (p. 44).

If one examines the summaries of the NRID models in Table 2.1, one cannot help but notice further striking similarities in stage content across the various models. If one were to be particularly investigative, one would also find that even though the models appeared in the literature around the same time, virtually none of the authors cross-referenced the others. Nor were any of the models developed in the same geographical location. Cross, Parham, and Helms (in press), in their historical overview of the Nigrescence literature, explain the multiplicity of models as follows:

Anyone who takes the time to interview some of the key actors will readily discover each was working independently of the other, and the similarity in their writings is not the product of a "copy-cat" phenomena, but the reflection of the fact that whether observed in Watts (Charles Thomas), Chicago (William Cross), Albany, New York (Bailey Jackson), New Orleans (Ivory Toldson and Albert Pasteur) or Pittsburgh (Jake Milliones), the dynamics of Black identity change were basically the same all across America. The similarity, then, is not so much with the models, but in the phenomena being observed. (pp. 4–5)

Cross et al. (in press) seem to be suggesting that by whatever particular NRID model one chooses to investigate Black racial identity development, one potentially contributes to the understanding of a significant common developmental process. Be that as it may, because the various models have been published in a variety of disparate outlets, it has been possible for the old models to exist and new models to accumulate unbeknownst to Black identity theorists and researchers, other than the originator and those fortunate enough to discover her or him.

Thus, though the first models to appear in the counseling (Parham & Helms, 1981) and psychotherapy (Butler, 1975; Milliones, 1980) literature were based on either the Cross (1971) model alone or combined with the Thomas (1971) model, the non-inclusion of the other models was probably more accidental than intentional. Parham and Helms, for instance, were only aware of the Cross and Thomas models at the time of their initial work and selected the former for empirical investigation because its propositions could be more readily operationalized.

Nevertheless, though the Cross (1971, 1978) model and modifications thereof are the theoretical foundations for the discussions of Black racial identity in this book, this focus is not intended to imply that the other models were not worthy of such investigation. In fact, as more empirical investigation of the various models occurs, it is quite likely that all of the NRID models will eventually be integrated into a single framework, comprised of the assets of the various models.

Yet because the Cross (1971, 1978, 1986) model, in toto or in part, has been the primary means of investigating racial identity in the counseling and psychotherapy process as broadly defined, his model, as amended by Helms and her associates (e.g., Carter & Helms, 1987a; Helms, 1984b, 1986, 1987; Parham & Helms, 1981), will be presented here in some detail. Furthermore, because it seems that issues related to racial identity development occur daily in the popular media (but without a theoretical model by which to explain them), wherever possible, examples from such sources as well as the author's therapy experiences will be used to illustrate the usefulness of analyzing Black personality from a Nigrescence perspective.

STAGES OF BLACK RACIAL IDENTITY DEVELOPMENT

Cross (1971, 1978) originally presented a four- or five-stage model of racial identity development in which each stage was characterized by self-concept issues concerning race as well as parallel attitudes about Blacks and Whites as reference groups. With respect to self-concept, he proposed that each stage had different implications for a person's feelings, thoughts, and behaviors. Where reference groups are concerned, his model implied that the individual, depending upon his or her stage of racial identity, makes complex choices as to whether Blacks and/or Whites will be treated as reference groups.

Helms (1986) amended Cross's model to suggest that each stage be considered a distinct "world view," by which she meant cognitive templates that people use to organize (especially racial) information about themselves, other people, and institutions. Additionally, Helms (1984b) suggested that an individual's stage or world view was the result of his or her cognitive maturation level in interaction with societal forces. In more recent writings, Helms (1989) has advised that it might be useful to think of each of the stages as bimodal, that is, as having two potentially distinguishable forms of expression. In this overview of the stages, bimodal descriptions of the stages will be presented, though it should be noted that in this instance as well as a few others, theoretical modification of Cross's model in particular or NRID theory in general has outstripped empirical investigation.

The stages, as originally conceptualized by Cross (1971, 1978) were Preencounter, Encounter, Immersion/Emersion, Internalization, and Internalization/Commitment, though the last stage has received less attention because of the measurement difficulty in differentiating it from the other stages.

Preencounter

Thomas's (1971) writings suggest that a person enters the first stage, Preencounter, from a state of "Negromachy," which if one liberally translates his construct, seems to be the absence of a self-concept or internally derived identity except as defined and approved of by Whites at a given moment. The general theme of the Preencounter stage is idealization of the dominant traditional White world view and, consequently, denigration of a Black world view. Because the dominant White world view in the United States considers Whiteness and White culture as superior to Blackness and Black culture, the Black person who espouses the Preencounter perspective must find some way to separate himself or herself from the devalued reference group in order to minimize the psychological discomfort that arises when one's cognitions are incompatible (see Festinger, 1957, chapter 4). In general, this disassociating occurs by artificially inflating one's personal identity, abandoning Blacks as a reference group while accepting Whites as such, and denying one's ascribed Black identity.

In attempting to explain how "ethnic" groups can tolerate their disadvantaged status, D. M. Taylor and McKirnan (1978; cited in D. M. Taylor, 1980) described ethnic identity development in terms of attribution theory (E. E. Jones & K. E. Davis, 1965). Attributions are typically considered to be either "external" or "internal," though presumably they actually vary along a continuum with these two dimensions anchoring the opposite extremes. Attribution theory roughly pertains to a person's beliefs concerning the reasons for one's own and other people's (perhaps including one's reference group's) rewards and punishments. Internal attribution means that the person believes that he or she (or, more generally, each individual) controls his or her own rewards and punishments; external attribution implies that the person believes that external forces such as luck, destiny, or fate control one's (or others') rewards and punishments.

Although the constructs underlying attribution theory are typically used to refer to individual personality characteristics, they may also be useful for describing how an individual relates to potential racial reference groups. As applied to one's racial reference groups, internal attribution might mean that the person believes that her or his racial group causes or is responsible for its own outcomes whereas external attribution means that she or he believes that external factors such as another racial group cause outcomes.

In D. M. Taylor and McKirnan's (1978) first stage, called "stable hierarchically organized intergroup relations," which seems to be approximately equivalent to the Preencounter stage of Black NRID theory, they suggest that the individual's personal identity and reference-group identity are internal. That is, the individual, in this instance, assumes that her or his own status as well as that of other Blacks and Whites is due to personal effort and ability or lack thereof. Consequently, if the individual achieves much in society, it is because he or she is a meritorious human being; if he or she achieves nothing, then it is because he or she is deficient in some way. Whites are assumed to hold advantaged status due to extraordinary effort and Blacks are assumed to occupy disadvantaged status because they have not expended equivalent effort. The person either does not acknowledge an ascribed racial identity or identifies with Whites. For the Preencounter person, exceptionality or deficiency is defined according to how well or poorly one fits into White culture and demonstrates those traits that the person *believes* typify White culture.

D. M. Taylor (1980) argues that a Stage 1 mentality can be maintained as long as the dominant racial group (read Whites) allows a few conforming "ethnic group" members (read Blacks) to be relatively successful. But the Preencounter person can then continue to believe that it is possible for her or him to be "just a person" (i.e., to have no ascribed identity) and not be deleteriously affected by her or his racial-group membership.

Recent empirical evidence (cf. Cross et al., in press) supports the existence of two forms of Preencounter, active (Mode 1) or passive (Mode 2). Nowadays one can find many examples of behavior representative of each kind of Preencounter. Passive Preencounter seems to be associated with healthier personal identity than active Preencounter.

Active. Active Preencounter was originally described by Cross (1971, 1978). In this form of Preencounter, the person deliberately idealizes Whiteness and White culture and denigrates Blacks and Black culture through behaviors as well as attitudes. In active Preencounter, the separation of personal identity from the other aspects of Self is quite evident.

The following paraphrased and disguised excerpt from a therapy interaction between the author (Therapist) and a Black female client (Gloria) illustrates the active and apparently automatic assumption in Mode 1 that what one perceives to be "bad" is somehow due to the person's Blackness and anything "good" is due to her or his ability to be other than Black and/or the individual's *personal* attributes.

Therapist: "Well, Gloria, it looks like you have a lot of complaints about your husband. Could you tell me about some of them?"

Gloria: "He's not like us."

Therapist: "How do you mean?"

Gloria: "He's loud. When he gets excited about something or when he gets angry about something, he raises his voice and you can tell how he feels just by listening to him. He's not calm and logical like us."

Therapist: "Where does your idea come from that it's bad to show your emotion in your voice?"

Gloria: "I don't know. I just learned it. That's how those ghetto Blacks behave on television. If you want to get ahead in this world, you have to be calm, cool, and totally in control of yourself."

Perhaps the bifurcation of identity, which occurs when one possesses an active Preencounter identity, is maintained by the person's ability to project his or her anger or feelings of rejection by particular Blacks or Whites onto Blacks in general and accounts for why Blacks might not be used as a reference group or source of ascribed identity except by exclusion. Thus, it is not unusual to hear "successful" Blacks argue that they reject other Blacks as a reference group because their values or behaviors are so different. Very often these differences are described, perhaps unwittingly, in language saturated with racial stereotypes (e.g., "*They* didn't like *me* because I couldn't dance as well as they could," or "I can't help it if I'm smarter than them."). Existing empirical evidence (e.g., Parham & Helms, 1985a; 1985b; Taylor, 1986) suggests that active Preencounter, relative to some of the subsequent stages, is associated with poor self-concept, low self-esteem, and high anxiety and depression. These findings seem to indicate at least some interrelationship between personal identity and racial identity and suggest that psychosocial adjustment may be least healthy when one is in the earlier phase of Preencounter.

Passive. Persons whose racial identity resolution is passive Preencounter are often hard to recognize because their world views so clearly mirror that which is dominant in White society. Consequently, behavior that may not be healthy for themselves in the long run is reinforced by the dominant society as well as racial peers who are at the same stage of racial identity.

This second type of Preencounter person, sometimes called passive or assimilating (cf. Helms, 1989), because of advantaged status in their own racial group, comes to believe that personal effort guarantees "passage" into White culture. Such persons are highly motivated to be accepted by Whites and lead their lives in ways that they think will earn them such acceptance. On the other hand, the person in the passive mode of the Preencounter stage also accepts the negative stereotypes of Blacks and the positive stereotypes of Whites as promulgated by White society and institutions, though the fact that one is stereotyping may be outside of conscious awareness. In actuality, the person may engage in massive denial in order to maintain a fiction of racial equality. A conversation illustrative of the second mode of the Preencounter stage might go as follows:

Black Man: "You know, you're different from the women I usually go out with."
Black Woman: "How do you mean?"
Black Man: "Well, I prefer women with blue eyes and long hair."
Black Woman: "So, you're saying you prefer White women?"
Black Man: "Naw, naw, it's not like that. I just happen to like blue eyes and if I happened to meet a Black woman with blue eyes who met my other qualifications, I'd go out with her."

Even if the passive Preencounter person does not always believe in stereotypes, he or she dare not risk questioning them for fear of losing his or her actual or hoped-for acceptance by Whites and the anticipated advantages that accompany this status. Consequently, the person adopts an inflexible belief in internal causation, individualism, and a just world even in the face of evidence to the contrary. Furthermore, denial of Blacks as a reference group and source of ascribed identity is present. To persons who have progressed to more advanced stages of racial identity development, the person in Mode 2 of the Preencounter stage seems quite naive, since Mode 2 persons can apparently assert with great credulity that neither other Blacks nor their race have had any influence or significance in their lives.

This selection from *New York* magazine illustrates the manner in which rejection of a Black ascribed identity often contributes to the apparent naivete and/or self-centeredness of people in the second mode of the Preencounter stage.

[Black surgeon]: *I'm not sure what they [other Blacks mean] when they say he has an elitist attitude.* I have an elitist attitude toward what I do for people, that's true. Sometimes, I'll be told that so-and-so wants to know, "why aren't you in Harlem practicing in a storefront office, taking care of Medicare patients?" Now, that's nonsense. I grew up in Great Neck—Harlem isn't my background. Why should I be there? *I'm always surprised and dismayed to find that when I finally reached the ivory tower, there was not unanimous acceptance* [italics added]. (Hopkins, 1987, p. 23)

Although the persons portrayed in the selected passages seem to be of at least middle class, it is fair to say that equivalent examples can be found in the other socioeconomic classes as well (cf. Carter & Helms, 1988). To remain comfortable in the second mode of the Preencounter stage, the person must maintain the fiction that race and racial indoctrination have nothing to do with how he or she lives life. Additionally, one must continue to believe that social mobility is determined primarily by personal ability and effort.

It is probably the case that the Preencounter person is bombarded on a regular basis with information indicating that he or she cannot really be a member of the "in" racial group, but relies on denial to selectively screen such information from awareness. However, one of the ironies of American society is that the more successful Blacks and/or particular Black persons become, according to White standards of success, the easier it is for Whites and Blacks to point out how different that person is from other Blacks as well as Whites. Statements such as "I wouldn't mind living next door to you" clearly denote that the speaker considers himself or herself to have the right to make such decisions whereas the person addressed does not, believes that the person addressed is somehow different from and inferior to the speaker, and is willing to treat the person addressed as though he or she is superior to and different from the group from which the addressee is perceived to originate.

Similarly, statements such as "You talk like you're White" imply that the speaker has the right to judge what constitutes Black speech whereas the person addressed does not and, at the same time, that the person does not measure up to Black behavioral standards in some important way. In short, the Preencounter person comes to perceive that he or she does not really "fit" into either group unconditionally. The conscious acknowledgment of this devaluation of the person's Self accompanied by feelings of alienation initiates her or his movement into the Encounter stage.

Encounter

Although there is considerable controversy (e.g., Cross et al., in press; Ponterotto & Wise, 1987) concerning whether the Encounter stage is in fact a full-blown stage, autobiographical accounts (e.g., Malcolm X, 1973; McClain, 1983; Wilkins, 1982) indicate that experiences consistent with an Encounter stage can be quite long-lasting and that individuals recall them as such. Be that as it may, in a racist society it stands to reason that every Black person is bombarded with racial affronts and indignities regardless of whether or not she or he is involved in actual interaction with Whites. After all, racism may be either direct (e.g., verbal and/or physical abuse) or indirect (e.g., the virtual absence of African history prior to slavery in "American history" textbooks while European history during the relevant periods is covered extensively), and individual-, other-, or group-focused. What is more relevant here is that during the Preencounter stage, the person expends considerable mental energy in rationalizing such occurrences and/or pretending that they have no implications for the well-being of Black people in general and/or herself or himself in particular; that is, attributions of responsibility and causation are internal, as required for membership in White American society (cf. D. W. Sue, 1980).

Nevertheless, for many people, at some point in their lives, it becomes impossible to deny the reality that they cannot become an accepted part of "the White world." Usually this awareness seems to be aroused by an event(s) in the environment that touches the person's inner core and makes salient the contradiction that no matter how well he or she personally or other Black individuals conform to White standards, most Whites will always perceive him or her as Black and therefore inferior.

The conscious awareness that the old Euro-American or White world view is not viable and that one must find another identity constitutes the first phase of Encounter. Lenita McClain (1983), the first Black editorial writer for *The Chicago Tribune*, describes a series of what appear to be her Encounter events as they occurred during the successful campaign and election of a Black mayor in Chicago:

A jubilant [Black] scream went up. . . . We had a feeling, and above all we had power. . . . So many whites unconsciously had never considered that blacks could do much of anything, least of all get a black candidate this close to being mayor of Chicago. My [primarily White] colleagues looked up and realized, perhaps for the first time, that I was one of "them." I was suddenly threatening. (p. C1)

As the person struggles to "discover" a new identity, she or he oscillates between the recently abandoned Preencounter identity and an as yet unformed Black identity. The struggle that follows constitutes the second phase of Encounter and is comprised of a mixture of feelings including confusion, hopelessness, anxiety, depression, and eventually anger and euphoria. McClain (1983) describes the struggle as follows: "In one day my mind has sped from the naive thought that everything would be all right in the world if people would just intermarry, to the naive thought that we should establish a black homeland where we would never have to see a white face again" (p. C1).

Although in many ways the Encounter stage appears to be so fleeting and complex as to be immeasurable (cf. Cross et al., in press; Helms, 1989) existing evidence suggests that it may be related in a variety of ways to personal identity, reference-group orientation, and perhaps ascribed identity variables. In investigating personal identity correlates, McCaine (1986) found that Encounter attitudes were related to high trait anxiety, but Parham and Helms (1985a, 1985b) found that they were related to high self-esteem, low anxiety, and positive self-regard. Perhaps whether or not healthy personal identity variables are positively related to Encounter depends on whether respondents are in the earlier or latter phase. Euphoria, that is, the latter phase, is probably related positively to personal identity variables. Studies pertaining to reference-group orientation have shown that Encounter attitudes are not related to desire to affiliate with people of unspecified race (McCaine, 1986), but they are positively related to affiliative behaviors with other Blacks in various roles (e.g., Denton, 1986; Parham & Helms, 1981), and to acceptance of Whites who are sensitive to Black cultural issues (e.g., Pomales, Claiborn, & LaFromboise, 1986). Each of these affiliative tendencies may typify second-phase orientations.

Taken together, empirical evidence suggests that the Encounter stage may have implications for the personal identity and reference-group orientation components of adjustment. In particular, emotionality and sentiment might be most evident during this stage. Entry into Encounter may also represent the person's first deliberate acknowledgment of a Black ascribed identity.

In case it is not obvious, it should be noted that the encounter events that trigger movement into the Encounter stage are idiosyncratic to the individual. That is, one does not automatically assume that one common set of experiences leads every individual to the Encounter stage. Rather it is the common *psychological* experience of confronting "an identity-shattering something" that links individuals to this stage. However, the something varies according to the person's life circumstances.

The person's abandonment of the previous world view leaves her or him virtually "identity-less," a condition that is more uncomfortable than it is comfortable. One needs some cognitive framework for making sense of one's own emotions, the world, and one's place in it. Consequently, the person begins an active search for a Black identity, a search that Helms (1984b) describes as akin to a religious rebirth. Cross (1978) says of the search: "the proposed new identity is highly attractive, the person throws caution to the wind and begins a frantic, determined, extremely obsessive, motivated search for Black identity. At the end of the encounter stage the person is not Black yet, but he/she has made the decision to become Black" (p. 85).

Therefore, in the latter phase of Encounter, the person acts as though an externally defined Black identity exists if only one could find it. However, the person's recognition that a Black identity must be developed rather than found signals the entry into Cross's (1971, 1977) third stage, Immersion/Emersion.

Immersion/Emersion

Cross (1971, 1978) originally described the Immersion stage in two phases, Immersion and Emersion, respectively. Thus, the subsequent descriptions do not differ markedly from his original formulations.

Immersion. In Immersion, the person psychologically and physically, if possible, withdraws into Blackness and a Black world. He or she thinks, feels, and acts the way he or she believes "authentic" Blacks are supposed to, and judges and evaluates other Blacks on the basis of their conformance to these "idealistic" racial standards. Thus, a Black ascribed identity and a Black reference-group orientation dominate the person's personality often at the cost of one's personal identity. Furthermore, because until this point the person's primary descriptions of what it means to be Black have been defined by White society, the person often "acts" Black in very stereotypic ways. In other words, the person's Black reference-group orientation is externally defined.

Generalized anger is one affect or personal identity variable that appears to characterize Immersion. The person is angry at Whites because of their role in racial oppression, herself or himself for having been a party to such a system for however long, and at other Blacks whose eyes have not been properly opened yet. Thus, one's acknowledgment of Blackness is high though it is not internalized; the person seems to be conforming to a preconceived notion of Black identity. Some research comparing characteristics of Preencounter and Immersion (Parham & Helms, 1985a; 1985b) suggests that they are similar in that they both appear to be reactions to environmental circumstances, but dissimilar in that hostility seems to be measurably associated with Immersion/Emersion.

Cross (1978) postulated that "either/or thinking" (i.e., dichotomous thinking) characterized the cognitive development of persons in Immersion, in that such persons typically idealize Blackness and African heritage, but denigrate everything thought to be White and of White Western heritage. He described their emotional functioning as follows: "Euphoria, rage, inordinate amounts of artistic and/or political energy, perturbation, effrontery, high risk taking, a destructive mood in constant tension with dreams of revitalization and an intense sense of intimacy toward Black life also characterize behavior in this stage" (p. 85).

Coping strategies that seemingly correspond to the Immersion phase appear to occur quite often among Black adolescents who find themselves adrift in White educational settings. Latimer (1986) decried Black students' avoidance of certain academic endeavors in which they were obviously talented (e.g., journalism, sailing, etc.) in favor of "hanging out" because the latter was accepted as "Black" behavior whereas the former were not.

Anson (1987) describes the demise of a Harlem youth (Eddie) following his attendance at an elite predominately White prep school in the East. In retrospect, one can virtually trace the youth's progression from Encounter to Immersion. Consider, for example, his comments following the deaths of Martin Luther King and John and Robert Kennedy as reported by his mother: "Mama, white people are the Devil . . . because they kill all the people who are trying to help us" (p. 37). Or his junior year abroad in Spain, which he described as the only place he had ever been where he was not being judged as a Black person. Or his frustrating nonromance with a White classmate. Could these events have comprised his Encounter?

After a period of apparent euphoria (typical of the last phase of Encounter), Anson (1987) describes a series of events that seem to reflect Eddie's movement into Immersion: (a) teachers noted a "growing ferocity," hostility, belligerence, and anger in demeanor; (b) he reportedly denounced the (Black) nonviolent civil rights movement as "accommodating white racism" and chastised his classmates via angry speeches; (c) he began to act like "a slick, fast-talking, uncompromising ghetto resident, a real hustler" (p. 41), though by all accounts such traits were the antithesis of his personality formerly. Taken together, Anson's description of Eddie appears to portray a youth who was mired in Immersion at the time of his early death.

Emersion

Though Eddie was seemingly fixated at the Immersion phase, Cross's (1971) model offers Emersion as a possible escape from Immersion. Entry into Emersion requires the opportunity to withdraw into Black community and to engage in catharsis within a supportive environment. During Emersion, one often finds individuals engaging in "rap" sessions, political action groups, exploration of Black and African culture, discussions of racial issues with Black elders whose experiences were formerly ignored, "hanging out" with other Blacks in a spirit of kinship, and so forth.

However one's experience of positive Black/African culture occurs, participation in the Emersion phase allows the person to develop a positive nonstereotypic Afro-American perspective on the world. Involvement in cathartic as well as educative activities allows the person's emotions, particularly anger, to level off and her or his cognitive strategies to become more flexible. Total acceptance of Blackness as defined by others is no longer necessary for the person to feel self-worth, and he or she begins to sort out the strengths and weaknesses of Black culture and being Black. As the person begins to feel greater control over herself or himself, he or she moves into the Internalization stage.

Internalization

The main theme of the Internalization stage is the internalization of a positive personally relevant Black identity. That is, one blends one's personal identity (i.e., what makes one unique) with a Black ascribed identity (i.e., acknowledgment that one's Blackness influences who one is). Furthermore, Blacks become the primary reference group to which one belongs, though the quality of one's belongingness is no longer externally determined. However, because in developing a stable Black identity the individual can face the world from a position of personal strength, it now becomes possible to renegotiate one's positions with respect to Whites and White society. Thus, although the Internalizing person rejects racism and similar forms of oppression, he or she is able to reestablish relationships with individual White associates who merit such relationships, and to analyze Whiteness and White culture for its strengths and weaknesses as well.

Cross (1971, 1978) originally suggested that a fifth stage, Internalization/Commitment, followed Internalization. The primary distinction between the two stages was that Internalization/Commitment reflected a behavioral style characterized by social activism and Internalization reflected one's level of cognitive development. However, subsequent theorists (e.g., Helms, 1989; Parham & Helms, 1985b) have recommended that Internalization/Commitment be considered the second mode or phase of the Internalization stage because of the difficulty in distinguishing motivation from behavior. With this latter view in mind, Internalization behavior may involve participation in social and political activities designed specifically to eliminate racism and/or oppression regardless of the race of the perpetrators and victims. However, it may also involve performance of everyday activities according to one's Black perspective. In either case, the limited available evidence does seem to suggest that an activist orientation may be associated with Internalization attitudes (cf. Carter & Helms, 1987). One can find many examples of the former type of activism in Civil Rights literature. For instance, Martin Luther King's focus on the economy and the Viet Nam war during the latter years of the Civil Rights Movement of the 1960s seems to illustrate the Internalization/Commitment Stage (cf. J. Williams, 1987).

Ordinary everyday experiences do not frequently capture media attention, and the individual who attempts to make sense of such experiences from an Internalizing perspective risks misinterpretation and rejection by individuals who do not, cannot, or will not understand the Internalizing person's frame of reference. Consider, for instance, this exchange in which a Black male transracial adoptee and a social worker attempt to explain to a television audience and other panel members the importance of a Black reference-group orientation to Black children's racial identity development.

[Adoptee:] ... I agree with you that there needs to come a time, and there will come a time, when black children will be able to interact with whoever it is, whoever they're living with, but the reality is ... for most of the people that I know ... who were interracially adopted ... and I was, too, the reality is

Table 2.2
Summary of General Characteristics of the Black Racial Identity Stages

Stages	General Theme	Emotional Themes	Identity Components		
			Personal Identity	Reference Group Orientation	Ascribed Identity
Preencounter					
Active	idealization of Whiteness	anxiety, poor self-esteem	negative	White/Euro-American	White
Passive	denigration of Blackness	defensiveness	idealized positive	White/Euro-American	none (non-Black)
Encounter					
events	consciousness of race	bitterness, hurt, anger	positive	White/Euro-American	none
experience		euphoria	transitional	Black	Black
Immersion/	idealization of Blackness	rage, self-destructiveness	none	Black	Black
Emersion	denigration of Whiteness	impulsivity; euphoric	positive	Black	Black
Internalization/	racial transcendence	self-controlled calm, secure	positive	bicultural	Black
Commitment		activistic	positive	pluralistic	Black/pan-African

that when you're in it, it's a blissful experience, when you're in it it's fantastic. *It's not until you evolve out of it and are able to look back on it, that you realize . . . [what you missed]*. The kind of camaraderie that you miss in a family situation where you have black sisters and black brothers who understand everything that you're going through . . . [italics added].

[Panelist:] "But that's nonsense."

[Researcher:] "That's not so, that's not so."

[Social Worker:] "There are some experiences that black children have that white folks do not have, have not had experience in, and cannot pass on lessons to them, and—"

[Panelist:] "You mean, like being called a nigger?"

[Social Worker:] "Well, like being called a nigger."

[Researcher:] "Every ethnic group in this society has been called names, it isn't unique." ("Oprah Winfrey Show," July 9, 1987, p. 12)

In identifying the Internalization stage, it is important to recognize that *what* the person feels, believes, or thinks is not as important as *how* he or she believes. In other words, though two Internalizing individuals may not share the same point of view on a particular issue, they should be similar in that each maintains a positive Black racial identity, that is, does not deny the merit of her or his Blackness as he or she confronts the issue. Moreover, in the Internalization stage one will find a variety of individuals expressing themselves in a variety of ways. Internalization frees the person to be.

Furthermore, persons in Internalization no longer need judge people by their cultural group memberships (e.g., race, gender, nationality). Rather they are concerned with common peoplehood. Consequently, the Internalizing person can find value in people who do not look like her or him. One might say that Internalization also frees the person to let other people be as long as by so doing one does not encourage oppression and victimization.

CONCLUDING REMARKS

In summary, then, four distinct stages of Black racial identity have been proposed. In general, these stages are proposed to differ in emotional, behavioral, and cognitive expression. Within each stage, personal identity, reference-group orientation, and ascribed identity are thought to vary. Table 2.2 summarizes the stages with respect to these components as previously outlined. Theoretically, each person can potentially progress from the least developed stage (and phase) to the most developed. However, recent theorists (Parham, 1989) have begun to speculate that every person may not enter the developmental cycle at the same place and that recycling through the stages may occur as the person moves through the lifespan.

3

The Measurement of Black Racial Identity Attitudes

JANET E. HELMS

The attempt to measure racial and/or cultural identity in adult populations is a relatively new phenomenon, though theoretical speculation about such issues has been around for quite some time (cf. Cross et al., in press). Although NRID theory speculates that the stages of racial identity can be defined by different cognitions, feelings, and/or behaviors, with occasional exceptions (e.g., Davidson, 1974), measurement has focused on cognitions in general and attitudes in particular. Moreover, four measurement approaches have characterized attempts to discover the effects of racial/cultural attitudes on clients involved or potentially involved in the therapy process. Three of these can be called "ascribed" identity approaches because they used some observable racial characteristics to infer psychological affiliation or connectedness. The fourth approach evolved directly from the NRID theories.

ASCRIBED IDENTITY APPROACHES

The first and most prevalent approach, which might be called an "imposed" ascribed identity approach, equated a person's racial identity with her or his self-described or observer-designated racial membership group (e.g., Black or Afro-American rather than White or Anglo-American). Some of the most egregious examples of this approach can be found in the counseling and psychotherapy literature pertaining to the effects of race on the counseling and psychotherapy process when it involves visible racial/ethnic groups (i.e., Asians, Blacks, Hispanics, and/

or Native Americans). (See Atkinson, 1983, and Sattler, 1977, for reviews of this literature.)

As it became evident that the imposed ascribed identity approach was *assuming* common racial attitudes among Black people rather than *measuring* their attitudes, researchers began to search for alternative racial attitudinal measures; measures that would reflect the variability inherent in Blackness. Following Vontress's (1971a, 1971b) speculation that Black racial attitudes could be categorized according to three types (see chapter 2), efforts to measure Black racial attitudes became somewhat more direct. Rather than inferring racial-group membership from physical appearance or demographic designation, a few researchers began to ask research participants about the extent of their identification with the relevant racial/ethnic groups.

Where Blacks are concerned, two additional versions of the ascribed identity approach appeared. In the first, quality of identification with Blackness was inferred from one's preferred racial self-designation (e.g., "Black" versus "Negro"). Using the self-labeling approach, G. G. Jackson and Kirschner's (1973) pioneering study represented the first attempt to quantify racial identity types in a manner that was potentially useful as a diagnostic tool. They did find that Black client surrogates' racial self-designation determined whether they preferred same-race therapists, whereas later findings by Gordon and Grantham (1979), Parham and Helms (1981), and Morten (1984) indicated little or no relationships between racial self-designation and preference for therapists of the same race. In explaining their inability to replicate G. G. Jackson and Kirschner's findings, Parham and Helms suggested that racial labels might be transitory indicants of the current social climate rather than accurate descriptors of the person's crystallized identity.

In the second ascribed identity approach, quality of Black identification was inferred from one's choice from among four mutually exclusive categories: commitment to Black culture, White culture, neither, or both. Using such an approach, Atkinson, Furlong, and Poston (1986) asked subjects to indicate their level of commitment (ranging from strong to weak) to Anglo-American and Afro-American cultures. However, they analyzed their data in such a way as to obscure the potentially differing responses of those groups most analogous to the Preencounter (i.e., strong commitment to Anglo-American culture, weak commitment to Afro-American culture) and Immersion/Emersion (strong commitment to Afro-American culture, weak commitment to Anglo-American culture) stages of identity. For that reason, their failure to find evidence that quality of Black identification contributed to differences in preferences for counselors' "ethnicity" is equivocal.

Interestingly, neither of the three ascribed identity approaches has consistently been shown to be differentially related to personal identity or reference-group orientation variables, though the self-labeling approach showed some promise early on. Racial identity is a complex construct that, perhaps, cannot be adequately assessed via single-item measures.

NRID MEASUREMENT APPROACH

The fourth measurement approach, based on Black racial identity developmental models, actually has been advocated in substance if not in form by several writers including Butler (1975), G. G. Jackson (1977), and Milliones (1980). Each of these authors suggested that stagewise models of racial identity development might form the basis for matching treatment interventions to clients' treatment needs. Each in his own way suggested that if therapists could differentially match their interventions to clients' levels of racial identity development, then clients would be more apt to benefit from the psychotherapy process.

For the matching approach to have heuristic value, some means of quantifying identity development was necessary. Although Cross and his associates (e.g., Hall, Cross, & Freedle, 1972) originally used interviews and Q-sort methodology to assess stages of identity, these techniques are generally too time consuming and expensive with respect to personnel to permit them to be readily adopted for use in therapy settings. More economical and transportable methods of assessment were needed if the models of racial identity were ever to gain a foothold in the counseling and psychotherapy diagnostic literature.

To date, two attitudinal scales have been developed for the purpose of operationalizing stage models of racial identity in adolescent and adult samples. They are Milliones's (1980) Developmental Inventory of Black Consciousness (DIBC) and Parham and Helms' (1981) Black Racial Identity Attitude Scale (RIAS-B). The former, developed on a Black male college sample, was designed to measure stages associated with an integrated version of Cross (1971) and Thomas's (1971) stage models of racial identity. The latter, developed on Black female and male college student samples, was designed to convert Hall, Cross, and Freedle's (1972) Q-sort items into a transportable paper-and-pencil measure. The development of the RIAS-B is described in detail elsewhere (Helms & Parham, in press). So, in the remainder of this chapter, theoretical and methodological issues related to the development and use of the RIAS-B will be discussed.

The RIAS-B, a rationally constructed scale, was originally designed to measure the general themes of four of the five stages of racial identity proposed by Cross (1971): Preencounter, Encounter, Immersion/Emersion, and Internalization. The fifth stage, Internalization/Commitment, was not operationalized because it described a style of behaving with respect to identity issues that did not seem to be unique to a single stage, but might be present in some of the earlier stages, albeit due to different motivations. In other words, weaning the underlying motivations from the observable behavior proved to be too subtle a measurement task.

Recall that the Preencounter stage (and consequently Preencounter scale items) reflects some manner of identification with a Euro-American world view, including belief in derogatory stereotypes of Blacks as a reference group. The Encounter stage marks the person's decision to adopt a Black perspective and is characterized by feelings of euphoria as well as confusion with respect to racial identity issues. The Immersion/ Emersion stage describes those persons who have psychologically and/ or physically withdrawn into a Black world in an effort to define a Black identity. The Internalization stage is one in which one's racial identity becomes crystallized.

In discussing how the identity stages might be adapted for counseling and research purposes, Helms (1989) recommended usage of racial identity attitudes as one convenient *product* of racial identity stages, though not a complete measure of them. If one uses a racial-identity-attitude-measurement approach, then according to Parham and Helms (1981, 1985a, 1985b), stage of racial identity per se is not determined by whether or not a person has a certain type of racial identity attitudes (since everyone is assumed to have some of each type in some amount). Instead one determines the amount of attitudes associated with each stage.

Yet the extent to which one type of attitudes predominates over the others at a particular time theoretically has some implications for other variables. Thus, a person who might be diagnosed as being in the Internalization stage, defined according to behavior, attitudes, emotions, and so forth, presumably has a predominance of Internalization attitudes, but she or he conceivably has some attitudes that correspond to some of the earlier stages as well. However, in this case the attitudes associated with the earlier stages should not be as strong as the Internalization attitudes. Nevertheless, to the extent that the person possesses some of the precursor attitudes, then these attitudes also might be expected to influence the Internalization person's behavior in some way. Therefore, it is important to use assessment procedures that allow one to measure each type of racial identity attitudes so that their moderating effects on one another can be ascertained.

THEORETICAL CONSIDERATIONS

At least three theoretical assumptions are implicit in the racial identity developmental models and, consequently, are inherited by any measure that purports to operationalize the models. The assumptions, not necessarily in order of importance, are (a) racial identity development occurs

Table 3.1
Summary of Grace's Intercorrelations among Black Racial Identity Attitude
Scales

Scales	P	E	I	In
Preencounter (P)		-.16*	-.15*	-.04
Encounter (E)			.62**	.17**
Immersion/Emersion (I)				.04
Internalization				

* p < .05

** p < .01

via a stagewise process that can be assessed, (b) racial identity is bidimensional such that a Black person incorporates attitudes about Blacks as well as Whites into her or his identity, and (c) racial identity is relatively stable (though not necessarily permanent). It seems important to consider how the RIAS-B does and does not address the foregoing assumptions.

Racial Identity as a Stagewise Process

As mentioned previously, one question that arises with respect to the RIAS-B is whether it can be said to measure a stagewise process. When examining this question with respect to the individual attitudinal subscales, it should be the case that if the subscales are developmentally related, then to the extent that they are correlated at all, adjacent scale scores (with the possible exception of Preencounter and Encounter) should be positively correlated, and scales measuring conflicting or exclusive attitudes should be negatively correlated. Data abstracted from Grace's (1984) study may help to clarify this point.

Table 3.1 summarizes the correlations between RIAS-B scales that she obtained. Notice that the highest positive correlation ($r = .62, p < .001$) occurred between scales measuring Encounter and Immersion/Emersion attitudes. This relationship is consistent with the theoretical descriptions of the respective stages, in which the former is presented as a stage of psychological entry into Black/Afro-American identity issues and the latter is portrayed as a stage of immersing oneself in these racial identity issues. In addition, notice that Preencounter attitudes are negatively correlated with the other three types of attitudes. Again, these relationships are consistent with theoretical descriptions of the relevant stages, in that Preencounter attitudes are the conceptual opposites in beliefs about Blacks as well as Whites. The minute (and nonsignificant) correlations between Internalization attitudes and Preencounter and Immersion/Emersion attitudes support the descriptions of these attitudes as representing conceptually different stages. Similar correlations have been reported by Parham and Helms (1981) and Carter (1984).

The Bidimensionality of Racial Identity

Implicit in the stage theories of identity is the premise that identity varies along a two-dimensional continuum, one emphasizing attitudes incorporated from Euro-American culture and the other emphasizing attitudes incorporated from Afro-American culture. Insofar as one can tell, this aspect of the stage models has not been tested empirically.

In Figure 3.1, the results of a multidimensional scaling analysis of the short form of the RIAS-B are shown. The purpose of this analysis was to determine the nature of the structure underlying the items. In particular, I wanted to discover whether the clustering of items seemed to represent two parallel world views, one Black and one White, the former ranging from anti-Black to pro-Black, the latter ranging from idealized White to reasoned acceptance of Whites.

In fact, four dimensions seemed to account for the common variance among items ($R^2 = .89$). The first two dimensions, illustrated in Figure 1, seem relatively consistent with theoretical descriptions of the stages of identity. The dimension represented by the vertical axis seems to represent a quality of rational acceptance (top) versus anti-White sentiment (bottom). The horizontal dimension illustrates the contrast between anti-Black (left) and positive-Black (right) feelings.

One gets a sense of the possible evolution of racial identity attitudes if one examines in a counterclockwise direction the clusterings of items within quadrants formed by the two dimensions. Quadrant 1 contains the majority of the Preencounter items, seven of nine. The first cluster of items here (Items 12, 25, and 17) seem to be those that advocate the abandonment of a Black world view or reference-group orientation in favor of a White world view. The second cluster (Items 8 and 4) seems to assess White idealization and Black denigration, and the third cluster (Items 9 and 24) measures negative feelings about Blacks. Quadrant 2 contains the remainder of the Preencounter items and two of the Immersion/Emersion items. These clusters seem to be equivalent to societal stereotypic views in the case of Cluster 4 (Items 29 and 21), and Black separatist views in the case of Cluster 5.

Thus, the left half of the figure describes identity (as measured by the RIAS-B items) as a process in which one abandons or denies Black identity and adopts a White world view, which may carry with it idealization of Whites and denigration of Blacks, negative feelings about

Figure 3.1
Multidimensional Scaling Analysis of the Short Form of the Black Racial Identity Attitude Scale

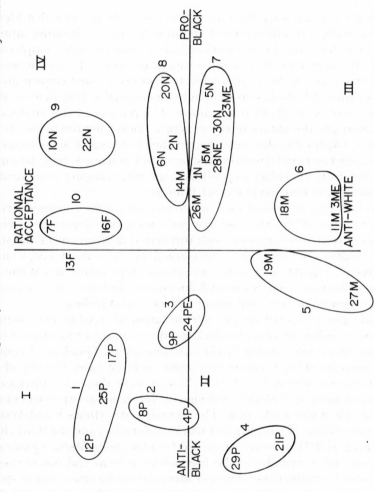

P = Preencounter; E = Encounter; M = Immersion/Emersion; N = Internalization; F = Filler.

Blacks, and acceptance of societal stereotypes about Blacks (e.g., Blacks are inferior to Whites intellectually). The first step toward developing a Black identity may be to withdraw from the White world and to immerse oneself in a Black world. This step, according to Cross (1971), represents the beginning of the Immersion/Emersion stage.

As one moves into Quadrant 3, one finds the majority of the Immersion items, five out of eight. Cluster 6 (Items 3, 11, and 18) suggests that one aspect of Immersion may be anger, as revealed through anti-White stereotyping combined with a Black perspective. The other cluster in Quadrant 3, Cluster 7, is comprised of a mixture of Immersion (Items 23 and 26), Encounter (Items 23 and 28), and Internalization (Items 28, 1, 5, and 30) items. The themes that these items have in common are positive feelings about being Black, an embracing of Black identity, and a commitment to Black causes. Across the horizontal axis into Quadrant 4, one finds Cluster 8, the first primarily Internalization cluster (Items 2, 6, and 20); it also contains a single Immersion item (Item 14). These items seem to reflect an activistic orientation and actually may be equivalent to Cross's (1971) Internalization/Commitment phase of identity.

The remaining items (10 and 22), located in Cluster 9, measure the rational or intellectualized approach to racial identity issues that is theorized to be typical of the Internalization stage. Other items in Figure 3.1, not previously discussed, are filler items and are included in the figure because they seem to help clarify the meaning of the dimensions and clusters. However, they have not been used in the most recent versions of the Racial Identity Attitude Scale because they do not contribute markedly to subscale reliabilities.

Then, to summarize the identity process as illustrated by the right half of the figure, it appears that the development of a positive Black identity may initially require a certain amount of anger and anti-White sentiment. These feelings may be eventually replaced by positive, possibly euphoric feelings about one's Blackness. Positive feelings about one's Blackness allow one to be socially committed on a humanistic level rather than merely a racial level which, in turn, allows one to develop a world view and behavioral style that is not restricted by one's own racial attitudes.

In general, the results of the multidimensional scaling analysis confirm Cross's (1971, 1978) early views of the identity development process in that the items do tend to align themselves in a pattern that could be indicative of a stagewise process. Missing from the pattern is a clearly discernable collection of Encounter items; possibly because this stage represents a period of transition and confusion, it is difficult to construct a set of items that can capture the essence of this stage adequately. On the other hand, the bidimensionality of attitudes present in Quadrant 2 may reflect a measurement version of the wavering between White and Black identities that characterizes Encounter.

Stability of Racial Identity Attitudes

Whether or not one conceptualizes stages and attitudes as synonymous, an important measurement question is whether either approach describes a relatively stable linear process as Cross (1971) proposed. If the process is linear and unidirectional, then a person should be able to move forward along the developmental continuum, but not backwards. Thus, for instance, a person with a preponderance of Immersion/Emersion attitudes and/or who is in the Immersion/Emersion stage could possibly remain at this level of development, or he or she could potentially move forward into Internalization, but the person should be incapable of moving back to the developmentally less sophisticated stages, Preencounter or Encounter.

The assumption that racial identity is relatively stable means that a person's racial identity attitudes are enduring personality characteristics that consistently influence the person's interactions within various environments, rather than transitory states likely to shift and to be triggered by the vicissitudes of changing environments. To address the theoretical issue of whether racial identity does proceed according to a relatively stable linear process, longitudinal studies of racial identity development, in which people's levels of identity are measured at more than one point in time, are needed. Since such studies do not exist currently, resolution of this theoretical issue must probably await the birth of such studies.

METHODOLOGICAL ISSUES

While it is customary to *think* about developing and standardizing personality measures on large, representative samples similar to the population on which the measure is to be used, this ideal is rarely reached in practice. When measurement construction ideals are not met, questions can always be raised about the general applicability of the resulting measure. With respect to this point and the RIAS-B, four general methodological issues seem important to consider. They are (a) sampling and scale development procedures, (b) evidence of scale reliability, (c) evidence of scale validity, and (d) the rationale for scoring procedures.

In developing the RIAS-B, we have attempted to anticipate concerns about the generalizability of the scale via the manner in which the RIAS-B has been constructed. Three versions of the RIAS-B have existed. Table 3.2 shows the items comprising the short form of the Racial Identity Attitude Scale, called RIAS-B (short form). The long form of the scale consists of an additional 20 items and is called RIAS-B (long form). Different versions of the scale have evolved as psychometric information about the properties of the scale has accumulated.

Sample. Psychometric analyses have been conducted on successive and

Table 3.2
Items Comprising the Black Racial Identity Attitude Scale (RIAS-B)

Item	Type of Attitude	Cluster
1. I believe that being Black is a positive experience.	Int	7
2. I know through experience what being Black in America means.	Int	8
3. I feel unable to involve myself in White experiences, and am increasing my involvement in Black experiences.	Enc/Im	6
4. I believe that large numbers of Blacks are untrustworthy.	Pre	2
5. I feel an overwhelming attachment to Black people.	Int	7
6. I involve myself in causes that will help all oppressed people.	Int	8
7. I feel comfortable wherever I am.	Filler	10
8. I believe that White people look and express themselves better than Blacks.	Pre	2
9. I feel very uncomfortable around Black people.	Pre	3
10. I feel good about being Black, but do not limit myself to Black activities.	Int	9
11. I often find myself referring to White people as honkies, devils, pigs, etc.	Im	6
12. I believe that to be Black is not necessarily good.	Pre	1
13. I believe that certain aspects of the Black experience apply to me, and others do not.	Filler	
14. I frequently confront the system and the man.	Im	8
15. I constantly involve myself in Black political and social activities (art shows, political meetings, etc.)	Filler	10
16. I involve myself in social action and political groups even if there are no other Blacks involved.	Filler	10

Table 3.2 (continued)

Item	Type of Attitude	Cluster
17. I believe that Black people should learn to think and experience life in ways which are similar to White people.	Pre	1
18. I believe that the world should be interpreted from a Black perspective.	Im	6
19. I have changed my style of life to fit my beliefs about Black people.	Im	5
20. I feel excitement and joy in Black surroundings.	Int	8
21. I believe that Black people came from a strange, dark, and uncivilized continent.	Pre	4
22. People, regardless of their race, have strengths and limitations.	Int	9
23. I find myself reading a lot of Black literature and thinking about being Black.	Enc	7
24. I feel guilty and/or anxious about some of the things I believe about Black people.	Enc/Pre	3
25. I believe that a Black person's most effective weapon for solving problems is to become a part of the White person's world.	Pre	1
26. I speak my mind regardless of the consequences (e.g., being kicked out of school, being imprisoned, being exposed to danger.	Im	7
27. I believe that everything Black is good, and consequently, I limit myself to Black activities.	Im	5
28. I am determined to find my Black identity.	Int	7
29. I believe that White people are intellectually superior to Blacks.	Pre	4
30. I believe that because I am Black, I have many strengths.	Int	7

Note: Pre = Preencounter; Enc = Encounter, Im = Immersion/Emersion; In = Internalization. Cluster numbers refer to Figure 1.

43

combined samples as additional samples have been obtained. So, for instance, Parham and Helms (1981) did the original item analyses and reliability studies of the scale using a sample of 58 Midwestern university students. Helms and Parham (in press) did a factor analytic study and additional reliability investigations of the scale using a sample of 250 university students, approximately half from the first study and the remainder from Parham's (1982) sample of university students. Subsequent item additions and deletions have occurred as new samples have been added to our data base.

Thus, the current versions of the scale, RIAS-B (short) and RIAS-B (long), have been developed using a diverse sample of college and university students. The diversity is reflected in terms of the samples' age (ranging from 17 to 72 years), gender (approximately balanced), geographical regions (North, South, East, West), type of educational institution (private colleges as well as state universities and community colleges), and racial composition of the respondents' environments (predominantly Black versus predominantly White). Therefore, it seems reasonable to assume that the RIAS-B can be appropriately used to assess the racial identity of Black male and female college/university students. Whether it can be appropriately used to assess the identity of noncollege populations remains to be determined.

Reliability Evidence. A minimum criterion for using the scale is that it possess internal consistency, that is, that the subscales of the inventory assess different types of attitudes consistently. So far, a series of reliability studies have been designed to examine this property of the individual subscales. In each of these studies, Cronbach's alpha has been used to calculate reliability estimates for the subscales. Obtained reliabilities for the short form subscales have been reported as follows: Preencounter = .69; Encounter = .50; Immersion/Emersion = .67; Internalization = .79. The long form represents an attempt to improve the reliabilities of the subscale by adding more items of similar content. Reliability estimates of the longer version have been reported as follows: Preencounter = .76; Encounter = .51; Immersion/Emersion = .69; Internalization = .80 (Helms & Parham, in press).

In general, the obtained reliabilities are moderate and compare favorably with those obtained for non-culture specific personality measures (Anastasi, 1982). Notice also that although lengthening the inventory did improve the reliability of three of the four subscales somewhat, the reliability of the Encounter scale was quite modest (approximately equaling the median reliability of .54 reported by Anastasi for other personality measures). This finding seems to be attributable to the dynamic changeable nature of these attitudes. It is difficult to measure a phenomenon consistently if the phenomenon itself is not consistent.

Validity Evidence. In a sense, most of the empirical studies of which the present book is composed address the issue of the validity of the RIAS-B. In anticipation of these studies, it seems fair to state that the scale generally seems to predict characteristics that should be related to racial identity according to theory, but does not predict those that should not be related. Examples of the former are self-esteem, affective states, and preference for therapists' race. An example of the latter is social class as variously measured.

Two other studies provide direct evidence about the validity of the RIAS-B. The first, which assesses the construct validity of the scale, was a factor analytic study conducted by Helms and Parham (in press). In several separate analyses, they found that four orthogonal factors essentially explained the RIAS-B (short form) items, and these factors seemed to reflect the four types of racial identity attitudes.

The second validity study examined the relationship between the original RIAS and Milliones's (1980) DIBC, also a measure of racial identity development. In this study, Grace (1984) found that parallel scales on the two measures were appropriately correlated with respect to direction. Thus, although it still seems advisable to consider the RIAS-B to be an experimental scale, evidence does exist to suggest that it predicts racial identity constructs in a manner consistent with racial identity development theory.

Scoring. Considerable controversy exists concerning how the RIAS-B should be scored and the solution to this issue is tied, in part, to one's manner of operationalizing the construct of stage. On the one hand, if one considers stage to be a discrete category into which a person should be placed and further assumes that attitudes and stages are synonymous, then it makes sense to devise a scoring plan whereby a person's highest mean score on a single scale can be used to so place her or him. The first version of the Racial Identity Attitude Scale initially was based on this scoring premise (Parham & Helms, 1981).

On the other hand, if one considers stages to contribute to types of attitudes, all of which are held by a person to some extent, then it makes sense to use scoring procedures that allow the scale administrator to make use of the scale-taker's scores on all four subscales. This latter philosophy underlies recent usage of the scale and seems appropriate given the previous discussion concerning the complexity of stages of identity as well as the subscales that purport to measure them. Be that as it may, different scoring procedures are likely to permit different interpretations of one's results.

IMPLICATIONS FOR COUNSELING AND PSYCHOLOGY

Whether one uses a personality measure such as the RIAS or relies on clinical interviewing techniques, the evidence presented in the present discussion points the way toward some fruitful avenues to explore in route to diagnosing a client's racial identity. First of all, an assessment of all three components of the client's racial world view(s) (i.e., personal identity, reference-group orientation, ascribed identity) seems in order, since it may provide clues about important affective and behavioral issues.

For instance, the person whose attitudes are primarily Preencounter may also have adapted either a Black-deprecatory or assimilationist world view as far as reference-group orientation and ascribed identity are concerned. It appears that painful feelings may be associated more with the former adaptation than the latter. Yet the latter, which also may be dysfunctional in the long run, is not easily recognized because it so closely matches White behavioral norms. Thus, the therapist's task may be to discover how these attitudes are expressed symptomatically.

The Immersion person whose world view has become separatist may express attitudes, feelings, and behavioral styles that are potentially self-defeating. It is not unusual, for example, for the person to direct feelings of anger and hostility inward rather than outward and/or to displace such feelings. In such cases, it may be the therapist's task to help the person to accept those feelings that are her or his due and to relinquish those that are not. Likewise, psychological and/or physical withdrawal may not always be a feasible alternative for people whose attitudes are primarily Immersion, and often they become angry with themselves or feel guilty because of self-perceived disloyalty to their reference group, other Blacks. The therapist's assessment responsibility once he or she determines that a person's attitudes are primarily Immersion is to help the client discover how his or her attitudes and feelings are currently being expressed as well as how they can be expressed more beneficially.

The end of the Immersion stage is Emersion. During this phase, the person's world view is Black, but it is proactive rather than reactive. The therapist's diagnostic task here is primarily to determine whether the client has access to environmental resources that will further the developmental process.

In a diagnostic interview, the distinction between the rationality of Internalization attitudes and the denial characteristic of Preencounter attitudes is often subtle. The primary difference seems to be that when pressed about his or her viewpoints, it is clear that the Internalization person is certain and confident of his or her own Blackness, whereas the Preencounter person seems confused about whether or not he or she is Black and can more easily get in touch with dissimilarities rather than similarities between herself or himself and other Blacks. It is also the case that Preencounter clients more often seem to be coping with self-generated uncomfortable feelings regarding racial matters, whereas if Internalization clients are dealing with such feelings, they typically have been triggered by some environmental events. Thus, the task of the therapist in the case of the Internalization person is to help clarify the nature of the environmental presses; the therapist should also seek to determine whether the Internalizing person's rational approach to life prevents him or her from acknowledging his or her feelings about the injustices that happen in life.

SUMMARY

The RIAS-B is a rationally constructed scale that was designed to measure attitudes specific to a particular theory of racial identity, Cross's (1971) Negro-to-Black self-actualization model. Development of the scale has been an ongoing process in which successive samples have been used to explore the psychometric properties of the scale. For the most part, it appears that the subscales of the RIAS typically "behave" in a manner consistent with theory. However, to date, the scale has been used with college and university samples exclusively and thus one must ask whether it has heuristic value for other types of populations. In addition, issues remain concerning whether the theory describes a stagewise process that actually occurs in reality and, consequently, whether the RIAS-B is appropriately sensitive to such a process. Nevertheless, therapists may be able to use the RIAS-B and/or clinical interviews to formulate hypotheses about relevant therapy issues.

4

Toward a Model of White Racial Identity Development

JANET E. HELMS

The development of White identity in the United States is closely inter-
twined with the development and progress of racism in this country.
The greater the extent that racism exists and is denied, the less possible
it is to develop a positive White identity. J. M. Jones (1972, 1981) has
identified three types of racism: (a) individual, that is, personal attitudes,
beliefs, and behaviors designed to convince oneself of the superiority of
Whites and the inferiority of non-White racial groups; (b) institutional,
meaning social policies, laws, and regulations whose purpose is to maintain the economic and social advantages of Whites over non-Whites; and
(c) cultural, that is, societal beliefs and customs that promote the assumption that the products of White culture (e.g., language, traditions,
appearance) are superior to those of non-White cultures.

Because each of these three types of racism is so much a part of the
cultural milieu, each can become a part of the White person's racial
identity or consciousness ipso facto. In order to develop a healthy White
identity, defined in part as a nonracist identity, virtually every White
person in the United States must overcome one or more of these aspects
of racism. Additionally, he or she must accept his or her own Whiteness,
the cultural implications of being White, and define a view of Self as a
racial being that does not depend on the perceived superiority of one
racial group over another.

Thus, the evolution of a positive White racial identity consists of two
processes, the abandonment of racism and the development of a non-
racist White identity. Because White racism in the United States seems

to have developed as a means of justifying the enslavement of Black Americans during the slavery eras of the 1700s and 1800s (cf. Comer, 1980; Cross et al., in press; Giddings, 1984), Blacks and/or Black culture have been the primary "outgroup" or reference group around which White racial identity development issues revolve. Thus, as is the case with Black racial identity, White racial identity contains parallel beliefs and attitudes about Whites as well as Blacks.

For the most part, theories or models of White racial identity development have focused on defining racism. Some of these perspectives are summarized in Table 4.1. As shown in Table 4.1, most of these models are typologies, that is, they assume that racists can be classified according to various categories. Moreover, most of these early perspectives were fueled by the implicit assumption that racism was only damaging to the victims of the resulting oppression but did not consider their effects on the beneficiaries or perpetrators of racism.

Only recently have theorists begun to speculate about the harmful consequences of racism on the perpetuators of racism, which include the absence of a positive White racial identity. In presenting the case for the need to help Whites develop a positive White identity, various authors have discussed the defense mechanisms by which Whites pretend that they are not White. For instance, J. Katz and Ivey (1977) noted that when faced with the question of their racial identification, Whites merely deny that they are White. They observed: "Ask a White person what he or she is racially and you may get the answer "Italian," "English," "Catholic," or "Jewish." *White people do not see themselves as White*" (p. 486). Relatedly, Terry (1981) commented, "To be white in America is not to have to think about it. Except for hard-core racial supremacists, the meaning of being White is having the choice of attending to or ignoring one's own Whiteness" (p. 120). If these authors' surmises are accurate, then it appears that most Whites may have no consistent conception of a positive White identity or consciousness. As a consequence, Whites may feel threatened by the actual or presupposed presence of racial consciousness in non-White racial groups.

In exploring the emotional consequences of racism to Whites, Karp (1981) indicated that major concomitants of racism and Whites' distorted views of racial identity are negative feelings such as "self-deception," "self-hate," and "guilt and shame, along with feeling bad about being white (sometimes expressed as a flip side—rigid pride in 'superiority')" (p. 89). She further suggests that these feelings can contribute to distorted behaviors as well as distorted views of the world. Dennis (1981) discussed the many "selves" into which a White person must compartmentalize her or his feelings and thoughts in order to be accepted by other Whites. In passing, it should be noted that theorists and researchers have viewed similar symptoms (e.g., racial denial, self-hate, feelings of

Table 4.1
Summary of White Racial Identity Models

Author	Model Type	Components Name		Description	
Carney & Kahn (1984)	Stage	1.	Stage 1	1.	Knowledge of ethnically dissimilar people is based on stereotypes.
		2.	Stage 2	2.	Recognizes own cultural embeddedness, but deals with other groups in detached scholarly manner.
		3.	Stage 3	3.	Either denies the importance of race or expresses anger toward her/his own cultural group.
		4.	Stage 4	4.	Begins blending aspects of her/his cultural reference group with those of other groups to form a new self-identity.
		5.	Stage 5	5.	Attempts to act to promote social equality and cultural pluralism.
Ganter (1977)	Stage	1.	Phase 1	1.	Protest and denial that Whites are patrons and pawns of racism.
		2.	Phase 2	2.	Guilt and despair as racism is acknowledged.
		3.	Phase 3	3.	Integrates awareness of Whites' collective loss of human integrity and attempts to free oneself from racism.
Hardiman (1979)	Stage	1.	Acceptance	1.	Active or passive acceptance of White superiority.
		2.	Resistance	2.	Person becomes aware of own racial identity for the first time.
		3.	Redefinition	3.	Attempts to redefine Whiteness from a non-racist perspective.
		4.	Internali-zation	4.	Internalizes non-racist White identity.
Helms (1984)	Stage	1.	Contact	1.	Obliviousness to own racial identity.
		2.	Disinte-gration	2.	First acknowledgment of White identity.

Table 4.1 (continued)

Author	Model Type	Components		
			Name	Description
		3.	Reinte-gration	3. Idealizes Whites/denigrates Blacks.
		4.	Pseudo-In-dependence	4. Intellectualized acceptance of own and others' race.
		5.	Immersion/Emersion	5. Honest appraisal of racism and significance of Whiteness.
		6.	Autonomy	6. Internalizes a multi-cultural identity with non-racist Whiteness as its core.
Kovel (1970) Gaertner (1976) Jones (1972)	Type	1.	Dominative racist	1. Openly seeks to keep Black people in inferior positions and will use force to do so.
		2.	Aversive Dominative Racist	2. Believes in White superiority, but tries to ignore the existence of Black people to avoid intrapsychic conflict.
		3.	Aversive Liberal racist	3. Despite aversion to Blacks, uses impersonal social reforms to improve Blacks' conditions.
		4.	Ambivalent	4. Expresses exaggeratedly positive or negative responses toward Blacks depending on the consequences to the White person.
		5.	Non-racist	5. Does not reveal any racist tendencies.
Terry (1977)	Type	1.	Color blind	1. Attempts to ignore race; feels one can exonerate self from being White by asserting one's humanness; equates acknowledgment of color with racism.
		2.	White Blacks	2. Abandons Whiteness in favor of overidentifying with Blacks; denies own Whiteness; tries to gain personal recognition from Blacks for being "almost Black".
		3.	New Whites	3. Holds a pluralistic racial view of the world; recognizes that racism is a White problem and attempts to eliminate it.

Note: Gaerther (1976) and J. M. Jones (1972) elaborated the typology originally proposed by Kovel (1970).

inferiority, etc.) as cause for alarm and serious psychological intervention in Black communities. However, it does not seem that similar enthusiasm has been expended in promoting healthy White racial identity development.

Implicit in much of the contemporary writings on White racial identity development is the awareness that, in spite of the pervasive socialization toward racism, some White people do appear not only to have developed a White consciousness, but one that is not predominated by racial distortions. Some authors have even loosely described an orderly process by which a White person can move from a racist identity to a positive White consciousness. In describing the process by which some Whites have overcome racism, Dennis observed: "one sees them moving from 'knowing' Blacks to knowing Blacks, from deracialization to reracialization, toward a more 'objective' approach to race with a clearer understanding of the role of race and culture in society" (p. 74). Karp (1981) described the process as follows: "Whites [must address] their feelings of oppression [must seek out] accurate information, [must discharge] feelings related to racism, and [consequently change] their attitudes and behaviors" (p. 88). Thus, Dennis essentially proposes a cognitive process of White identity development, whereas Karp emphasizes the interrelatedness of emotions, attitudes, and behaviors.

At least two of the White identity typologists (Pettigrew, 1981; Terry, 1981) have speculated more systematically about the relationship of White racial identity to Whites' psychological health. Applying Jahoda's (1958) trichotomy of "sick," "not healthy," and "well" to describe the psychological consequences to Whites of racism, Pettigrew (1981) concluded that roughly 15 to 75% of Whites were in the categories of sick or not healthy as a consequence of internalizing some form of personal racial bigotry. Terry's (1977) categorical system recognized that there were different ways that one could acknowledge and, consequently, be White (see Table 4.1), just as there were different ways that one could be racist. However, from none of the typological perspectives is it clear how or whether a person can shift from one type of identity or category to another.

Working independently, in separate places and at different times, Hardiman (1979) and Helms (1984b) proposed developmental models of White racial identity development. Both models are similar in that they propose a linear process of attitudinal development in which the White person potentially progresses through a series of stages differing in the extent to which they involve acknowledgment of racism and consciousness of Whiteness. They differ in the particulars of some of the stages, though both agree that the highest stage involves an awareness of personal responsibility for racism, consistent acknowledgment of one's Whiteness, and abandonment of racism in any of its forms as a defining aspect of one's personality. Hardiman's theoretical model is summarized in Table 4.1. However, since Helms's model has been subjected to empirical investigation and (to the author's knowledge) Hardiman's has not, Helms's model is the primary theoretical basis for the subsequent presentation of White racial identity development. Consequently, it will be presented in some detail.

STAGES OF WHITE RACIAL IDENTITY DEVELOPMENT

One of the concomitants of being a White person in the United States is that one is a member of a numerical majority as well as the socioeconomically and politically dominant group. One result of this racial status is that, as Dennis (1981) points out, even if one has few resources oneself, as long as one has White skin in America, one is entitled to feel superior to Blacks. This sense of entitlement seems to be a basic norm of White society.

Perhaps more importantly, as previously noted, if one is a White person in the United States, it is still possible to exist without ever having to acknowledge that reality. In fact, it is only when Whites come in contact with the idea of Blacks (or other visible racial/ethnic groups) that Whiteness becomes a potential issue. Whether or not this initial contact has any implications for racial identity development depends upon the extent to which it is unavoidable. Thus, if the Black (in this instance) presence "intrudes" into the White person's environment, and the intrusion cannot be ignored or controlled, then the White person is likely to be forced to deal with White racial identity issues somewhat. However, to the extent that such intrusions can be avoided, which may still be the case in much of White America, one can avoid resolving White racial identity issues. That is, one can choose to be oblivious to race and the differential effects of race on how one is perceived and treated by society at large; or one can decide to remain fixated at one of the identity stages to be described subsequently.

There are two primary ways by which one can become aware of the presence of Blacks as an outgroup: vicariously or directly. Vicarious awareness occurs when significant persons in one's life (e.g., media, parents, peers) inform one of the existence of Blacks as well as how one ought to think about them. Dennis (1981) does an excellent job of describing how Whites are socialized directly and indirectly to fear and devalue Blacks. Direct awareness occurs when the White person interacts with Blacks himself or herself. These two means of awareness are not necessarily exclusive, as Dennis points out. Nevertheless, though one's own initial experiences with Blacks may be pleasant and non-individually racist, significant White persons in one's environment may use the socialization pressures available to them to ensure that the White person learns the rules of being a socially accepted White person. A number of autobiographical accounts (e.g., McLaurin, 1987; L. Smith, 1961), usually written from a Southern perspective, describe how Whites are taught to develop individual racism.

Recall that institutional and cultural racism are so much a part of the White (or Black) individual's world that he or she is often blind to their presence. Thus, the White person's developmental tasks with regard to development of a healthy White identity, according to both Hardiman's (1979) and Helms's (1984b) perspectives, require the abandonment of individual racism as well as the recognition of and active opposition to institutional and cultural racism. Concurrently, the person must become aware of her or his Whiteness, learn to accept Whiteness as an important part of herself or himself, and to internalize a realistically positive view of what it means to be White.

Helms (1984) originally proposed that White racial identity development occurred via a five-stage process, each involving attitudes, emotions, and behaviors in which Whites as well as Blacks are referents. More recently, she has included a sixth stage, Immersion/Emersion, to reflect Hardiman's (1979) contention that it is possible for Whites to seek out accurate information about their historical, political, and cultural contributions to the world, and that the process of self-examination within this context is an important component of the process of defining a positive White identity.

Thus, presently, Helms conceptualizes a two-phase process of White identity development. As illustrated in Figure 4.1, Phase 1, the abandonment of racism, begins with the Contact stage and ends with the Reintegration stage. Phase 2, defining a positive White identity, begins with the Pseudo-Independent stage and ends with the Autonomy stage.

Contact

As soon as one encounters the idea or the actuality of Black people, one has entered the Contact stage of identity. Depending somewhat upon one's racial (particularly) familial environment, one will enter Contact with either naive curiosity or timidity and trepedation about Blacks and a superficial and inconsistent awareness of being White. When one is in Contact, if one exhibits individual racism, it is probably exhibited in a weak and unsophisticated form since the person is just beginning to try her or his racial wings. Nevertheless, the person in Contact automatically benefits from institutional and cultural racism without necessarily being aware that he or she is doing so.

Oddly enough, the person in Contact may enjoy being a racist more than persons at the other stages simply because he or she has not had to confront the moral dilemmas resulting from such an identification. The Contact person's White racial identification is equally subtle. Thus,

Figure 4.1
Stages and Phases of White Racial Identity Development

Phase I: Abandonment of Racism

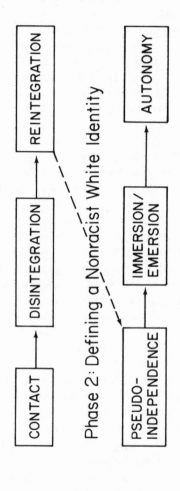

Phase 2: Defining a Nonracist White Identity

although such a person evaluates Blacks according to White criteria (e.g., White physical appearance, standardized tests, etc.), he or she does so automatically without awareness that other criteria are possible, and that he or she might be as legitimately evaluated according to other racial/ cultural groups' criteria.

Behaviors thought to characterize Contact people are limited interracial social or occupational interaction with Blacks, unless the interaction is initiated by Blacks who "seem" White except for skin color or other "Black" physical characteristics. In such interactions, the White person uses the Black person to teach him or her about what Black people in general are like and often uses societal stereotypes of Blacks as the standard against which the Black person is evaluated. Comments such as "You don't act like a Black person," or "I don't notice what race a person is," are likely to be made by Contact persons.

Affectively, Contact persons can be expected to have positive self-esteem because they have not yet learned to compartmentalize and differentially value their different selves (cf. Dennis, 1981). They should generally have positive feelings about the "idea" of Blacks and fair treatment of Blacks; though trait anxiety should be low, state anxiety or arousal may be present when actual interactions with Blacks are experienced or anticipated.

One's longevity in the Contact stage depends upon the kinds of experiences one has with Blacks and Whites with respect to racial issues. For instance, as the White person becomes aware of Blacks, if this awareness is based on vicarious information rather than actual experiences, then he or she is likely to remain in the Contact stage, particularly the aspect of the stage associated with fearfulness and caution. This supposition is based on the common observation (e.g., Karp, 1981; Reid, 1979) that the bulk of information available to Whites (and Blacks) about Blacks is negative. In such cases, the person is likely to continue to engage in minimal cross-racial interaction, is unlikely to be forced to rethink her or his racial perspective, is tolerated by her or his racial peers if he or she makes known her or his Contact perspective, and, of course, is warmly accepted if he or she remains silent about it.

On the other hand, if the Contact person continues to interact with Blacks, sooner or later significant others in the person's environment will make it known that such behavior is unacceptable if one wishes to remain a member in good standing of the "White" group (cf. Boyle, 1962; L. Smith, 1961). Where Blacks are concerned, if Whites in the Contact stage continue to interact with them, sooner or later the Contact person will have to acknowledge that there are differences in how Blacks and Whites in the United States are treated regardless of economic status. Sometimes this awareness may occur because the Black person points out the differences; sometimes it occurs because of obvious acts of discrimination (e.g., cab drivers who pass by Blacks regardless of how they are dressed, but stop for their White associates). Moreover, many Blacks will not join the Contact person in pretending that he or she is also Black (see Terry, 1980). When enough of these "socialization" experiences penetrate the White person's identity system, then he or she can enter the Disintegration stage.

Disintegration

Entry into the Disintegration stage implies conscious, though conflicted, acknowledgment of one's Whiteness. Moreover, it triggers the recognition of moral dilemmas associated with being White as described by Dennis (1981). If some of his dilemmas are reworded to refer to Whites regardless of religion or geographic origin, then they can be summarized as follows:

(a)   the desire to be a religious or moral person versus the recognition that to be accepted by Whites one must treat Blacks immorally;

"[b]   the belief in freedom and democracy versus the belief in racial inequality";

"[c]   the desire to show love and compassion versus the desire to keep Blacks in their place at all costs";

(d)   the belief in treating others with dignity and respect versus the belief that Blacks are not worthy of dignity or respect;

"[e]   the belief that each person should be treated according to his or her individual merits versus the belief that Blacks should be evaluated as a group without regard to individual merits and talents" (p. 78).

Accompanying the conflicted White identification is a questioning of the racial realities the person has been taught to believe. It is probably during this stage, for instance, that the person first comes to realize that in spite of mouthings to the contrary, Blacks and Whites are not considered equals and negative social consequences can besiege the White person who does not respect the inequalities. Moreover, the Disintegration stage may be the time in which the person comes to realize that the social skills and mores he or she has been taught to use in interacting with Blacks rarely work. Thus, the person in Disintegration may not only perceive for the first time that he or she is caught between two racial groups, but may also come to realize that his or her position amongst Whites depends upon his or her ability to successfully "split" her or his personality.

Self-actualization personality theorists such as Rogers (1951) suggest that emotional discomfort, which Rogers calls "incongruence," results when one must markedly alter one's real self in order to be accepted by significant others in one's environment. The feelings of guilt, depression, helplessness, and anxiety described by various authors (e.g., J. Baldwin, 1963; Karp, 1981; J. Katz, 1976) as correlates of Whiteness probably have their origins in the Disintegration stage.

Festinger (1957) theorized that when two or more of a person's cognitions (e.g., beliefs or feelings about oneself) are in conflict, an uncomfortable psychological state that he calls "dissonance" likely results. He suggests that when dissonance is present, a person will not only attempt to reduce it, but will also take steps to avoid situations and information that are likely to increase it. Thus, if one thinks of the uncomfortable feelings resulting from White moral ambivalence as previously described as dissonance, then it seems plausible that the same sorts of strategies used to reduce dissonance in general may also be used to reduce race-related dissonance.

Festinger proposed three ways of reducing dissonance: (a) changing a behavior, (b) changing an environmental belief, and (c) developing new beliefs. Accordingly, the person in the Disintegration stage might reduce discomfort by (a) avoiding further contact with Blacks (changing a behavior), (b) attempting to convince significant others in her or his environment that Blacks are not so inferior (changing an environmental belief), or (c) seeking information from Blacks or Whites to the effect that either racism is not the White person's fault or does not really exist (adding new beliefs). Additionally, as a means of avoiding an increase in dissonance, the person may selectively attend only to information that gives him or her greater confidence in the new beliefs and/or he or she will interact only with those who can be counted on to support the new belief.

Which alternative the White person chooses probably depends on the extent to which her or his cross-racial interactions are voluntary. It seems likely that the person who can remove herself or himself from interracial environments or can remove Blacks from White environments will do so. Given the racial differences in social and economic power, most Whites can choose this option. If they do so, they will receive much support in an exclusively White environment for the development of individual racism as well as the maintenance of cultural and institutional racism.

Attempts to change others' attitudes probably occur initially amongst Whites who were raised and/or socialized in an environment in which White "liberal" attitudes (though not necessarily behaviors) were expressed. However, due to the racial naiveté with which this approach may be undertaken and the person's ambivalent racial identification, this dissonance-reducing strategy is likely to be met with rejection by Whites as well as Blacks.

To the extent that cross-racial interaction is unavoidable, the White person will attempt to develop new beliefs. However, the desire to be accepted by one's own racial group and the prevalence in the White group of the covert and overt belief in White superiority and Black inferiority virtually dictates that the content of the person's belief system will also change in a similar direction. As this reshaping of the person's cognitions or beliefs occurs, he or she enters the Reintegration stage.

Reintegration

In the Reintegration stage, the person consciously acknowledges a White identity. In the absence of contradictory experiences, to be White in America is to believe that one is superior to people of color. Consequently, the Reintegration person accepts the belief in White racial superiority and Black inferiority. He or she comes to believe that institutional and cultural racism are the White person's due because he or she has earned such privileges and preferences. Race-related negative conditions are assumed to result from Black people's inferior social, moral, and intellectual qualities, and thus, it is not unusual to find persons in the Reintegration stage selectively attending to and/or reinterpreting information to conform to societal stereotypes of Black people. Cross-racial similarities are minimized and/or denied.

Any residual feelings of guilt and anxiety are transformed into fear and anger toward Black people. Much of the person's cross-racial behavior is motivated by these feelings. Though the feelings may not be overtly expressed, they lie just below the surface of the person's awareness, and it only takes an event(s) that can be characterized (whether or not it actually is) by the White person as personally threatening for these feelings to be unleashed.

Behaviorally, people in the Reintegration stage may express their beliefs and feelings either passively or actively. Passive expression involves deliberate removal of oneself and/or avoidance of environments in which one might encounter Black people. In this instance, honest discussion of racial matters is most likely to occur among same-race peers who share or are believed to share a similar view of the world. Active expression may include treating Blacks as inferior and involve acts of violence or exclusion designed to protect White privilege.

In this society, it is fairly easy to remain or fixate at the Reintegration stage, particularly if one is relatively passive in one's expression of it. A personally jarring event is probably necessary for the person to begin to abandon this essentially racist identity. Again, the event can be direct or vicarious; it can be caused by painful or insightful encounters with Black or White persons. Changes in the environmental racial climate may also trigger transition from the Reintegration stage. For instance, the Civil Rights Movement of the 1960s and the Vietnam War caused some Whites to question their racial identity, though hopefully the catalyst for such self-examination does not have to be so major. Be that as it may, once the person begins to question her or his previous definition of Whiteness and the justifiability of racism in any of its forms, then he or she has begun the movement into the Pseudo-Independent or Liberal stage.

Pseudo-Independent

Pseudo-Independent is the first stage of redefining a positive White identity. In this stage, the person begins actively to question the proposition that Blacks are innately inferior to Whites. Instead, in this stage, the person begins to acknowledge the responsibility of Whites for racism and to see how he or she wittingly and unwittingly perpetuates racism. Consequently, he or she is no longer comfortable with a racist identity and begins to search for ways to redefine her or his White identity. Usually the redefining process takes the form of intellectual acceptance and curiosity about Blacks.

The Pseudo-Independent stage is primarily a stage of intellectualization in which the person attempts to submerge the tumultuous feelings about Whiteness that were aroused in previous stages. To the extent that feelings concerning racial identity issues are allowed to emerge, they are apt to be feelings of commiseration with Blacks and perhaps disquietude concerning racial issues in White peer groups.

Nevertheless, though the person in the Pseudo-Independent stage is abandoning the belief in White superiority/Black inferiority, he or she may still behave in ways that unwittingly perpetuate this belief system. That is, though the person may seek greater interaction with Blacks, much of this interaction involves helping Blacks to change themselves so that they function more like Whites on White criteria for success and acceptability rather than recognizing that such criteria might be inappropriate and/or too narrowly defined. Furthermore, cultural or racial differences are likely to be interpreted by using White life experiences as the standards. Moreover, the Pseudo-Independent person still looks to Black rather than White people to explain racism and seeks solutions for it in hypothetical Black cultural dysfunctionalities.

Although the person in the Pseudo-Independent stage no longer has a negative White identity or consciousness, neither does he or she have a positive one. The paucity of White models of positive Whiteness means that the person usually has no visible standards against which to compare and/or modify himself or herself. Additionally, such a person is likely to be met with considerable suspicion from other Whites as well as Blacks.

Many Whites will treat the Pseudo-Independent person, who actively expresses this identity, as though he or she has violated White racial norms. Many Black people will be suspicious of the motives of a person who devotes so much attention to helping Blacks rather than changing Whites. Consequently, the Pseudo-Independent person may not feel entirely comfortable with her or his White identity, but overidentification with Blacks is also not likely to be very comfortable. Thus, the person may come to feel rather marginal where race and racial issues are concerned. However, if the personal rewards (e.g., self-esteem, monetary, etc.) are great enough to encourage continued strengthening of a positive White identity, then the person may begin the quest for those positive aspects of Whiteness that are unrelated to racism. The quest for a better definition of Whiteness signals the person's entry into the Immersion/Emersion stage.

Immersion/Emersion

Redefining a positive White identity requires that the person replace White and Black myths and stereotypes with accurate information about what it means and has meant to be White in the United States as well as in the world in general. The person in this stage is searching for the answers to the questions: "Who am I racially?" and "Who do I want to be?" and "Who are you really?"

Often such a person will immerse herself or himself in biographies and autobiographies of Whites who have made similar identity journeys. He or she may participate in White consciousness-raising groups whose purpose is to help the person discover her or his individual self-interest in abandoning racism and acknowledging a White racial identity. Changing Black people is no longer the focus of her or his activities, but rather the goal of changing White people becomes salient.

Emotional as well as cognitive restructuring can happen during this stage. Successful resolution of this stage apparently requires emotional catharsis in which the person reexperiences previous emotions that were denied or distorted (cf. Lipsky, 1978). Once these negative feelings are expressed, the person may begin to feel a euphoria perhaps akin to a religious rebirth. These positive feelings not only help to buttress the newly developing White identity, but provide the fuel by which the person can truly begin to tackle racism and oppression in its various forms.

Autonomy

Internalizing, nurturing, and applying the new definition of Whiteness evolved in the earlier stages are major goals of the Autonomy stage. In this stage, the person no longer feels a need to oppress, idealize, or denigrate people on the basis of group membership characteristics such

Figure 4.2
A Workshop Activity on Self-Assessing White Racial Identity

For each of the subsequent items, use the following scale to indicate the extent to which the item is true of you.

4 - Strongly Agree
3 - Agree
2 - Disagree
1 - Strongly Disagree

Write the numbers of your responses on the line next to the item. Add together your responses to the item precededs by the same combination of letters and plot your scores on the graph. Draw a line to connect your C total, R total, D total, P total, E total, and A total. Draw another line to connect the totals preceded by double letters (e.g., CB). This will give you a racial identity profile.

C1. _____   There is no race problem in the United States.

C2. _____   Racism only exists in the minds of a few Black people.

C3. _____   I personally do not notice what race a person is.

_____   C TOTAL

CB1. _____   I have asked or would ask a Black person to help me understand how I might be prejudiced.

CB2. _____   I contribute or would contribute money or time to social programs to help Blacks.

CB3. _____   I participate or would participate in an activity to help Blacks overcome their poor environment.

_____   CB TOTAL

R1. _____   I believe that White culture or Western civilization is the most highly developed, sophisticated culture ever to have existed on earth.

R2. _____   Africans and Blacks are more sexually promiscuous than Europeans and Whites.

R3. _____   The White race will be polluted by intermarriage with Blacks.

_____   R TOTAL

RB1. _____   When a Black male stranger sits or stands next to me in a public place, I move away from him.

RB2. _____   I live or would live in a segregated (White) neighborhood.

RB3. _____   The people I do my non-business related socializing with either are Whites or Blacks who "act White."

_____   RB TOTAL

D1. _____   American society is sick, evil, and racist.

D2. _____   There is nothing I can do to prevent racism.

D3. _____   I avoid thinking about racial issues.

_____   D TOTAL

Figure 4.2 (continued)

P1. _____ It is White people's responsibility to eliminate racism in the United States.

P2. _____ Eliminating racism would help Whites feel better about themselves.

P3. _____ White people should help Black people become equal to Whites.

_____ P TOTAL

PB1. _____ I have boycotted a company or its products because of its racist programs.

PB2. _____ For Martin Luther King's Birthday, I attend or would attend a commemorative event.

PB3. _____ I have tried to help Whites understand Blacks.

_____ LB TOTAL

E1. _____ White culture and society must be restructured to eliminate racism and opposition.

E2. _____ Whites and White culture are not superior to Blacks and Black culture.

E3. _____ A multi-cultural society cannot exist unless Whites give up their racism.

_____ E TOTAL

EB1. _____ I have studied the history of White and Western European people.

EB2. _____ I meet with Whites to discuss our feelings and attitudes about being White and White racism.

EB3. _____ I have conducted activities to help Whites overcome their racism.

_____ EB TOTAL

A1. _____ I accept that being White does not make me superior to any other racial group.

A2. _____ Being a member of a multi-racial environment is a must for me.

A3. _____ My Whiteness is an important part of who I am.

_____ A TOTAL

AB1. _____ I speak up in a White group situation when I feel that a White person is being racist.

AB2. _____ I express my honest opinion when a Black person is present without worrying about whether I appear racist.

AB3. _____ I attempt to explain to White friends and relatives the relationship of racism to other forms of oppression.

_____ AB TOTAL

Figure 4.2 (continued)

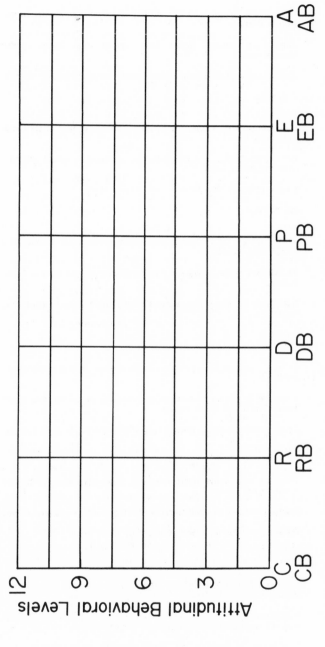

This workshop activity is adapted from Hardiman (1979) and Helms (1984). These items are not from a validated scale and are presented here for the reader's possible self-exploration. Abbreviations are: C = Contact attitudes, CB = Contact behavior, R = Reintegration attitudes, RB = Reintegration behavior, D = Disintegration attitudes, DB = Disintegration behavior, P = Pseudo-Independent attitudes, PB = Pseudo-Independent behavior, E = Emersion attitudes, EB = Emersion behavior, A = Autonomy attitudes, AB = Autonomy behavior. Higher scores indicate higher levels of the attitudes/behaviors.

as race because race no longer symbolizes threat to him or her. Since he or she no longer reacts out of rigid world views, it is possible for him or her to abandon cultural and institutional racism as well as personal racism. Thus, one finds the Autonomous person actively seeking opportunities to learn from other cultural groups. One also finds him or her actively becoming increasingly aware of how other forms of oppression (e.g., sexism, ageism) are related to racism and acting to eliminate them as well. Terry's (1977) description of the characteristics of the New White (see Table 4.1) seems to describe the Autonomous person.

Although Autonomy represents the highest level of White racial identity and might be thought of as racial self-actualization or transcendence, perhaps it is best to think of it as an ongoing process. It is a process wherein the person is continually open to new information and new ways of thinking about racial and cultural variables. Nevertheless, reaching the Autonomy stage does not necessarily mean that the person is perfect with respect to all aspects of her or his identity. Chances are if the person had a grouchy personality (i.e., personal identity) before he or she began movement through the racial identity development process, then he or she will still be a grouch once the process is completed. It is just that his or her grouchiness will no longer be governed by cultural or racial determinants. In other words, one might find a variety of personality characteristics and styles among people who have reached the Autonomy stage.

CONCLUSIONS

As might be apparent, each of the White racial identity stages is hypothesized to have its own unique effect on attitudes, behaviors, and emotions. Nevertheless, it is probably not the case that each of these develops at the same rate. In fact, studies of symbolic racism (e.g., McConaghy & Hough, 1976) suggest that attitudes (at least racist attitudes as opposed to White identity attitudes) may change faster than behaviors. As an example of how this is possible, the reader might wish to try out the workshop exercise in Figure 4.2. It seems reasonable to speculate that the greatest discomfort occurs for those individuals whose attitudes, emotions, and behaviors are not in harmony.

5

Development of the White Racial Identity Inventory

JANET E. HELMS
AND ROBERT T. CARTER

An increasing amount of speculation and some theoretical models recently have been developed to explain the racial identity development of White Americans in the United States. Hardiman (1979), in an unpublished paper, summarized several of these models, most of which had grown out of theorists' attempts to characterize the various styles by which Whites could express racism. However, most of the models did not explain how Whites themselves are affected by their racism and, consequently, how it was possible for any of them to develop a healthy non-racist White identity in an essentially racist society.

Working independently, Hardiman (1979) and Helms (1984b) proposed developmental models of White racial identity that were quite similar in many respects. Both suggested that White identity development occurred via a stagewise process in which the White individual moved from a stage of naivete with respect to race or racism to a sophisticated stage of biculturalism or racial transcendence. The primary difference in the two models was that Hardiman placed more emphasis on racism as the catalyst for identity development whereas Helms placed more emphasis on moral dilemmas in social interactions.

DESCRIPTION OF THE WHITE RACIAL IDENTITY ATTITUDE INVENTORY

The White Racial Identity Attitude Scale (WRIAS) was developed to assess attitudes related to the original five stages of White racial identity development proposed by Helms (1984b). Similar to the Black scale, a basic premise underlying the WRIAS scales is that attitudes about Whites, Whiteness, and White culture as well as attitudes about Blacks, Blackness, and Black culture propel the person's racial identity development, though not always consciously. Thus, each stage is characterized by attitudes about Whites and oneself as a White person and attitudes about Blacks and one's relationship to them. The stages, and consequently attitudes reflective of the stages, are aligned from least sensitive to race and racism to most aware or conscious of race and racism. Implicitly, they are also aligned from least to most healthy.

Specifically, the scale measures attitudes hypothesized to derive from membership in the following five stages:

1. Contact—obliviousness to racial/cultural issues. A person in the Contact stage typically approaches the world with a color-blind or cultureless perspective and general naivete about how race and racism impact on herself or himself as well as other people. Such a person generally views Blacks with curiosity and/or trepidation. The person rarely thinks of herself or himself in racial terms.

2. Disintegration—awareness of the social implications of race on a personal level. During this stage, the person may feel caught between White and Black culture, oppression and humanity. On the one hand, she or he does not want to assume responsibility for discrimination by acknowledging his or her Whiteness and the benefits that result therefrom; on the other hand, because one and (usually) one's social environment are not Black, one cannot identify entirely with Blacks or Black culture.

3. Reintegration—idealization of everything perceived to be White and denigration of everything thought to be Black. Anger covertly or overtly expressed as well as projection of one's feelings characterize the person in this stage.

4. Pseudo-Independence—internalization of Whiteness and capacity to recognize personal responsibility to ameliorate the consequences of racism. The person has an intellectual understanding of Black culture and the unfair benefits of growing up White in the United States.

5. Autonomy—bicultural or racially transcendent world view. He or she has internalized a positive, nonracist White identity, values cultural similarities and differences, feels a kinship with people regardless of race, and seeks to acknowledge and abolish racial oppression.

Scale Construction

The WRIAS is a rationally derived scale based on Helms's (1984b) model of White racial identity development. Each of five subscales is measured by 10 items, each of which had a minimum item-total subscale correlation with its own scale of .30 in the original pilot study of the measure. In addition, none of the items correlated significantly with the

Crowne and Marlowe (1964) Social Desirability scale, a measure used to explore the possibility of a social desirability response set.

Scoring

For each of 50 attitudinal statements, respondents are instructed to use five-point Likert scales (1 = Strongly Disagree, 5 = Strongly Agree) to describe themselves. Scores are calculated by adding the point values of the responses marked by respondents for each of the subscales. Each subscale sum is divided by 10 to maintain the scale metric. Zero values are included in the total scores because, according to the theory on which the measure is based, until the person has reached the relevant stage of development, some items may appear to be meaningless. The higher the score, the more descriptive of the respondent is the subscale. Although the attitudinal scales are based on a model that proposes discrete stages of racial identity, it is probably best to use all five of a respondent's scores to form a profile rather than single scores to assign her or him to single stages.

Table 5.1 presents means and some preliminary percentiles broken down by gender for use in comparing each attitudinal scale across samples. Comparison of female and male respondents' mean scores on each of the subscales indicated that the two groups did not differ significantly on any of the subscales. However, males tended to have higher scores on the Autonomy (F (1,504) = 3.59, p = .06) and Pseudo-Independent (F (1,504) = 2.94, p = .09) subscales.

Reliability

In the pilot study of the WRIAS (see Carter, 1984), reliabilities in the .90s for each scale were found. Since then, reliabilities have been calculated in three studies, and are summarized in Table 5.2. Using an amended version of the scale (4 items for each subscale), Westbrook (1986, personal communication) found reliabilities via the Spearman-Brown prophecy formula ranging from .67 (Contact) to .82 (Reintegration). For this chapter, Helms and Carter (Study 1) used the full scale to investigate the racial identity attitudes of a larger sample (N = 506). The Study 1 sample consisted of a combination of samples of White university students attending predominantly White universities in the Eastern United States (cf. Carter, 1987; Carter, Fretz, & Mahalik, 1986; Helms & Carter, 1987). In Study 1, we found reliabilities ranging from .55 (Contact) to .77 (Disintegration).

As shown in Table 5.2, Helms and Carter (1987) found reliabilities ranging from .65 (Pseudo-Independence and Autonomy) to .76 (Disintegration) among participants in a counselor preference study (Study

Table 5.1
Preliminary Means (M), Percentiles (%ile), and Standard Deviations (SD) for the White Racial Identity Attitude Scale

Scale	Females (n=339)		Males (n=167)		Total (N=506)	
	M	SD	M	SD	M	SD
Contact	30.77	4.53	31.16	4.17	30.9	4.17
Disintegration	25.18	5.48	24.91	5.31	25.09	5.42
Reintegration	25.10	5.88	25.02	5.94	25.07	5.89
Pseudo-Independent	35.82	4.88	36.63	5.31	36.08	5.04
Autonomy	33.43	4.93	34.29	4.46	33.71	4.79

	Raw Scores									
%ile	Con		Dis		Rnt		Psu		Aut	
	F	M	F	M	F	M	F	M	F	M
90	36	36	31		31	31	42	43	39	39
80	35	35		30	30	30	40	41	37	
70	33	34	30	28	29	29	39		36	37
60	32	32	27	27	27	27	38	39	35	
50		31	25	25	25	25	36	37	34	35
40	30	30	24	24	23	23	35	36	32	33
30	29	30	22	22	22	22	33	34		32
20	28	28	21	21	20	21	31	32	30	
10	25	26	18	18	18	17	30	30	28	30

Note: Con = contact; Dis = Disintegration; Rnt = Reintegration; Psu = Pseudo-Independent; Aut = Autonomy. F = Female, M = Male.

2). Thus, overall, each scale has been found repeatedly to exceed the median reliability coefficient of .54 reported by Anastasi (1982) for personality tests in general. Therefore, the measure seems to have adequate reliability to warrant further experimental use.

Validity

The WRIAS is a relatively new measure, and thus only limited validity information is presently available. However, the available information is of three types: content, construct, and criterion validity.

Table 5.2
Summary of Studies of the Reliability of the White Racial Identity Attitude
Scale

Scale	Reliability Studies		
	Westbrook	Helms & Carter	
	(N = 350)		
		Study 1	Study 2
		(N = 506)	(N = 176)
Contact	.67	.55	.67
Disintegration	.75	.77	.76
Reintegration	.82	.80	.75
Pseudo–Independence	.77	.71	.65
Autonomy	.74	.67	.65

Content

The measure seems to include items identified by other authors as
being important components of White racial identity development,
though more systematically than is typically the case. However, it is not
intended to be a racism or prejudice scale per se, and therefore, less
emphasis on racism and the measurement of racism is inherent in the
items than is typically the case. As compared to other models of White
racial identity development (see chapter 4), the greatest similarity of the
WRIAS items (and the theory on which they are based) to other theoretical models occurs with respect to one or more of the stages from

Reintegration through Autonomy. Thus, visual examination and logical analysis of the subscales suggests that the items do seem to reflect identity issues considered by White identity theorists (e.g., Hardiman, 1979; Terry, 1977) to be important aspects of White identity development.

Construct

For the WRIAS, construct validity concerns the adequacy of the scale in measuring the hypothetical construct of White racial identity. One strategy for investigating the construct validity of the WRIAS was to examine the interrelationships or correlations among the WRIAS sub-scales. A second strategy for exploring the construct validity of the scale was to factor analyze the 50 items. Both of these analyses are discussed in this section.

Patterns of Correlations

Examination of the patterns of subscale correlations suggests that they are consistent with theory. If one reads horizontally across Table 5.3, then it seems fairly clear, for instance, that Contact attitudes represent weakly positive racial identity attitudes that are most similar to Pseudo-Independent or intellectualized racial attitudes. Disintegration attitudes are most strongly related to Reintegration attitudes, which confirms the notion that these are both related to discomfort with racial issues. Both Disintegration and Reintegration attitudes are related in a negative direction to the other three types of attitudes. Finally, though Pseudo-Independent and Autonomy attitudes are both positively related to Contact attitudes, their strongest positive relationship is with each other.

None of the interscale correlations are high enough to suggest that the scales are redundant. However, the pattern of correlations does seem to confirm that two general "styles" of White racial identity attitudes might exist; one characterized by reactivity and general discomfort with racial issues, the other characterized by positivity and intellectual and/or emotional comfort with racial issues.

Criterion Validity

In assessing the criterion validity of the WRIAS, each of the scales has been correlated with measures of other personality constructs. Evidence of validity is a pattern of correlations in the direction hypothesized by identity theory.

Contact attitudes. Some feelings and/or attitudes have been found to be related to Contact attitudes. McCaine (1986) found that for a sample of White females and males, higher Contact attitudes were associated with

Table 5.3
Summary of Matrix of Correlations among the White Racial Identity Attitude Scale

Scales	2	3	4	5
Contact (1)	-20	-32	49	39
Disintegration (2)		72	-52	-63
Reintegration (3)			-55	-49
Pseudo-Independence (4)				63
Autonomy (5)				

Note: Decimal points omitted. All correlations are significant at or beyond the .01 significance level (degrees of freedom = 181).

lower levels of anxiety. Westbrook (1986, personal communication) found that the following attitudes were more likely to be endorsed if one's Contact attitudes were high: "a family of the same socioeconomic status can move in next door regardless of their race," "it is easy to understand Blacks' complaints about racism on campus," and "Blacks and Whites should room together, even if Whites object." Higher Contact attitudes were related to stronger disagreement with the attitudinal statement, "government and news media respect Blacks too much."

Two studies indirectly support the proposition that Contact attitudes may be related to interpersonal behaviors. In the study by McCaine (1986), White males' and females' Contact attitudes were found to relate to interpersonal style as measured by the Fundamental Interpersonal Relationship Orientation scale (FIRO-B; Schultz, 1958). Specifically, the higher one's Contact attitudes, the less likely one was to report a desire to initiate social contact with others.

Carter (1987) found that Contact attitudes were related to clients' reactions to therapist interventions in a counseling simulation. In his study, the higher their Contact attitudes, the more likely clients were to report reactions of "felt supported" and "understood"; the less likely they were to report reactions of felt "relief" and "no reaction." Reactions were measured via Hill, Helms, Spiegel, and Tichenor's (1988) Client Reactions measure.

Thus, in general, Contact attitudes appear to be related to interpersonal receptivity as long as the person does not have to initiate the interaction himself or herself. However, the theory underlying the scale would suggest that this receptivity may be due to a lack of awareness rather than genuine comfort with cross-racial interactions.

Disintegration attitudes. Westbrook (1986, personal communication) found that Disintegration attitudes were related to several attitudinal statements designed to assess symbolic racism. Higher Disintegration attitudes were related to the beliefs that "government and news media respect Blacks too much" and "Blacks need extra help to graduate"; they were also related to an inability to "understand the anger of Black people in America."

Some evidence suggests that Disintegration attitudes may be related to how White individuals experience the counseling process. For instance, Helms and Carter (1987) found that higher Disintegration attitudes were related to stronger preferences for White female counselors and that White females tended to have higher Disintegration attitudes than White males. In his study of counseling simulations involving discussion of racial issues, Carter (1987) found that when clients' Disintegration attitudes were high, they were more likely to report feeling "challenged" by the counselors' interventions.

So far, overall findings concerning Disintegration attitudes may support the theory's description of these attitudes as reflecting discomfort with interpersonal interactions and a consequent desire to reaffiliate with people who are White like oneself.

Reintegration attitudes. On an attitudinal level, Reintegration attitudes have been found to be related to a number of symbolic racism attitudes that seem to reflect three basic themes: (a) attitudes toward interracial, Black–White, intimacy; (b) beliefs about Blacks' character; and (c) beliefs about social–political policy (Westbrook, personal communication, 1986). Examples of the first category are bias against Black–White dating and disapproval of Black–White marriage. The second category includes beliefs that Blacks are intellectually inferior to Whites. In the last category are beliefs that government and other systems favor Blacks over Whites (e.g., "affirmative action gives Blacks too many jobs").

McCaine (1986) also found that Reintegration attitudes were related to increased levels of anxiety for White men, but not White women, and less desire to initiate affiliative activities with others. In his counseling simulation study, Carter (1987) found that the higher clients' Reintegration attitudes were, the less likely they were to report feeling "challenged" by the counselors' interventions.

In general, validity studies seem to support the description that Helms (1984) offered for the Reintegration stage. That is, Reintegration attitudes seem to be related to idealization of Whiteness and denigration of Blackness. Furthermore, they seem to reflect low desire to engage or interact with others (especially Blacks), possibly because such interaction engenders anxiety.

Pseudo-Independent attitudes. Pseudo-Independent attitudes have been found to be related to "liberal" attitudes with regard to racial issues. In particular, Westbrook (personal communication, 1986) found that they were related to approval of the ideas of interracial dating and marriage. On the other hand, Helms and Carter (1987), in their counselor preference study, found that Pseudo-Independent attitudes acted as suppressor variables. That is, when these attitudes were examined via simple correlations, they appeared to be negatively related to preference for White counselors, indicating that as these attitudes increased, preferences for White counselors decreased. However, when they were adjusted for their overlap with the other racial identity attitudes via multiple regression analysis, then Pseudo-Independent attitudes were positively related to preference for White counselors. Thus, it is possible that Pseudo-Independent attitudes represent an intellectualized way of expressing racial discomfort, as proposed in chapter 4. Also supportive of this intellectualization explanation is the finding that Pseudo-Independent attitudes have not been found to be related to levels of affect or reactions to discussions of racial issues (Carter, 1987; McCaine, 1986).

Autonomy. In Westbrook's data (personal communication, 1986), Autonomy attitudes were related to the belief that Blacks are not more likely than Whites to be involved in campus crime. They were also related to a position in support of full racial integration. Autonomy attitudes have been found to be negatively related to preference for White counselors (Helms & Carter, 1987). Carter (1987) found that surrogate clients' Autonomy attitudes were negatively related to their feelings of being supported by counselor interventions. That is, the higher this type of racial identity attitude, the less supported clients felt. Thus, for the most part, evidence at hand seems to support the description of Autonomy attitudes as the most racially accepting and flexible of racial identity attitudes.

Factor Analysis

In conducting the factor analysis, the authors used principal components analysis to examine the responses of the Study 2 (n = 506) sample of White male and female students attending predominantly White colleges and universities in the eastern United States.

Initially, 11 factors had eigenvalues greater than one and accounted for 56.2% of the item variance. These factors were rotated via varimax rotation. Table 5.4 summarizes the resulting factors. Factor loadings were considered significant if their absolute value exceeded .32.

Nineteen items loaded significantly on Factor 1. The item with the largest loading (.71) was from the Reintegration scale ("I believe Blacks are inferior to Whites"), as were seven of the positively loading items. The remainder of the positive items were from the Disintegration scale. These were contrasted against three negatively loading Contact, three Pseudo-Independent, and two Autonomy items. The general theme of the positively loading items is White superiority (or Black inferiority) and avoidance of Blacks. The theme of the negatively loading items is endorsement of racial equality.

On Factor 2, eleven items had significant Factor loadings. This was primarily a Disintegration factor. The highest loading (.65) was for a Disintegration item ("I feel depressed after I have been around Black people"), as were four of the seven positively loading items. These items were contrasted against four Pseudo-Independent and Autonomy items. The theme underlying all of the positive items seems to be anxiety or insecurity around Blacks. The negative items seem to reflect positive interpersonal relationships with Blacks as "just people."

Factor 3 consisted of six positively loading items which, with two exceptions, were from the Contact scale. This factor appears to capture the naivete or curiosity hypothesized to characterize the Contact stage of identity. Item 16 ("I think it is exciting to discover the little ways in which Black people and White people are different") had the highest (.77) loading.

Factor 4 also consisted of only positively loading items. Of the five items, three were from the Disintegration scale and two were from the Reintegration scale. The theme of this factor seems to be captured by the highest loading (.68) Disintegration item ("I don't understand why Black people blame all White people for their social misfortunes"). This factor seems to assess anger and frustration.

Eight items loaded on Factor 5. Again the positively loading items on this factor are mostly from the Reintegration and Disintegration scales. A Reintegration item ("Society may have been unjust to Blacks, but it has also been unjust to Whites") had the highest loading (.69). Thus, this factor may measure perceived injustices to Whites.

Factor 6 is an Autonomy factor, although only three items loaded significantly on it. This factor seems to pertain to knowledge about Black culture. The highest loading item (.72) was "I think I understand Black people's values."

Table 5.4
Summary of Factor Analysis of the White Racial Identity Attitude Scale Items

Item's Stage	Factor Loadings										
	1	2	3	4	5	6	7	8	9	10	11
1. Contact					-40				52		
2. Disintegration				58							
3. Reintegration				59							
4. Pseudo-Independent	-44									43	
5. Autonomy					-53						
6. Contact			51							-39	
7. Disintegration		65									
8. Reintegration	55										
9. Pseudo-Independent											
10. Autonomy										58	
11. Contact	-44		47								
12. Disintegration		50									
13. Reintegration	52	44									
14. Pseudo-Independent		-48	33								
15. Autonomy		-45						33			34
16. Contact			77								
17. Disintegration	38			32				-34			
18. Reintegration	66										
19. Pseudo-Independent	-46		33								
20. Autonomy					35		42				
21. Contact									74		
22. Disintegration	48							-37			
23. Reintegration	40			60							
24. Pseudo-Independent								67			
25. Autonomy								65			
26. Contact			73								

Table 5.4 (continued)

	1	2	3	4	5	6	7	8	9	10	11
27. Disintegration	52				41						
28. Reintegration					69						
29. Pseudo-Independent					-60						
30. Autonomy						70					
31. Contact		37									
32. Disintegration		60									32
33. Reintegration	56	48									
34. Pseudo-Independent								54			
35. Autonomy						72					
36. Contact	-34										63
37. Disintegration	46	47									
38. Reintegration	71										
39. Pseudo-Independent							80				
40. Autonomy						54					
41. Contact									49		32
42. Disintegration					41						
43. Reintegration					67						
44. Pseudo-Independent		-52									
45. Autonomy	-66										
46. Contact	-50										
47. Disintegration				68							
48. Reintegration	65										
49. Pseudo-Independent	-65										
50. Autonomy	-36	-39									
% of Variance	21.6	7.2	5.1	4.4	3.6	3.0	2.6	2.3	2.3	2.1	2.0

Note: For item content, see Appendix II. Decimal points for factor loadings have been omitted to conserve space.

Two items loaded on Factor 7: "In many ways Blacks and Whites are similar, but they are also different in some important ways," and "there are some valuable things that White people can learn from Blacks that they can't learn from other Whites." It is possible that this factor assesses willingness to inform oneself about Black culture. However, given that the two items had a negligible correlation ($r = .17$) with each other, it is also possible that the factor represents error of some sort.

Factor 8 consists of two positively loading Autonomy items ("It is possible for Blacks and Whites to have meaningful social relationships with each other," and "When a Black person holds an opinion with which I disagree, I am not afraid to express my viewpoint"), and two Pseudo-Independent items ("There are some valuable things that White people can learn from Blacks that they can't learn from other Whites," and "Blacks and Whites can have successful intimate relationships"). Two Disintegration items loaded in a negative direction. Items with positive loadings on Factor 8 assess belief in racial equality in interpersonal relationships with Blacks whereas items with negative loadings assess negative attitudes about racial integration.

Factor 9, with three positively loading items ("For most of my life, I did not think about racial issues," "I hardly ever think about what race I am," and "I think it's okay for Black and White people to date each other as long as they don't marry each other"), is a Contact factor. This factor comes closest to measuring the racial obliviousness or lack of awareness postulated by Helms's (1984b) model.

Two of the three items loading on Factor 10 were either from the Pseudo-Independent ("I feel as comfortable around Blacks as I do around Whites") or Autonomy ("I seek out new experiences even if I know a large number of Blacks will be involved in them") scales. The only item with a negative loading was from the Contact scale ("I find myself watching Black people to see what they are like"). This factor appears to relate to comfort with bi-racial interpersonal situations.

Finally, Factor 11 is also primarily a Contact factor, with four positively loading items. The item with the highest loading (.63), "I was raised to believe that people are people regardless of their race," signals the general theme of this factor. That is, Factor 11 appears primarily to concern familial influences on racial obliviousness.

In summary, with the exception of Item 9, every item loaded significantly on at least one factor. However, it appears that the items as well as subscales are quite factorially complex. Nevertheless, items from the same subscales tended to have factor loadings in the same direction, though often the items were dispersed across more than one factor (e.g., Factors 10 and 11). Also, when items from a variety of subscales loaded on a factor, it was the case that those from adjacent scales loaded in the same direction. The patterns of factor loadings suggest that White identity development is complex and many of the items seem to be assessing multidimensional White racial identity. However, if future analyses confirm these findings, it might be advisable to reassign some Disintegration and Reintegration items and some Pseudo-Independent and Autonomy items. As for the Contact items, although they also appear to reflect a complex phase of identification, they tended to load on factors distinct from the other scales. Therefore, the Contact items probably can continue to be used as a single scale.

CONCLUSIONS

In summary, the reliability and validity data to date are consistent enough and strong enough to support the idea that usage of each of the five scales seems warranted. Nevertheless, those intending to use the measure should calculate reliability estimates on their own samples as recommended by Dawis (1987) with regard to Likert scales in general. Since it is likely that differences in the racial circumstances of an environment will influence individuals' manner of expressing their racial identity, then it is possible that future investigators' findings will differ from those reported in this chapter with respect to reliability coefficients and/or factor structures. However, as the empirical studies of White racial identity begin to proliferate, they will eventually converge on the important aspects of this developmental process.

PART II
PSYCHOLOGICAL CORRELATES OF RACIAL IDENTITY

6

The Beginnings of a Diagnostic Model of Racial Identity

JANET E. HELMS

Racial identity theories were not originally designed to be used to gather diagnostic information in the amount of detail typically desired by professional helpers. Rather they were intended to explain reactions to a social environmental anomaly, that is, how many Black people were able to develop healthy racial identities though surrounded by a racist environment. It should be noted that inquiry about how or whether White people develop healthy racial identities in the midst of a racist environment has only recently begun to occur (see chapter 4).

Consequently, a major difficulty in using the racial identity models to "diagnose" clients' (or counselors') internal dynamics and observable behavior is that because they were not originally intended for this purpose, none of the racial identity models for either race provides a systematic framework for discerning the important influences on the individual's racial identity development. Therefore, both practitioners and researchers concerned with racial identity interventions are often at a loss as to what type of racial/cultural information should be collected as well as how to use such information once it is collected.

The various models *do* suggest that other personality characteristics such as feelings, beliefs, and behaviors can be affected by the particular stage of racial identity in which the person finds himself or herself. However, one cannot tell from the models the mechanisms by which one comes to exhibit one stage of identity rather than another, or whether the same internal and external factors contribute to the person's racial identity development regardless of her or his race.

Nevertheless, theoretical discussions of the reasons for White prejudice and Black victimization (For reviews see Amir, 1976; Chesler, 1976; and J. M. Jones, 1972) point to similar causative and/or correlational agents for both races. These include systemic factors (such as labor force or economic fluctuations), physical attributes (such as skin color), and personality characteristics (such as level of intelligence).

Recall that in earlier chapters, the term "White racism" was hypothesized to encompass the first three stages of White racial identity (Contact, Disintegration, Reintegration) in some form; Black reactions to racial victimization were thought to be encompassed by the first three stages of Black identity (Preencounter, Encounter, Immersion/Emersion) in some form. To the extent that these formulations of the stages are valid, then it seems likely that the same forces that influence the development of the global constructs of racism and/or victimization also influence the development of these constructs in more differentiated form, namely, stages of racial identity for the respective racial groups.

Thus, by combining some of the factors gleaned from the racism literature in social psychology and Helms's (1986) notion of stages of identity as world views, then it is possible to propose a framework by which practitioners and researchers can explore the racial identity issues of individuals. Figure 6.1 illustrates the skeleton of the psychodiagnostic model incorporating both intrapsychic and extrapsychic components as influences on Self or identity development.

THE PSYCHODIAGNOSTIC MODEL

World Views

In the center of the figure (i.e., Box IV), are a variety of types of world views or strategies one might use for interpreting social information from one's environment. Several general personality theorists have proposed a variety of strategies for organizing and/or interpreting information. As shown in Figure 6.1, examples of these include cognitive styles such as field-independence/dependence (Witkin & Goodenough, 1969), value orientations (Kluckhohn & Strodtbeck, 1961), sex role orientation (Bem, 1974), and so on. The examples are intended to be illustrative of the many constructs present in the personality literature rather than exhaustive. Although racial differences in usage of many of these organizational strategies have been used to support the existence of distinctive Afro-centric (i.e., having its locus in classical African traditions) and Euro-centric (i.e., having its roots in classical European traditions) world views (cf. Carter & Helms, 1987; Nobles, 1980; Shade, 1982), in fact, virtually none of the constructs from traditional psychol-

Figure 6.1
A Psychodiagnostic Model of Racial Identity Development

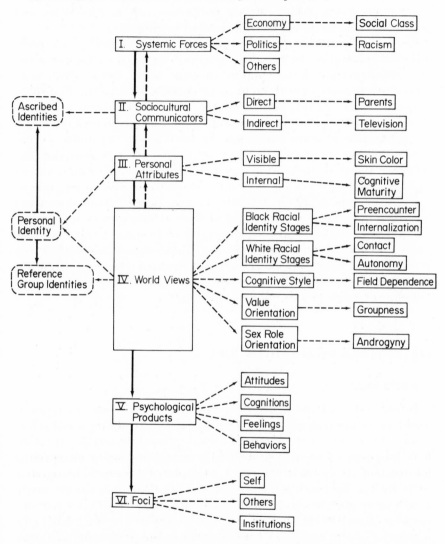

The individual's racial identity is composed of three interacting components (personal, ascribed, and reference-group identities). The components are influenced by and influence external factors with environmental reactions to proximal characteristics (e.g., physical attributes) having the strongest influence in racial identity development.

ogy explicitly addresses the relevance of race to the individual's satis-
factory development.

In his argumentation concerning the appropriateness of Afro-centric
theory for describing the life circumstances of Black Americans, Nobles
(1976) does distinguish between African and European world views on
three dimensions: (a) psychobehavioral modalities, (b) values and customs, and (c) ethos. Accordingly, one dichotomy that distinguishes Africans from Europeans on the first dimension is groupness rather than
individuality; one distinction in values and customs is cooperation rather
than competition; and on the ethos dimension, Africans are distinguished from Europeans because of their greater belief in "survival of
the tribe" rather than "survival of the fittest."

Nobles (1976) does concede that in the United States, classical African
and European world views do not exist in unadulterated form, but he
further argues that remnants of these world views do differentially influence Black and White personality. Moreover, his perspective moves
us somewhat closer to understanding how ancestral cultures and modern
socialization experiences can lead to different manners of interacting
with one's environment(s). For instance, in the case of Blacks, he con-
tends that European domination and imposition of the European
world view on non-European people has led Blacks to reject, deny, or
devalue their own African perspectives. In response to this domination
and self-devaluation, many Blacks are said to have developed pseudo-
personalities (e.g., the Negro personality) in which they actively attempt
to discard any remnants of their African roots and/or world views. Par-
enthetically, one might argue that Whites also have developed pseudo-
personalities (e.g., the "color-blind" person) as a result of their participation in the domination of other groups and denial of such involvement.

Nevertheless, in neither the case of Blacks nor Whites does Nobles's
(1976) theoretical approach contribute to a ready identification of the
factors leading a person to perceive the world through African or European eyes or a mixture of both. The psychodiagnostic model presented
in this chapter represents an attempt to begin to outline those factors
that might be expected to shape a person's view of the world in one
direction or another.

In the proposed model, Cross's (1971) stages of Black identity are used
to represent Black racial world views, and Helms's (1984b) stages of
White identity are used to represent White racial world views, though
presumably any of the other previously mentioned racial identity models
could be substituted here. In this diagnostic model, "world views" can
be defined as not necessarily conscious patterns or templates for processing or organizing social (especially racial) information about one's
world. Racial information can include the attitudes, cognitions, feelings,
and behaviors concerning race that are communicated to the person via

her or his social environment(s) (i.e., Box II). The quality of the information received by the individual is determined primarily by influential sociocultural communicators in her or his environment, who, in turn, influence the nature of the person's world view.

Diverse world views cause persons to selectively attend to information and to perceive similar information differently, though the same kinds of information are potentially available to each person regardless of race. Thus, both the White and Black racial identity models propose that the earlier stages (or the mono-racial types) are associated with poorer adjustment than later stages (or pluralistic racial types) because in the earlier stages, the person has to expend considerable energy in screening out or denying potentially identity-shattering information.

Sociocultural Influences

Significant sociocultural influences in the person's environments potentially include parents, family, peers (especially cohorts), schools, churches, media, and other institutions. In discussing adolescent identity development in general, theorists such as Erikson (1968) and Marcia (1980) suggest that different sociocultural influences matter at different times in a person's life. Thus, during infancy and early childhood, parents are most important; during late childhood and adolescence, peers or cohorts and nonfamilial institutions (e.g., school, media) become increasingly more important. Therefore, if racial identity follows the same course of development as other aspects of identity, one would suspect that parents and adult authority figures are most influential early on, followed by peers or cohorts and social institutions in later years.

Be that as it may, what possibly makes racial identity development different from other aspects of identity development, with perhaps the exception of gender, is that most of the focus of sociocultural communications from the environment to the person are about group-related appearance rather than the individual's own abilities, interests, and so on. On a national level, to the extent that the person appears to share the group characteristic of Whiteness, he or she is considered to be superior to others who do not share that characteristic and, conversely, to the extent that the person shares the group characteristic of Blackness, he or she is considered to be inferior to those who do not share the characteristic. A person's first knowledge of how her or his racial characteristics are likely to be evaluated by society is transmitted by these various communicators.

An individual develops a view of the racial aspect of herself or himself (ascribed racial identity) primarily on the basis of how these sources react to that aspect of the person. To the extent that the person is socialized in multi-racial environments in which significant role models consider race to be a normal and desirable part of themselves as well as others, it is likely that the person, so influenced, will develop a positive and pluralistic racial identity.

On the other hand, to the extent that the person is raised in an environment in which he or she is taught to idealize or denigrate the value of her or his racial group or others' racial group, it is likely that the person will develop a less healthy racial identity. Because they usually are raised in an environment that is automatically structured so as to be friendly to Whites, it is easier for White persons to develop a positive (albeit inflated) view of their own racial group and themselves because they belong to the "favored" group (i.e., ascribed and reference-group identities).

However, local or immediate sociocultural influences might communicate messages about race to the individuals that are in contrast to the prevailing norm. In fact, Barnes (1980) theorizes that those Blacks who successfully develop a positive Black identity do so because Black parents, family, and community have actively modeled and provided sources of positive identification who are Black and delegitimized the racist messages of White society. Also, individuals may have views of the personal identity aspects of themselves that differ from the prevailing racial norms.

When the individual receives many and/or conflicting messages about race, then it is necessary for her or him to work harder to make sense of the information. Consequently, for such individuals, racial identity world views become a more important part of the person's personality structure and, therefore, govern a broader range of the person's attitudes, cognitions, feelings, and behaviors. Thus, for Blacks in general, it follows that racial identity will obviously influence a wider range of personality and related behaviors than is the case for Whites who are less frequently subjected to contradictory racial information about themselves or others.

Psychological Products

According to the proposed diagnostic model, sociocultural experiences focused on individuals' racial attributes are used by these individuals to develop a racial identity world view. In virtually all of the racial identity perspectives, racial identity world views are thought to generate in a predictable fashion specific types of racial identity attitudes as well as cognitions, feelings, and behaviors.

Drawing from the various racial identity models, the objects or foci (Box VI of the diagnostic model) of these psychological products can be the person's Self (personal identity), as well as other people (reference groups and/or social institutions). Thus, by way of illustration, idealization of one's own racial group accompanied by devaluation of another's group leads one to perceive one's Self as superior, to look only to one's "own kind" for suitable values and beliefs, and/or to act in ways that maintain hierarchical statuses between the two racial groups such that one's own racial group enjoys the most benefits.

Personal Attributes

In the model shown in Figure 6.1, personal attributes include internal mechanisms (e.g., cognitive maturity, life coping skills) as well as physical attributes (e.g., skin color, physiognomy) that are visible to the individual and perceivers in his or her environment. Personal characteristics, particularly those that are visible to observers, receive the brunt of communications about the person's worth to her or his sociocultural environment. Such communications are usually accompanied by the supposition that the (usually) visible physical characteristics mean something about the person's internal psychological characteristics. Thus, the person's level of commitment to a particular group (i.e., ascribed identity) results in large part from her or his transactions with powerful sociocultural communicators. The transactions may be direct as is the case when a child's parents tell the child how to interact with other racial groups; they can be vicarious as is the case when the child sees how people of her or his racial group are treated and construes meaning from such treatments; they can also be indirect as is the case when media consistently present one racial group as the "good guys" and the other as the "bad guys."

Systemic Forces

Yet the sociocultural influences may, themselves, be influenced by larger systemic factors (Box I), including economic and political forces (e.g., racial discrimination, fluctuating economy, quality of interracial interaction). One finds a variety of theoretical explanations as to how these factors influence racial groups and, consequently, global attitudes pertaining to these groups. Here, one example of relevant theories is the economic analyses of White prejudice (e.g., Tobin, 1965; Willhelm, 1971), in which it is suggested that Whites' perceived or actual competition with Blacks for economic resources lead Whites to exhibit more prejudice and, presumably, Blacks to exhibit more symptoms of victimization.

Also relevant here are the theories of intercultural contact (e.g., Amir, 1976). In outlining favorable conditions for reducing prejudice/victimization via interracial contact, Amir speculated that prejudice (and victimization) should be reduced when members of the interacting groups are of equal status or the Blacks (in this case) are of higher status than the Whites. Yet other authors (e.g., Dennis, 1981; Horowitz, 1936) have contended that Whites' prejudiced attitudes are influenced not so much by the amount or quantity of contacts with Blacks as by their own self-perpetuated thoughts about Blacks.

Conclusions. Using the proposed diagnostic model, it should be possible to form some working hypotheses about how the person is and/or how he or she came to be that way with respect to racial identity. For example, the White person who has frequent interaction with high-status Black persons in an economically secure environment (systemic factors), and whose parents and other role models exhibit and advocate positive racial identities (sociocultural communicators), is likely to acknowledge membership in his or her own societally designated racial group (ascribed identity), and have a self-conception that is neither enhanced nor hampered by race (personal identity) because the person does not have to advocate racism.

Additionally, the person will adopt one of the world views typical of the advanced stages of White racial identity. Which one will depend on which kinds of attitudes are exhibited by the person's significant role models as well as her or his own level of cognitive maturity. Her or his feelings, attitudes, and behaviors should then be consistent with his or her particular mode of racial identification. One would expect similar outcomes for Blacks in analogous racial circumstances with respect to Black identity. However, in both cases, such uniformly positive outcomes are not very likely without considerable personal effort since the individual—whether Black or White—must often work against omnipresent societal norms in order to bring them about.

RESEARCH IMPLICATIONS

With the possible exception of Garza and Lipton's (1982) sociocultural interaction model, theorists typically have not speculated about how the combination of societal role models, economic and political forces, and physical attributes affect the individual's identity development. Thus, counseling and psychotherapy researchers typically have not had a systematic framework by which to guide their explorations of the influence of cultural/racial factors on clients' internal dynamics.

However, non-theory guided investigations of sociocultural influences on racial attitudes have begun to appear in mental health literature. For the most part, the focus of these empirical investigations has been Black people. Therefore, in addressing the question of the validity of the proposed diagnostic model, more (though not much) information is available for Blacks than for Whites.

In presenting the information relevant to the psychodiagnostic model, it might be beneficial to point out that the Black and White stages of racial identity are, in fact, hypothetical constructs. That is, though they can be used for explanatory purposes, they cannot themselves be measured or observed directly, but rather must be inferred from "products" such as attitudes, behaviors, and so on, hypothesized to evolve from the racial identity stages.

The "truth" of the constructs, then, results from whether the products operate in a manner consistent with racial identity theory. In the empirical literature, racial and/or occasionally racial identity attitudes have generally been used to operationalize racial identity, though such attitudes are not direct measures of racial identity types or stages but rather products thought to evolve from them. So, in this section of the chapter, literature will be discussed in which participants' racial attitudes, particularly those from which some aspect of racial identity can be inferred, have been examined in some form.

The model proposes that racial identity development occurs in response to transactions among a variety of factors. The strategy here will be to discuss those transactions or linkages in the model for which some racial identity attitudinal information, broadly defined to include both explicit and indirect measures, is presently available. Let us focus the presentation even further by limiting it to those studies that have investigated linkages between variables included in the psychodiagnostic model and racial (identity) attitudes. Some relevant empirical information exists for the following categories: (a) systemic forces (Box I); (b) parental attitudes (Box II); (c) physical characteristics (Box III); (d) products resulting from other world views (Box V); and (e) self-perceptions (Box VI).

Systemic Forces

Social class and environmental racial composition are the variables most often used to operationalize systemic forces. In such studies, racial preference typically has been the attitudinal variable from which racial identity is inferred. Even so, both of these systemic factors have received surprisingly little attention in studies of either Black or White participants. One does find a bias in such studies such that investigators have typically questioned how social class or environmental racial composition is related to Whites' attitudes toward Blacks while generally ignoring how it is related to Whites' attitudes toward Whites, whereas in the case of Blacks and systemic forces, investigators have focused on a greater variety of within and outgroup racial attitudes.

Whites. The guiding hypothesis in studies of White participants has been that Whites of lower social classes are likely to have stronger negative attitudes toward Blacks than are Whites from higher social classes.

The often implicit hypothesis is that economic deprivation or competition breeds contempt toward the group with which one is competing.

Yet empirical evidence has consistently supported neither of these hypotheses. In reporting the results of a nationwide survey, Campbell (1971), for instance, reported that lower-class White workers' attitudes toward Blacks were no more negative than those of Whites from other social classes. However, he did not examine their attitudes toward Whites.

The available evidence concerning the effect of interracial contact on the racial attitudes of Whites has also been inconclusive. Sorce (1979) found that White preschoolers from segregated communities developed racial awareness earlier than those from integrated communities, a finding seemingly supported by Palmer's (1970) findings that preschoolers' and nine and ten-year-olds' preference for their own racial group was mitigated by living in an integrated neighborhood. Yet J. Moore, Hauck, and Denne (1984) found that White children, in grades six through ten, demonstrated greater prejudice in situations requiring prolonged interracial contact rather than minimal contact.

Blacks. Studies of Black participants have often addressed attitudes that seem to have some bearing on racial identity development. In such studies various indicators of social class and measures of racial identity have been used, though environmental composition is usually limited to whether or not the environment is integrated. Previously used social class measures can be broadly classified as "objective" or "subjective." Objective refers to researcher or societally defined indicants of class such as income, education, areas of residence, and so on. Subjective indicators include respondents' self-definitions of their social class standing.

In studying the effects of social class on a Black adult sample's "Emersion or Internalization-like" attitudes, Barnes (1980) used income and education to represent social class and solicited interviewees' reactions to a variety of self-report measures. He found that higher social class was related to more frequent conceptualization of "Black power" as requiring political rather than militant activity, and endorsement of the teaching of Black/African history and language in elementary school.

Several other studies (e.g., Campbell & Schumann, 1968; Dizard, 1970; Marx, 1967; and Tomlinson, 1970) in which educational level was used to assess social class also found that "militant" (perhaps Immersion) attitudes and/or attachment to Black identity were more indicative of higher levels of education (e.g., some high school) than lower levels (e.g., some elementary school). Moreover, Dizard found that attachment to Black identity was lowest among the occupational groups of craftsmen, service workers, and proprietors/managers, relative to other lower and higher status occupational groups.

Although it is usually impossible to find a consistent definition of what investigators mean by "high" and "low" income groups with respect to Black samples, there appears to be some evidence that low-income groups are more likely to advocate "Preencounter-like" attitudes than their economically better-off counterparts (Caplan & Paige, 1968; Brink & Harris, 1966). For instance, Caplan and Paige found that lowest income Blacks tended not to endorse measures of Black pride, but did endorse deprecatory stereotypes of Blacks.

In possibly the only study to investigate the relationship of social class to a variety of racial identity attitudes per se, Carter and Helms (1988) used a combination of objective and subjective social class measures to predict each of the four types of racial identity attitudes as measured by the Black Racial Identity Attitude Scale (see chapter 3). Their sample was college students. None of the attitudes were significantly predicted by any of the social class indicants.

In his study of environmental contributors to racial identity development, J. A. Banks (1984) found that upper-middle-class children, ranging in age from 8 to 18, who were socialized in predominantly White suburban communities, developed bi-racial attitudes with a slightly pro-Black bias. Palmer (1970) found that neighborhood segregation level had no effect on children's color preference, though Scott and Mc-Partland (1982) found that desegregation did contribute to more tolerant racial attitudes for both Blacks and Whites.

Conclusions. Though not enough empirical evidence exists to warrant definitive conclusions concerning social class and environmental composition and racial identity, some tentative themes are present. For Whites, it appears that attitudes toward Blacks may not show consistent differences in patterns due to social class. However, in agreement with the interactional theories (e.g., Amir, 1976), increased interracial interaction does seem to moderate White children's anti-Black attitudes, at least on a superficial level. This greater positivity may be enhanced when the interracial contact occurs in an interracial residential environment.

On the other hand, virtually no evidence exists concerning the effects of environmental composition and/or social class on Whites' attitudes toward Whites as a reference group or Whites relative to Blacks. However, according to racial identity theory, racial identity constructs cannot be adequately assessed in the absence of measurement attention to Whites' attitudes toward both racial groups as well as themselves as members of one of these groups.

The evidence concerning Blacks' social class and/or environmental racial composition and racial identity suggests that if there is a relationship, it is not necessarily linear. For instance, the evidence does seem to suggest that the middle range of Black social class (wherever that may be) is more likely to demonstrate attitudes consistent with a positive Black identity and the lower range is more likely to demonstrate attitudes consistent with a Euro-American identity. This seems to be more true of preschoolers and elementary school children than of older student samples or Black adults. In the latter two groups, racial identity attitudes have not been found to be consistently related to social class. As was the case for Whites, more studies are needed in which Blacks' attitudes toward Whites and/or Black racial identity per se is investigated. Where environment is concerned, racial composition of the environment seems not to be a determining factor in how Blacks feel about themselves or their racial group, but may influence their level of positive feelings toward Whites.

Oddly enough, most of the social class/racial composition and racial identity studies to date are not particularly germane to the proposed psychodiagnostic model. The model proposes that sociocultural communicators act as mediators between systemic forces and the individual. Therefore, according to the model, the individuals' racial identity should be more influenced by the messages he or she receives from others (such as parents) concerning systemic factors than her or his objective social class or the number of Whites or Blacks in the person's neighborhood. Thus, relevant research would include investigations of differential communication patterns concerning race when social class or environmental racial composition are varied.

Parental Attitudes

It is now a commonly accepted assumption that children recognize color differences and/or different racial categories by the time they are three or four years old (P. A. Katz, 1976). Yet it is not clear how children come to evaluate the racial groups differently or decide to which group they prefer to belong. Possibly the most common assumptions have been, (a) children's racial identities are the result of direct parental instruction, (b) children learn their identities by imitating their parents, and (c) parental lifestyles implicitly convey which manner of racial identification is appropriate. In general, one of these forms of instruction is assumed to have occurred when parents and children express similar racial attitudes.

Blacks. Much of the information concerning parental influences on Black people's racial identity development is impressionistic or qualitative and comes from consideration of the adjustment of transracial adoptees (Ladner, 1977; McRoy & Zurcher, 1983; McRoy, Zurcher, Lauderdale, & Anderson, 1984; Morin, 1977). These writings indicate that at least through adolescence, Black adoptees of White parents seemed to exhibit ascribed and reference-group racial identities that were congruent with those of their adoptive parents. Thus, if the parents denied the child's Black racial-group membership (e.g., "he's not Black, he's mixed," or "she belongs to the human race") and/or stressed how different the child was from other Blacks, then the adoptees tended to follow suit. Similarly, if the White parents raised the child within the context of an integrated lifestyle including Black neighbors, friends, and educational experiences and communicated the positive value of the child's racial ancestry, then the child exhibited a bicultural identity based on positive feelings about her or his Blackness.

Empirical studies of parental attitudes and children's racial identity have yielded intriguing, but not always anticipated results. Seemingly age of the child may determine her or his susceptibility to parental influence, with children becoming more independent as they age. This trend is consistent with general developmental theory.

Two studies (Floyd, 1969; Branch & Newcombe, 1980) examined the relationship of Black parents' activism in the Civil Rights Movement and Black preschoolers' racial attitudes. Both found some evidence that the children of the *more* active parents had *more* pro-White attitudes on at least one measure. Branch and Newcombe (1986) also found that Black four- and five-year-olds exhibited *stronger* pro-White preferences on a multiple choice doll test when their parents exhibited pro-Black child-rearing practices, but six- and seven-year-olds exhibited *stronger* pro-Black preferences if their parents' attitudes were pro-Black. In addition, parents' and children's attitudes in both groups varied in the same directions when responses to structured interviews were the measures of attitudes.

Carlson and Iovini (1985) compared Black adolescent boys' racial attitudes to their fathers' actual attitudes and perceived attitudes. Their findings indicated that the Black youths' attitudes were less anti-White than they perceived their fathers' to be, but that the fathers' actual attitudes were less biased than their sons thought they were. Also, Black fathers' and sons' attitudes were not significantly correlated.

Whites. More often than not White (and Black) children's racial identity attitudes are inferred from their responses to racial preferences measures such as the various versions of the K. B. Clark and M. P. Clark (1939) Doll Test. Although many empirical studies concerning White children's racial preferences currently exist (for reviews see Katz, 1976, and Pushkin & Norburn, 1983), few of these studies have examined parental influences on these racial preferences. Moreover, with all too infrequent exceptions (Roebuck & Neff, 1980; Ward, 1985), qualitative analyses, other than autobiographical accounts of single individuals' racial identity development (e.g., Griffin, 1961), are rare.

Ward's (1985) qualitative analysis is unique in that it examines the long-term effects of White parental attitudes on White adult racial attitudinal development. Ward interviewed the adult children of fathers who had been interviewed about their racial attitudes in 1962. The primary indicator of parental anti-Black attitudes in Ward's study was fathers' opposition to miscegenation; the primary indicators of adult children's anti-Black attitudes were responses to symbolic racism items (e.g., position on bussing for integration).

Ward (1985) found that 71% of adult children whose fathers opposed miscegenation opposed measures designed to eliminate the effects of racism, whereas 69% of those whose fathers were in favor of miscegenation approved of such tactics. Ward interprets the findings to mean that rather than communicating to their children the exact content or cognitive structure of racial attitudes, parents may transmit their attitudinal affect. In other words, adults may structure the content of their attitudes to match the emotions they learned during childhood from their parents in a manner that does not conflict too much with the contemporary social norms of their racial group regarding race.

Carlson and Iovini (1985), in the previously cited study, also examined White male adolescents and their fathers' anti-Black attitudes. Theirs was essentially a study of whether or not the content of White youths' attitudes was similar to that of their fathers. Although they found significant positive correlations between fathers' and sons' actual attitudes, they found stronger relationships between the adolescents' actual attitudes and their perceptions of their fathers' attitudes. However, as was the case with Black adolescents, White youths overestimated the level of their fathers' anti-outgroup attitudes. Thus, Carlson and Iovini's findings may provide support for Dennis's (1981) idea that Whites' racial identity development is more a function of their thoughts about race than objective reality.

Conclusions. Surprisingly few studies of parental influences on the racial identity development of either race have been conducted. Of those that do exist, most have used the questionable methodology of doll preference to infer racial identity attitudes. This particular methodology has been excoriated (e.g., W. C. Banks, 1976; W. C. Banks, McQuater, & Ross, 1979; Brand, Ruiz, & Padilla, 1974; P. A. Katz, 1976) and defended by many authors (e.g., J. E. Williams & Morland, 1979). Major criticisms include: (a) lack of evidence concerning the reliability of the methodology (e.g., Would respondents duplicate their preferences if they were retested at a later date or via a different methodology?); (b) lack of demonstrable validity (e.g., Doll preference may not generalize to other kinds of behaviors); and (c) researchers' ethnocentric interpretation of Black and White children's responses (e.g., exclusive preference for one's own racial group may not necessarily be an ideal).

Of the three criticisms, the one having the most implications for racial identity theory concerns how preference responses are interpreted. An extremely robust finding is that most White children state a preference for characteristics signifying Whiteness (e.g., White dolls, figures, hair texture, etc.) during the preschool years and these preferences generally increase in strength as the children age (cf. P. A. Katz, 1976; Pushkin & Norburn, 1983). On the other hand, Black children's preferences apparently are less rigid. For instance, in their reanalysis of existing preference studies involving children, Banks and his associates (e.g., W. C. Banks, 1976; W. C. Banks, McQuater, & Ross, 1979) found that the majority of studies demonstrated no racial preference among Black children. Whereas some authors (J. E. Williams & Morland, 1979) have argued that the White children's behavior of virtually always preferring their own racial group is healthier than the Black children's non-preference, racial identity theory seems to suggest an opposite interpretation. That is, people who do *not* judge others solely on the basis of physical attributes such as race may in fact be demonstrating the highest levels of racial identity according to either the Black or White models.

Physical Attributes

Considering the import of physical attributes in this society, again one must be astonished by the minimal attention given to how they are related to indivduals' racial identity development. Of the many possible qualities that could be examined, skin color has received the most attention, though gender and physiognomy also have been investigated occasionally. Again, the majority of the inquiries have been focused on Blacks and not many of them have been empirical.

Whites. One theorist (Welsing, 1974) has specifically noted Whites' ambivalence about skin color and the significance of this ambivalence for their racial identity development. In this regard, Welsing notes such self-destructive and color-related behaviors as the tendency of Whites to sun tan in spite of considerable evidence that such behavior constitutes a major health risk. When questioned about this desire to darken their skin, it has been the present author's experience that Whites typically respond to this observation by explaining that they are trying to look affluent rather than Black. Of course, such a response begs the implicit racial identity question, that is, how a physical attribute (skin color) that is considered to be a negative aspect of Blackness has come to be associated with wealth in White culture? White racial identity theory might suggest that this type of "illogical" leap is conceivably more evident in those stages associated with ambivalent racial attitudes and feelings (e.g., Disintegration, Pseudo-Independent) than those stages in which one's attitudes are crystallized. Nevertheless, the interrelationship between Whites' skin color and racial identity has yet to be examined empirically.

Some available research evidence (e.g., Johnson & Buttny, 1982; Marwit, 1982; Palmer, 1973; K. H. Williams, J. E. Williams, & Beck, 1973) does support the premise that Whites use physical attributes, perhaps a wider variety than do Blacks, to differentiate among racial groups, though some contradictory evidence (P. A. Katz & Zalk, 1974) does exist. Again, when the differentiation effect is found, it seems to have developed by early childhood. For instance, Sorce (1979) found that three- to five-year-old White preschool children distinguished the races on the basis of hair characteristics and "physiognomic features" more often than skin color. Using approximately the same age group, Anderson and Cromwell (1977) found that with the exception of some rejection of a blond White doll, Whites tended to prefer dolls of their own race regardless of hair features or skin color.

Very little reseach has examined gender differences in White racial identity attitudes. The existing studies on this topic usually have occurred as a subsidiary part of a larger study. Nevertheless, these studies do suggest that White females enjoy the most favored status and dark males the least favored status among Whites (e.g., Sciara, 1983). White females also may experience greater tolerance (Bierly, 1985) as well as conflict (Helms & Carter, 1988) over racial identity issues than their White male counterparts.

Blacks. Much speculation exists concerning the importance of skin color on Black personality development. More often than not, the speculation centers around how others react to Blacks with light versus dark skin. Occasionally studies have examined the relationship of skin color to self-esteem and/or have inferred self-esteem and racial attitudes from Black respondents' reference-group skin color preferences. Yet few of these presentations have investigated the contribution of skin color to Blacks' racial identity development.

McCargo (1987) addressed this latter question indirectly when she asked Black male and Black female adolescents to estimate their own skin color and that of their parents and best male and female friends. She used differences in skin color perceptions to determine whether the racial identity attitudes of youths would be similar to the person who they most resembled in terms of skin color. Although her results indicated no significant differences in any of the four racial identity attitudes as measured by an abridged version of the Black Racial Identity Scale (Helms & Parham, in press) when those who most resembled parents were compared to those who most resembled peers, her results are not conclusive because respondents in the former group outnumbered the latter by a ratio of four to one.

Research conducted by the present author does suggest that the relationship between perceived skin color and the RIAS-B attitudes (Helms & Parham, in press) might be more complex than researchers have anticipated. In one study, 285 college students used a five-point skin color scale (1 = White or almost White; 2 = light; 3 = brown; 4 = dark; 5 = Black or almost Black) to describe their skin color as they perceived it and the RIAS-B to describe their racial identity attitudes. Multiple regression analyses, in which linear and curvilinear estimates of skin color were used to predict attitudes, indicated that only Encounter attitudes were *not* predicted by perceived skin color.

Preencounter attitudes were significantly predicted by the linear component of skin color such that the lighter respondents perceived themselves to be, the higher were their Preencounter attitudes, and the darker they perceived themselves to be, the lower were their Preencounter attitudes. Immersion/Emersion attitudes were predictable in a similar fashion. However, both linear and curvilinear components of skin color significantly predicted levels of Internalization attitudes. The linear trend indicated that the darker the person perceived herself or himself to be, the higher were her or his Internalization attitudes; but this was only true for the first three levels (white through brown) of the skin-color measure. The nature of the curvilinear trend was such that individuals who perceived themselves to be in the middle ranges of color (i.e., "brown") had higher Internalization attitudes than people at the extremes.

It seems then that people who perceive themselves to be either "white" or "black" may have more difficulty developing a positive racial identity, as indicated by level of Internalization attitudes, than people who believe that they are in the middle of the color continuum. Of these two groups, those of "white" skin color may have greater conflict over racial identity issues than those of "black" skin color, as indicated by the former group's higher levels of both Preencounter and Immersion/Emersion attitudes, which in the model are oppositional types of attitudes.

As far as the other physical attribute, gender, is concerned, for Blacks as well as Whites, rarely has it been the primary focus of a study. Incidental findings of studies in which the RIAS-B (Helms & Parham, in press) was used do suggest that males and females often do not differ in mean levels of the various attitudes (Helms & Parham, in press; Helms & Carter, 1987), but when differences were found (Parham & Helms, 1985b), Black women relative to Black men had higher levels of Internalization attitudes.

Conclusions. The empirical work necessary to clarify the associations among physical characteristics and racial identity development has not been conducted adequately for either group. As was true for other areas presented so far, one finds implicit racial and gender biases in the literature that does exist. One evidence of bias is that the same types of questions are not asked of both races. For instance, one occasionally sees studies of the implications of Black people's skin color for their attitudes toward Blacks and, by inference, themselves as Black people, but one never finds studies of the significance of White people's skin color to their own White reference-group identity, or, by implication, themselves. Moreover, gender effects on identity development are rarely investigated, though the limited information available suggests that racial identity development may be more conflictual for White females than White males and Black males than Black females.

Other World Views

Though the psychodiagnostic model shown in Figure 6.1 does not require interrelationships among different world views or cognitive processing strategies, one can reasonably postulate the presence of such relationships. In fact, racial identity models, for the most part, seem to assume a superordinate role for racial identity such that other aspects of the person are governed by her or his stage of racial identity development. One test of this assumption would be the accurate prediction of products (e.g., attitudes, feelings, etc.) resulting from other world views by racial identity attitudes.

Whites. Since White behavior is usually considered the standard for positive mental health in the behavioral and social science literature, a number of studies have examined racial differences between Whites and Blacks with respect to world views and/or cognitive styles (see chapters 7 and 8). Yet only a few investigators have examined the interrelationships between cognitive variables and racial attitudes.

In several therapy or therapy-like studies, investigators have attempted to modify Whites' racial attitudes by modifying their cognitive structures through active interventions. If one overlooks the methodological limitations of these studies (e.g., Haimowitz & Haimowitz, 1950; Pearl, 1954, 1955; Rubin, 1967), which have used some form of psychotherapy to change attitudes, they do provide some evidence that non-specific therapy interventions can decrease highly educated or professional clients' anti-outgroup attitudes, particularly if the clients are not too disturbed and the therapy is intensive. Presumably, the cognitive structure being modified in such studies is participants' Self-system or personal identity, since cognitive restructuring of *racial* attitudes rarely seems to be the explicit goals of such treatment.

A few experimental studies of cognitive development and racial attitudes have found results that imply a cognitive structure and racial identity linkage in children and adolescents. In a study of how White children develop conceptions of race, A. Clark, Hocevar, and Dembo (1980) found that preschool children's selection of White or Black playmates was related to their association of the color white with good and black with bad. Two studies (Gardiner, 1972; McCaine, 1986) have shown more direct relationships between cognitive structure and racial attitudes with late adolescent samples. McCaine attempted to classify White respondents into Harvey, Hunt, and Schroeder's (1961) four conceptual categories, which range from System 1, a concrete world view in which the person perceives the world in absolutes, to System 4, an abstract world view in which the person considers the complexities of the world. He also measured the first four of the attitudes assessed by the White Racial Identity Attitude Scale (see chapter 5). Although he had difficulty finding participants who were in categories other than System 4, he did find that System 1 respondents tended to have higher Pseudo-Independent attitudes than did the other conceptual categories. None of the other attitudes differed significantly by category. His findings may support the hypothesis that Pseudo-Independent attitudes represent the individual's initial transition from White racist to positive racial identity.

Gardiner (1972), who speculated that prejudice could be reduced by increasing individuals' cognitive complexity, developed interventions to enhance complexity. His intervention specifically focused on race relations and was administered to White high school students. He found some evidence that prejudice was reduced by his complexity interventions, but not immediately. Gardiner recommended that such interventions be matched to the individual's level of cognitive complexity.

Blacks. A number of studies (e.g., Livingston, 1971; Lunceford, 1973; Suggs, 1975), based on Nigrescence models, have attempted to modify Blacks' racial identity via therapy-like interventions designed to alter their personal identity and/or reference-group identity. Cross et al. (in press) reviewed these studies in detail. Again one has to ignore certain methodological limitations in analyzing these studies. From their review, Cross et al. concluded that the racial identity interventions have not been shown to influence personal identity, but have been shown to influence reference-group identity.

More direct examinations of the links between alternative world views and Black racial identity attitudes have yielded mixed results. McCaine (1986) did not find evidence that Black racial identity attitudes were differentially related to Harvey et al.'s (1971) conceptual systems. However, Carter and Helms (1987) found that these attitudes did differentially predict F. R. Kluckhohn and Strodbeck's (1961) value orientations. Moreover, they found that the orientations best predicted were those consistent with an Afro-centric world view.

Conclusions. While it is difficult to compare the studies across racial groups because of differences in methodology, questions addressed, and so forth, there seems to be at least a reasonable possibility that some world views are related to racial identity for both groups, though not necessarily the same ones. It may even be the case that a broader range of White racial identity attitudes than Black racial identity attitudes are related to a greater variety of world views, though this observation requires further substantiation.

Self-Evaluation

Historically, investigators have tended to assume that self-concept (personal identity) and racial identity (reference-group and/or ascribed identities) were synonymous. However, in several critical analyses of the racial identity developmental literature (Cross, 1987; Cross, 1986; Cross et al., in press), Cross has pointed out the absence of empirical support for such a viewpoint.

The proposed psychodiagnostic model posits differential linkages among the various racial identity stages of both races and indicators of personal identity. For instance, within the Black racial group, one might expect the highest stages of racial identity development to be associated with the highest levels of self-esteem and the earliest stages (e.g., Preencounter Phase 1) to be associated with deflated levels of self-esteem (as compared to the norms of the racial group under consideration).

Blacks. J. A. Baldwin (1979) reviewed the literature prior to 1980 concerning Black "self-hatred" and concluded that investigators typically had not given enough attention to racial-group heterogeneity and/or methodological rigor to sustain the hypothesis that Black people generally dislike themselves. In support of this viewpoint, several studies have found positive connections between some forms of racial identity and self-esteem.

In their review of the Nigrescence literature specifically, Cross et al. (in press) summarized the status of Black racial identity and personal identity variables. They concluded that the majority of the empirical studies (e.g., Parham & Helms, 1985a; Parham & Helms, 1985b; J. Taylor, 1986; R. L. Williams, 1974) based on Nigrescence theory and using measures of racial identity, have found deficiencies in personal identity (e.g., depression, low self-esteem, high anxiety, etc.) to be most characteristic of Preencounter attitudes, and strengths (e.g., positive self-esteem, low anxiety) to be associated with Encounter and/or Internalization attitudes.

Consistent with Cross et al.'s (in press) conclusion, Wright (1985) found that positive self-esteem was associated with Black high school seniors' endorsement of a positive Black ideology (i.e., positive reference-group identity), whereas M. L. Clark (1982) found some associations between general self-esteem and pro-Black racial attitudes when Black third- and fourth-graders were studied.

Whites. Some studies have examined correlations between Whites' self-attitudes and prejudicial attitudes toward non-Whites. More specifically, in his review of the pre–1970 literature, Ehrlich (1973) reported on three studies conducted by Tabachnick (1962) that showed negative relationships between self-esteem and bias against Blacks. Rubin (1967) also found that, among Whites, low self-acceptance was associated with high anti-Black attitudes. Thus, for Whites too, some evidence suggests that attitudes consistent with early stages of racial identity are related to poor feelings about themselves.

Conclusions. The clearest support for the model can be found in those studies examining the link between racial identity products (i.e., attitudes) and perceptions of Self. For both races, there seems to be fairly consistent support for the hypothesis that high levels of anti-Black attitudes coexist with poor feelings about oneself. Likewise, among Blacks, high levels of anti-White attitudes, as inferred from endorsement of Immersion attitudes, were related to more negative expressions of personal identity (cf. Parham & Helms, 1985a; Parham & Helms, 1985b). For Blacks, there also is some evidence suggesting that Black identification is related to positive self-feelings. However, there is no evidence concerning the relationship of positive White (as opposed to anti-Black) identification to Whites' self-feelings. The territory of positive White identity remains largely unexplored.

Counseling Implications

It may be clearer now why the psychodiagnostic model is considered to be skeletal. Although there seems to be enough research and theory to suggest a tentative structure, this information is not sufficient enough to confirm what is related to what and in what directions components are related. In fact, the model raises enough questions to keep a researcher (or practitioner) busy for quite awhile looking for answers.

Still, while we are waiting for answers, the practitioner may be able to use the framework to structure interventions concerning racial issues. In the long run, perhaps a practitioner's effectiveness depends upon a willingness to assess the client's racial identity and/or related functioning as well as the practitioner's own. Adequate assessment may require familiarity with or willingness to gather information about factors that perhaps appear to be extraneous to the immediate counseling situation.

Gunnings and Simpkins's (1972) systemic counseling approach advocates the importance of assessing the client–environment interaction. The psychodiagnostic model suggests some aspects of the client's environment that might be fruitfully explored. Generalizing from the model to the diagnostic interview, it is recommended that the practitioner collect information about as many of the components of the model as seems pertinent to the client's particular circumstances. Since one of the implications of the model is that clients, even from the same racial group, may have been exposed to qualitatively different life experiences, it would be a mistake to proceed with a client on the basis of racial stereotypes. Be that as it may, sometimes the requisite information can be inferred from what the client says about herself or himself if the practitioner can remain open enough to hear the client. Sometimes the practitioner may have to probe for such information.

Furthermore, the hypothesis that racial identity attitudes evolve in response to a variety of environmental influences may have some implications for how one interprets a client's circumstances. If it is the case that racial identification is a fluid process whose overt manifestations differ depending upon how the person's identity has evolved, then a person whose predominant racial identity attitudes are bi-racial has had qualitatively different and perhaps more diverse life experiences than the person whose racial identity attitudes are mono-racial. Thus the astute practitioner should attempt to determine which of the proposed factors are most significant to the particular client.

Moreover, if fluidity does describe the expression of racial identity attitudes, then a possible counseling implication is that counselors ought not to be overly concerned with exactly determining which single set of attitudes best characterize a client (or practitioner). Instead, the practitioner can devote more attention to identifying the types of attitudes that oscillate in the person's personality profile; each type is theorized to contribute to the client's being in some way. The practitioner's task is to determine what aspects of the client's life have influenced the development of which racial identity attitudes and how the attitudes are maintained. Ideally, the more information the practitioner collects about the client's racial identity and correlates, the better should be the counseling offered.

7

White Racial Identity Attitudes and Cultural Values

ROBERT T. CARTER
AND JANET E. HELMS

Helms (1984b) has noted that prior to the development of her White racial identity development model, few theories existed that attempted to explain how Whites developed attitudes toward their racial-group membership (White) rather than their *ethnic* group (e.g., Greek, Italian, German, etc.). Yet, though Whites may exhibit cultural differences if they belong to different ethnic groups, they all may be similar in some ways because they belong to the same *racial* group. Considerations of ethnicity, for the most part, have not included analyses of how White individuals' racial heritage is related to their attitudes about other cultural or racial groups or themselves as racial/cultural beings (McGoldrick, Pearce, & Giordano, 1982; Papajohn & Spiegel, 1975).

When White racial attitudes defined as Whites' prejudice toward other racial/cultural groups have been considered, usually Blacks rather than Whites have been the focus of these discussions. That is, investigators have studied what Whites believe, feel, or think about Blacks, but not what they feel, think, or believe about Whites. With respect to this point, Helms (1984b) observed, regarding the use of prejudice to understand Whites' racial attitudes, "[investigation of] prejudice provides no information about how Whites feel about themselves as racial beings" (p. 155).

Relatedly, J. Katz and Ivey (1977) have suggested that White Americans possess a culture that derives from their racial-group membership. White American culture seems to exist over and above its members' ethnic origins or identifications. J. Katz and Ivey argue that Whites, who deny their racial-group membership, consequently deny the values, attitudes, and other characteristics associated with their race/culture group and fail to develop an awareness or understanding of their cultural heritage as White Americans.

Thus, both Helms (1984) and J. Katz and Ivey (1977) are proposing that White Americans' racial identity, independent of their ethnic origin, might be associated with particular cultural characteristics that stem from their unique sociopolitical history. Although some people might argue that White ethnic groups have retained their ethnic identity, most White ethnic groups in America have also assimilated into what is considered to be mainstream American culture, and have consequently become more identified with the dominant White American middle-class culture than a particular ethnic group or culture.

Carter and Helms (1987) hypothesize that racial identity is related to other cultural characteristics such as cultural value orientations. Cultural value orientations are characterized by those dimensions that members of a particular group consider important and desirable. What a group considers important and desirable, that is, what it values, guides the behavior of its individuals, forms the basis for group norms, and dictates lifestyles that are deemed appropriate for group members. These guiding forces, when used in reference to an individual, are usually referred to as values. For cultural or racial groups, these values form a complex set of guiding principles known as value orientations or cultural values (C. Kluckhohn, 1951).

In a study of the relationship of Black racial identity to value orientations, Carter and Helms (1987) found that racial identity attitudes predicted Black Americans' cultural values. However, they also found that only those stages of racial identity attitudes that were associated with identification with Black culture predicted Black Americans' value-orientation preferences. Based on their findings, it seems reasonable to assume that White Americans' racial identity may also be related to their value orientations or cultural values.

The cultural value theory used by Carter and Helms (1987) was F. R. Kluckhohn and Strodtbeck's (1961) theory of variation in value orientations. F. R. Kluckhohn and Strodtbeck's theory holds that (a) value orientations represent a limited number of common human problems, (b) the need to find solutions to these common human problems is shared by all cultures, and (c) cultures are limited in the number and variety of solutions that are possible.

F. R. Kluckhohn and Strodtbeck's (1961) problems or orientations involve five aspects of human life: (a) human activity, (b) social relations, (c) time perspective, (d) person/nature relationships, and (e) the innate character of human nature. Each problem or orientation has three possible solutions or alternatives. Therefore, although each human society, culture, and possibly racial group theoretically must solve common problems, the differential solutions chosen by each is alleged to account for variation between and within cultural and racial groups. Table 7.1 summarizes the value-orientation alternatives.

To test the theory of variation in value-orientations, F. R. Kluckhohn and Strodtbeck (1961) studied several cultural groups who shared geographic proximity. In general their results revealed differences in value-orientation patterns among the cultural groups studied. The White Americans, in their study, as compared to Spanish and Native Americans, preferred the Individual alternative of the Relational Orientation, the Doing alternative of the Activity Orientation, the Mastery position on the Person/Nature Orientation, the Future alternative of the Time/Sense Orientation, and the Mixed position on the Human Nature Orientation.

Other researchers (Trimble 1976; Szapocznik, Scopetta, & King, 1978; Szapocznik, Scopetta, Aranalde, & Kurtines, 1978; Graves, 1967; Price-Williams & Ramirez, 1974; Khoury & Thurmond, 1978; Chandler, 1971; Papajohn & Spiegel, 1971, 1975; Sue, 1982) have compared White American value-orientations to those of other cultural and ethnic groups. The majority of the studies have reported value-orientation patterns similar to those found by Kluckhohn and Strodbeck (1961). Thus, one might think of the Individualism, Doing, Mastery, and Future alternatives as White or Euro-centric alternatives when other racial/ethnic groups are used as comparison groups.

Although theorists (e.g., Rokeach, 1973) have recognized that there might be some heterogeneity in cultural value-orientations *within* the White racial group, empirical studies of within-group differences in cultural values among Whites have generally focused on demographic factors such as White Americans' age, social class, and/or gender (e.g., Gruen, 1966). Few, if any, studies have considered whether White American cultural values vary according to differences in psychological variables (e.g., White racial identity attitudes). The present study explored the relationship between White racial identity attitudes and cultural value-orientations for White Americans.

More specifically, the purpose of our study was to (a) determine whether White racial identity attitudes could be used to predict White respondents' value orientations, and (b) if so, which value-orientations were predictable. Also, the study attempted to determine which of F. R. Kluckhohn and Strodtbeck's (1961) value-orientations characterized a sample of White Americans independently of other racial/ethnic groups.

METHOD

Subjects

Subjects were 506 White students, freshmen through seniors, attending a university in the northeast region of the United States. The majority

Table 7.1
Kluckhohn and Strodtbeck's Value Orientations Model with Alternative Solutions

Human Nature	Evil: People are born with evil inclinations	Mixed: People are both good and bad at birth.	Good: People are basically good.
Person to Nature	Subjugation to Nature: People have little control over natural forces. Nature guides one's life.	Harmony with Nature: People are one with nature. Nature is one's partner in life.	Mastery over Nature: One is expected to overcome natural forces and use them for one's own purposes.
Time Sense	Past: Traditional customs are of central importance.	Present: The past and future are of little importance. Here-and-now events are most important.	Future: The temporal focus is on planning change for events that are to occur.
Activity	Being: Emphasis is on activity that is spontaneous; self-expression of emotions, desires, and impulses is most important.	Being in Becoming: Emphasis is on self-expression aimed at integration of the personality through control.	Doing: Emphasis is on action-oriented self-expression, which is measured by criteria external to the acting person (e.g., achievement).
Social Relations	Lineal: Lines of authority are clearly established and dominate subordinate relationships.	Collateral: Individual goals are subordinated to group goals (collective decision-making).	Individualism: People are autonomous of the group. Individual goals are more important than group goals.

Note: With permission of the American Association for Counseling and Development (AACD), this table is reproduced from "The relationship of Black value-orientations and racial identity attitudes" by R. T. Carter and J. E. Helms, 1987, *Evaluation and Measurement in Counseling and Development, 19(4), 187. Copyrighted by AACD.*

of subjects from the university were solicited through psychology classes and received credit toward course grades for participation in the study. Subjects ranged in age from 17 to 33 years; the sample consisted of 167 men and 339 women.

Instruments

The following instruments were used in this study: the White Racial Identity Attitudes Inventory (see chapter 5), the Intercultural Values Inventory (Kohls, Carter, & Helms, 1984, cited in Carter & Helms, 1987), and a personal data sheet constructed for this study.

Intercultural Values Inventory. The Intercultural Values Inventory (Kohls et al., 1984) measures the alternative solutions to the value orientations or problems described in F. R. Kluckhohn and Strodtbeck's (1961) model of value orientations. The inventory uses a yes/no format and contains five orientation scales, each of which is measured with three subscales consisting of 10 items each. The subscales correspond to alternative solutions. Subjects are instructed to indicate whether the sets of 30 statements reflect a value by which they would either live their lives or raise their children. Scores were calculated by summing the "yes" responses within each subscale. Carter and Helms (1987) reported internal consistency reliability coefficients for the 15 subscales ranging from .50 (Good Human Nature subscale) to .79 (Present Time subscale).

Personal data sheet. The personal data sheet was used to investigate subjects' personal characteristics and family background. Subjects were asked to provide a variety of information about themselves. However, for purposes of this study, only the demographic data concerning subjects' sex and race were used.

Procedure

The Intercultural Values Inventory (Kohls et al., 1984) and White Racial Identity Attitude Inventory were counterbalanced such that approximately half of the subjects completed the Intercultural Values Inventory first, and half of the subjects completed the White Racial Identity Attitude Inventory first. Subjects volunteered via posted sign-up sheets and were tested in small groups at the time indicated on the sign-up sheets. Upon reporting to the testing room, subjects were handed a questionnaire packet by an experimenter or a trained assistant. The packet contained the White Racial Identity Attitude Inventory, Intercultural Values Inventory, and the personal data sheet. Upon completion of the questionnaire packet, each subject received a debriefing sheet outlining the goals and hypotheses being tested in the study.

Analyses

Two preplanned sets of analyses were conducted. The first set of analyses concerned the ability of racial identity attitudes to predict the 15 value-orientation alternatives. The second set concerned the comparisons of value-orientation alternatives to each other. In addition, gender differences in value orientations were examined, though no a priori hypotheses or research questions concerning gender had been proposed.

To explore the question of whether White racial identity attitudes were differentially predictive of the students' value orientations, a series of 15 multiple regression analyses were performed. In these analyses, racial identity attitudes were the independent variables and each of the 15 value orientations served as successive dependent variables. Approximately one of these analyses would be expected to be statistically significant due to chance at the .05 level of confidence.

In order to compare alternatives or explore the pattern of value-orientation alternatives for the sample and determine if sex differences existed among the sample, treatment X subjects analyses of variance were conducted. In these analyses, the three types of alternatives within each value orientation were compared to one another (i.e., were the "subject" variable). Sex was treated as a between-group variable in these analyses, and the dependent variables were each of the value-orientation alternative scores.

RESULTS

As shown in Table 7.2, the multiple regression analyses revealed that racial identity attitudes significantly predicted the following value-orientation alternatives: the Evil ($R^2 = .11$; $F(5,500) = 12.45, p < .001$) and Mixed ($R^2 = .06$; $F(5,500) = 6.65, p<.001$) alternatives of the Human Nature Orientation; the Subjugation ($R^2 = .03$; $F(5,500) = 5.27, p<.001$), Harmony ($R^2 = .05$; $F (5,500) = 2.95, p<.01$), and Mastery ($R^2 = .07$; $F(5,500) = 7.60, p<.001$) alternatives of the Person/Nature Orientation; the Past ($R^2 = .02$; $F(5,500) = 2.79, p<.05$) and Future ($R^2 = .03$; $F(5,500) = 2.76, p<.05$) alternatives of the Time/Sense Orientation; and the Being ($R^2 = .06$; $F(5,500) = 5.89, p<.001$), the Being and Becoming ($R^2 = .02$; $F(5,500) = 2.41, p<.05$), and the Doing ($R^2 = .04$; $F(5,500) = 4.17, p<.001$) alternatives of the Activity Orientation.

An examination of the beta weights for individual variables comprising the significant regression models suggests that Disintegration (beta = .23; $T(1,500) = 3.30, p<.001$) and Reintegration (beta = .20; $T(1,500) = 2.98, p<.01$) attitudes were positively related to a belief in an Evil Human Nature. Disintegration (beta = .21; $T(1,500) = 2.87, p<.01$)

Table 7.2

Summary of Multiple Regression Analyses for Value Orientations and White Racial Identity Attitudes

Value Orientations	R	R^2	R^2 adj	F	P	Racial Identity Attitudes Predictive of Cultural Value Alternatives
Human Nature						
Evil	.33	.11	.11	12.45	.001	(+)D, (+)R
Mixed	.25	.06	.05	6.65	.001	(+)D, (+)R
Good	.12	.01	.04	1.45	.19	
Person-to-Nature						
Subjugation	.22	.05	.04	5.27	.001	(+)D,(+)R,(+)A
Harmony	.17	.03	.02	2.95	.01	(+)R
Mastery	.27	.07	.06	7.60	.001	(+)C,(+)D,(+)R,(+)P
Time Sense						
Past	.16	.02	.02	2.79	.05	(+)C, (+)R
Present	.15	.02	.01	2.17	.06	
Future	.16	.03	.02	2.76	.05	(+)D
Activity						
Being	.24	.06	.05	5.89	.001	(+)C
Being-in-Becoming	.15	.02	.01	2.4	.05	(+)C
Doing	.20	.04	.03	4.17	.001	(+)C,(+)R
Social Relation						
Lineal	.12	.01	.00	1.37	.24	
Collateral	.13	.02	.01	1.68	.14	
Individual	.12	.01	.00	1.37	.23	

Note: C = Contact attitudes; D = Disintegration attitudes; R = Reintegration attitudes; P = Pseudo-Independent attitudes; A = Autonomy attitudes. (+) = positive relationship; (−) = negative relationship.

and Reintegration attitudes (beta = .13; $T(1,500)$ = 1.96, $p<.05$) were positively related to a belief in a Mixed Human Nature, suggesting that confusion regarding racial issues and/or White supremacy seem to be associated with value orientations in which humans are viewed as inherently evil, with some potential for good.

All three alternatives of the Person/Nature Orientation were related to racial identity attitudes. Specifically, Disintegration (beta = .16; $T(1,500)$ = 2.15; $p<.05$), Reintegration (beta = .16; $T(1,500)$ = 2.26, $p<.05$), and Autonomy (beta = .13; $T(1,500)$ = 2.06, $p<.05$) attitudes were also significantly positively related to the Subjugation to Nature alternative. These findings suggest that confusion about Whites, idealization of Whites, and emotional and intellectual acceptance of Whites seemed to be associated with a belief that one is at the mercy of natural forces. Reintegration (beta = .14; $T(1,500)$ = 2.05, $p<.05$) attitudes were also significantly positively related to the Harmony with Nature alternative, suggesting that high levels of Reintegration attitudes are associated with the belief that one is part of nature or one's beliefs are what is natural. The Mastery alternative was found to be significantly positively related to Contact (beta = .10; $T(1,500)$ = 1.99, $p<.05$), Disintegration (beta = .14; $T(1,500)$ = 1.98, $p<.05$), Reintegration (beta = .06; $T(1,500)$ = 2.86, $p<.01$) and Pseudo-Independent (beta = .17; $T(1,500)$ = 2.67, $p<.05$) attitudes. Thus, all levels of White racial identity, with the exception of Autonomy attitudes, were associated with the belief that humans should master nature.

Two alternatives of the Time/Sense Orientation were related to racial identity attitudes. The Past alternative was found to be significantly positively related to Contact (beta = .10; $T(1,500)$ = 1.93, $p<.05$) and Reintegration (beta = .21; $T(1,500)$ = 2.98, $p<.01$) attitudes. The Future alternative was significantly positively related to Disintegration attitudes (beta = .16; $T(1,500)$ = 2.23, $p<.05$). This finding suggests that lack of awareness, denial of race, and active idealization of Whiteness were related to a belief in traditions and customs, whereas confusion regarding race was associated with a focus on events in the future.

For the Activity Orientation's alternatives, it was found that Contact attitudes (beta = .19; $T(1,500)$ = 3.56, $p<.001$) were significantly related to the Being alternative, and Contact attitudes were significantly positively related (beta = .12; $T(1,500)$ = 2.30, $p<.05$) to the Being-in-Becoming alternative of the Activity Orientation. The Doing alternative of the Activity Orientation was significantly positively related to Contact (beta = .17; $T(1,500)$ = 3.12, $p<.01$) and Reintegration (beta = .13; $T(1,500)$ = 1.94, $p<.05$) attitudes. Consequently lack of awareness of racial issues appears to have been associated with beliefs in spontaneous expression of emotions, and expression of an integrated personality. Naivete about race and attitudes of racial superiority were both related to an action-oriented lifestyle that is governed by external criteria of appropriateness. No racial identity attitudes were related to the Social Relations Orientation.

Value-Orientation Profile

The treatment X subjects analyses showed significant differences in five value orientations, each involving three alternative solutions (see Table 7.3). For the Human Nature Orientation, Whites in the sample

Table 7.3
Summary of Means (M) and Standard Deviations (SD) for Men's and Women's Value Orientations

Value-Orientation	Gender					
	Men (n=167)		Women (n=339)		Total (N=506)	
	M	SD	M	SD	M	SD
Human Nature						
Evil	3.38	2.14	3.08	2.02	3.18	2.06
Mixed	7.59	1.63	7.47	1.69	7.51	1.69
Good	7.22	1.78	7.73*	1.62	7.56	1.69
Person-to-Nature						
Subjugation	4.33	2.48	4.85*	2.39	4.69	2.43
Harmony	7.47	1.99	7.80*	1.95	7.69	1.97
Mastery	5.56*	2.05	5.17	1.98	5.30	2.01
Time Sense						
Past	3.97	1.85	3.92	1.74	3.94	1.77
Present	6.13	2.53	6.72	2.46	6.53	2.50
Future	7.14	1.77	7.17*	1.76	7.17	1.76
Activity						
Being	6.74	1.98	7.23*	1.87	7.07	1.93
Being-in-becoming	4.82	1.59	5.09	1.77	5.00	1.72
Doing	7.39	1.80	7.25*	1.74	7.29	1.76
Social						
Lineal	4.67	2.39	4.40	2.16	4.48	2.24
Collateral	5.71	1.76	6.08*	1.70	5.96	1.73
Individual	8.13	1.44	8.08	1.49	8.10	1.47

*$p \leq .05$

(disregarding gender) had higher scores on the Mixed and Good alternatives relative to the Evil alternative. On the Person/Nature Orientation, highest scores were on the Harmony-with-Nature alternative followed by Mastery and Subjugation. With regard to the Time/Sense Orientation, Whites in the study had highest mean scores on the Future alternative, followed by the Present and then the Past. Whites' mean scores on the Activity Orientation in descending order were Doing, Being, and Being-in-Becoming. With respect to the Social Relations Orientation, Whites had higher scores on the Individual alternative, followed by Collateral and Lineal.

General Differences

Gender differences were found for the five value orientations. White women in comparison to White men were found to have higher scores on the Good alternative of the Human Nature Orientation. This finding suggests that White women in comparison to White men had a stronger belief in humans' inherent goodness. On the Person/Nature Orientation, women, when compared to men, were found to have higher mean scores on the Subjugation to Nature alternative. This finding might suggest that women, in comparison to men, felt at the mercy of natural forces.

Men, relative to women, had significantly higher mean scores on the Mastery over Nature Orientation. This finding suggests that men more than women endorsed the notion that nature is to be shaped or changed for human needs. With regard to the Time/Sense Orientation, women endorsed the Present alternative more than men did, which suggests that women, in this sample, were more focused on here-and-now events than were the men.

Higher mean scores on the Being alternative of the Activity Orientation also characterized women relative to men. This finding suggests that women placed more value on emotional expressiveness than did men. On the Social Relations Orientation, when the genders were compared, women had higher mean scores on the Collateral Social Relations Orientation. Thus, women valued group or interpersonal relations more strongly than did men.

DISCUSSION

The present study was designed to investigate whether or not value orientations were predicted by White racial identity attitudes and to examine the pattern of White value orientations. When White racial identity attitudes were examined, in general, the findings of the present study indicate that racial identity attitudes were predictive of White Americans' cultural value orientations. More importantly, if it is accurate to think of racial identity attitudes and value-orientation alternatives as being reflective of different types of world views, as Helms (1984a, 1986; see chapter 6) does, then the results of the present study seem to confirm her opinion that White racial identity overlaps but does not necessarily subsume those world views that have no conscious or obvious racial components.

Person/Nature Orientation

In brief, it appears that with respect to the Person/Nature value orientations (world views), the various White racial identity attitudes reflect somewhat different preferences or cultural perspectives. Contact attitudes were uniquely related only to Mastery over Nature, whereas Disintegration attitudes reflected beliefs in Subjugation and Mastery over Nature. Perhaps the dual relationships present for Disintegration attitudes reflect the emotional and psychological correlates of movement from a stage of "innocence" (Contact), in which one thought one was master of one's fate, to a stage of "helplessness" (Disintegration), wherein one feels subjugated to others' wills. Perhaps one believes both things at some time when one's Disintegration attitudes are high.

Reintegration attitudes, on the other hand, were related to all three Person/Nature alternatives. This finding may suggest that Reintegration attitudes are associated with more complex views of one's social world than are the other attitudes. It may be that the complex emotions and beliefs required to hold negative attitudes toward Blacks and idealize Whites require a fluid world view so that the individual can process information that is inconsistent with her or his racial stereotype. Another possibility is that the Reintegration stage of racial identity reflects confusion and turmoil such that no clear value-orientation preference can be identified.

Pseudo-Independent attitudes appear to reflect a Mastery over Nature world view. This finding might support the hypothesis that this stage of racial identity involves the initial commitment to resolve racial conflict and belief that one can do so. Autonomy attitudes were only associated with Subjugation to Nature. By the time the person evolves to the Autonomy stage, perhaps he or she comes to recognize how much of the racial environment is beyond his or her control.

Time/Sense Orientation

Time/Sense Orientation pertains to how the individual perceives events over the course of time. Contact and Reintegration attitudes were predictive of a belief in a Past Time Orientation. The Past alternative of the Time/Sense Orientation reflects adherence to tradition and time-honored customs. Contact and Reintegration attitudes have in common a lack of acceptance of racial differences and similarities as they currently exist. It may be necessary for individuals at the Contact and Reintegration stages of racial awareness to believe in time-honored traditions and customs to justify their racial attitudes and/or to rely on past experiences and events to help them interpret their present circumstances.

The Future alternative of the Time/Sense Orientation was predicted by Disintegration attitudes. The Future Time alternative reflects a temporal focus that is based on planning for events that might occur. The Disintegration stage of racial identity was described as a self-threatened stage in which the individual becomes aware of herself or himself as a racial being and the social norms regarding race for the first time. It is possible that this discovery and the confusion associated with it lead one to value a time in the future when things might be different—and perhaps better. Consequently, persons with high levels of Disintegration attitudes may focus primarily on potential future events rather than life as it was or is.

Activity Orientation

The Activity Orientation concerns one's views about the appropriate mode of self-expression. The Activity Orientation alternatives, Being, Being-in-Becoming, and Doing, were predicted by Contact and Reintegration attitudes. Contact attitudes were predictive of all three alternatives. Reintegration attitudes were only predictive of the Doing alternative. The Being alternative reflects belief in spontaneous expression of one's personality, whereas Being-in-Becoming reflects spontaneous expression of an integrated personality. The Doing alternative reflects activity that can be evaluated by external criteria.

At first glance, it is puzzling that Contact attitudes were associated with all three activity alternatives. Yet if one conceptualizes the Contact stage as one in which the individual acknowledges no (racial) constraints on her or his self-expression, then the findings make some sense. That is, the Contact person may feel he or she is above any constraints on her or his behavior. With regard to the Doing alternative, since both Reintegration and Contact attitudes were associated with this alternative, some manner of need for social approval may be typical of the related stages of White racial identity.

SUMMARY

In general, for Whites, Contact, Disintegration, and Reintegration attitudes were most often related to cultural value-preferences (or world views), suggesting that these lower-stage racial identity attitudes may be more strongly predictive of White cultural characteristics than higher-stage racial identity attitudes.

Structure of Cultural Values

The analyses conducted to determine the pattern of cultural values for this sample of White Americans revealed highest preferences were shown for the Mixed and Good alternatives of the Human Nature Orientation. Thus the value-orientation structure of the White Americans (disregarding gender) examined in the present study suggests a view of human nature as essentially mixed and good. Respondents believed that one should be in harmony with nature, but that one should be active in developing one's personality and society. In addition, they viewed the world from an individualistic perspective and endorsed a future orientation. These findings appear to be consistent with previous research and theory regarding White Americans' value orientations. However, the structural analysis suggests that it is important to examine within racial-group characteristics such as racial identity as well as between-group characteristics such as gender in order to fully grasp the differential within-group and between-group complexity of cultural characteristics among White Americans.

Gender Differences

Women showed stronger preferences for Collateral Social Relations, Being activity, Present Time, and Subjugation to Nature orientations than did men. These findings appear to support recent theorists' (e.g., Gilligan, 1982) arguments that women and men have different world views that are likely due primarily to different gender socialization experiences. Because women generally are exposed to a greater amount of group- and relationship-oriented socialization, maybe the preferences for Collateral Social Relations and Being Activity are indicative of experiences in which group and/or family decision-making and emotional expressiveness were the norm. Until quite recently, the norm in our society has been for White women to subordinate their will to White men and to structure their lives around whatever was important to White men in the world. Perhaps the preferences for Present Time and Subjugation to Nature reflect the operation of socialization experiences by which these women were taught to feel that they should value here-and-now events and not their own personal futures. It might be difficult to value the past or foresee a future if one's cultural history reflects a theme of oppression and discrimination due to sex. More importantly, the findings with respect to gender differences may suggest the need for further investigations of sex roles as within racial-group influences on the development of world views.

Implications for Counseling and Psychotherapy

In spite of possible methodological limitations, the obtained results may have some implications for counseling and psychotherapy. The present study suggests that perhaps White Americans' racial identity attitudes do interrelate to various cultural values or "world views." Therefore, consideration of how racial identity development influences the White client's cognitions, affect, and behaviors may aid counselors in their interventions with such clients. Furthermore, although the White client's racial identity development may be most salient when the topic or issue in counseling involves racial/cultural issues, it is possible that racial identity issues are implicit in other world views or orientations as well. Therefore, counselors may wish to consider a variety of factors in attempting to "diagnose" clients' racial identity development. The results of the present study raise the possibility that racial identity attitudes, value orientations, and gender may be additional places to begin the search for ways to understand the world from the client's perspective.

8

The Relationship between Black Racial Identity Attitudes and Cognitive Styles

JANET E. HELMS
AND THOMAS A. PARHAM

Cognitive styles of Black people have been hypothesized to effect a variety of personality, academic, and vocational variables including interpersonal styles (Halpern, 1973; McAdoo, 1981; Nobles, 1976), academic performance (R. Cohen, 1969; Peterson & Magaro, 1969), intelligence test scores (Riley & Denmark, 1974), and vocational choice (E. Smith, 1980). A widely held assumption regarding cognitive styles is that Blacks process information in a manner that is different from other racial/ethnic groups in that their cognitive styles are more likely to be people-oriented rather than task-oriented, emotional and intuitive rather than objective and analytic, and concrete rather than abstract (Akbar, 1974; Hilliard, 1976; Nobles, 1976; Shade, 1982). For instance, based on her review of literature comparing cognitive styles and academic performance of Black and White students, Shade (1982) tentatively concluded that "the available evidence could lead to the conclusion that the difference in school success is attributable to the use of sociocentric, field-dependent, nonanalytic categorizing information processing strategies by many Afro-Americans" (p. 233). She also proposed that given that use of this style in educational settings has been described as dysfunctional by some authors (e.g., R. Cohen, 1969), then performance discrepancies between the two groups possibly could be attributable to cognitive style and environment incongruence. As a consequence of their acceptance of the viewpoint that Black people's cognitive styles are dysfunctional in non-Black environments, several authors have proposed remedial programs designed to teach Black students cognitive styles that are assumed to be more functional in academic and occupational settings (Barnes, 1980; Norman & Atlas, 1978; Bradley & Stewart, 1982).

Nevertheless, in spite of the relatively consistent descriptions of Black cognitive styles among a variety of theorists, most of the information on which their descriptions are founded comes from their personal life experiences, clinical observations, and/or impressionistic analyses of "Black culture." While such information cannot be automatically discarded, it is interesting to note that the limited number of empirical studies pertaining to Black people's cognitive styles presents a more diverse picture. It appears, for instance, that some Blacks do use analytic information-processing styles and that use of such styles facilitates their academic performance in a variety of areas (Stuart, 1967; Harrison & Nadelman, 1972; Vinson, 1974). Vinson, for one, found that Blacks who used analytic rather than concrete conceptual strategies tended to obtain better grades. It also seems to be the case that Blacks who use sociocentric styles do not necessarily exhibit the same sets of personality characteristics as do Whites who use similar styles. E. E. Jones (1978a), for example, explored the relationship between field-dependence and personality traits for Blacks and found that although his Black sample used a field-dependent perceptual style to a greater extent than did Witken and Goodenough's (1979) sample of Whites, they were also more dominant, socially poised, and power-oriented than were the Whites.

Harrell (1979), Shade (1982), and E. Smith (1980) have noted the absence in the cognitive literature of models to account for individual differences among Blacks with respect to cognitive styles. Efforts to attribute such differences to gender or to socioeconomic status have been contradictory and inconclusive at best (Gill, Herdtner, & Lough, 1968; Palmer, 1970; Perney, 1976). Harrell suggested that an adequate model for diagnosing Black cognitive styles must be specific to Black culture and must take into account the various coping strategies and systems Blacks may adopt as a means of surviving in a color-biased country. In fact, Harrell proposed a model for diagnosing Black people's cognitive styles in which he describes six distinctive potential styles. However, his model confounds information-processing strategies with the person's racial/cultural adaption. So, for instance, his "Black Nationalistic Alternative" is described as a cognitive style in which the person's actions and goals are oriented toward achieving (Black) group unity and cohesiveness. Thus, the person who relies on this style presumably has made a decision to align himself or herself with other Black people, that is, has a Black reference-group orientation. Yet, it seems possible that a person might use a group-centered or other directed-information processing strategy without necessarily having committed herself or himself to Blacks or Blackness as the focus of that strategy. A model is needed that allows one to measure cognitive style and racial/cultural identification independently of one another. One culture-specific model that seems amenable to the investigation of the influence of different cultural adaptations on cognitive tendencies is Cross's (1971, 1978) model of psychological Nigrescence.

Parham and Helms (1981, 1985a, 1985b) modified the Cross (1971, 1978) model by recommending that the stages be considered to be types of attitudes that develop at different rates and that a person might hold at different times in the course of her or his development, rather than discrete stages into which a person can be classified. The advantage of such a modification is that it is consistent with the viewpoint of those authors (e.g., W. M. Banks, 1980) who observe that a Black person might hold an assortment of racial attitudes simultaneously, some of which might be conflicting. In various studies designed to explore the relationship between racial identity and various affective states and sentiments, Parham and Helms (1981, 1985a, 1985b) found evidence to indicate that the attitudes as measured by their Racial Identity Attitudes Scale (Helms & Parham, in press) were differentially related to such variables.

The purpose of this study was to investigate the relationship between racial identity attitudes derived from Cross's (1971) model and cognitive styles, operationalized in the present study as decision-making styles of Black students. While it might not be readily apparent from the brief foregoing summary of Cross's (1971, 1978) Negro-to-Black conversion model, it seems possible that racial identity attitudes may influence the information-processing strategies used by Black people. When different attitudes are predominant, people may attend to different aspects of their environments. For instance, predominantly Preencounter attitudes may contribute to styles of information processing that are stereotypic, constricted, and rely on (probably White) authority figures for validation; predominantly Encounter attitudes may lead to impulsivity or confusion about which information to process given the individual's abandonment of the Euro-American world view and the absence of another world view with which to replace it; predominantly Immersion/Emersion attitudes may lead to the processing of only that information that is perceived to be consistent with a Black separatist perspective; predominantly Internalization attitudes, being the most flexible, should encourage the gathering, processing, and evaluation of information without its being prejudged according to the racial/cultural group from which it originates. Thus, in the language that has been previously used to describe Black people's cognitive styles, it seems that cognitive styles may vary from sociocentric to emotional to analytic, with the exact nature of a person's style depending upon her or his levels of racial identity attitudes.

Relatedly, to the extent that information processing and decision-making styles are synonymous, then one would expect different racial identity attitudes to be predictive of different types of decision-making styles.

Harren's (1976) decision-making model was used to operationalize decision-making styles in this study. Via his model, he proposed three potential styles: Rational, Intuitive, and Dependent. The Rational style reflects a logical, systematic, and objective approach to decision-making; Intuitive decision-making is characterized by a reliance on the use of fantasy, attention to present feelings, and self-awareness; the Dependent style is characterized by conformity to other people's expectations and opinions. Since this study was intended to be exploratory, no specific hypotheses were proposed. However, it seemed reasonable, based on the foregoing analyses of racial identity attitudes, to postulate that (a) Internalization attitudes might be positively related to a rational decision-making style, (b) Encounter attitudes might be positively related to an impulsive or intuitive decision-making style, and (c) Preencounter and Immersion attitudes might both be related to a dependent style, but in opposite directions.

METHOD

Subjects

Subjects consisted of 142 Black college and university students (91 females, 45 males, 6 of unspecified sex) who attended one of four institutions, two in the Midwest, one in the West, and one in the South. Ages of subjects ranged from 17 to 25 years, and their self-reported socioeconomic status was as follows: lower (n = 7), working (n = 39), middle (n = 67), upper middle (n = 21), and upper (n = 7).

Instruments

Instruments used in the study were Harren's (1979b) Assessment of Career Decision Making (ACDM) scale, Parham and Helms's (1981) Racial Identity Attitudes Scale, and a personal data sheet. All instruments formed a part of a larger questionnaire and were arranged in the following order: (a) Racial Identity Attitudes Scale, (b) ACDM, and (c) personal data sheet. Subjects used a computer-scorable answer sheet to record their responses.

Racial Identity Attitude Scale. The short form of the Racial Identity Attitude Scale consists of 30 items that are modifications of the Q-sort items that Hall, Cross, and Freedle (1972) developed to measure the stages of racial identity proposed by Cross (1971). Subjects responded to the items by using a 5-point scale (ranging from 1 = strongly disagree to 5 = strongly agree) and scores for each stage were obtained by finding the mean of responses to the appropriately keyed items. Helms and Parham (in press) recently factor analyzed their original items using a sample of 250 subjects and found that Preencounter, Encounter, Immersion/Emersion, and Internalization attitudes were characterized by nine, four, eight, and nine items, respectively. Cronbach's alpha was used to compute respective reliability coefficients of .69, .50, .67, and .79 for the four scales. In the present study, the Helms and Parham (in press) factor-derived version of the short form of the RIAS was used. Evidence of the validity of the scales can be found in Helms (1984b) and Helms & Parham (in press).

Assessment of Career Decision Making Scale (ACDM). Harren (1976) devised 30 items to measure three decision-making styles, Rational, Intuitive, and Dependent. Subjects obtained scores by indicating that they "agree" rather than "disagree" with an item keyed to a particular scale. A maximum score of 10 was possible for each of the three scales. Harren and his associates (e.g., Harren, Kass, Tinsley, & Moreland, 1978) reported no internal consistency reliability for the scales, but reported two-week test-retest reliability of .85, .76, and .85 for the Rational, Intuitive, and Dependent styles, respectively. D. A. Cook (1979) used the ACDM with a predominantly Black sample of university students enrolled in a special preparation program. She found that 64% of her sample could be classified into one decision-making category when highest score was used as the classification criterion. In the present study, however, all of the subjects' three scores were used as dependent variables.

Personal data sheet. The personal data sheet was developed for this study to obtain demographic information about subjects. A multiple-choice format was used to allow subjects to report their sex, age, class level, racial self-designation (e.g., Black, Negro, etc.) and socioeconomic status. Respondents indicated socioeconomic status by checking one of five categories (1 = lower class; 5 = upper class). Carter and Helms's (1988) study of the relationship between social-class variables and racial identity attitudes indicated that Black respondents were more willing or able to provide subjective estimates of social class than they were to provide traditional estimators of social class (e.g., parents' occupation or income). However, according to their data, for those subjects who provided both kinds of social-class information, self-reported social class was positively correlated with traditional measures and predicted racial identity attitudes to the same extent. Therefore, they recommended use of self-reported social class when minimizing the length of one's measures is of concern.

Procedure

Packets containing the questionnaires were mailed to Black colleagues located in higher education institutions in the geographical regions mentioned previously. These individuals solicited participation of Black students through the classes and subject pools to which they had access. With the exception of the subjects obtained from subject pools, who received points toward their course grades, no one received remuneration for his or her participation in the study. Subjects completed the measures during single class periods of approximately one hour.

RESULTS

Hierarchical multiple regression analysis was used to examine the relationship between racial identity attitudes and each of the three decision-making scales. Respondents' sex and self-reported social class were entered on the first step of the analysis to control for demographic factors, and the four racial identity attitude scale scores were entered on the second step. Thus, this analysis is tantamount to asking the question of whether or not racial identity attitudes account for any more of the variance in decision-making styles than can be explained by sex and social class. Prior to conducting the regression analyses, preliminary analyses of variance were conducted to determine whether subjects were similar with respect to those demographic variables that were not included in the regression analyses. When the overall F-ratios were significant, Tukey's HSD test was used to perform post hoc tests.

Demographic effects. To determine the effects of demographic characteristics on decision-making styles, several analyses of variance were conducted. In these analyses, academic class levels, racial self-designation, and geographic location were successively used as independent variables and the three decision-making scales were used as successive dependent variables. Groups formed on the basis of academic class levels did not differ significantly when either the Rational ($F(3,138 = .25, p = .86$) or Intuitive ($F(3,138 = .87, p = .46$) decision-making styles were the dependent variables. However, when the Dependent style was the dependent variable, juniors reported significantly higher levels than did sophomores. Neither racial self-designation nor subjects' geographic region led to significant between-group differences for any of the decision-making styles. Means and standard deviations for these preliminary analyses are presented in Table 8.1. Since there were no consistent between-group differences, the samples were combined for the subsequent regression analyses.

Regression analyses. The Rational decision-making style was significantly predicted by the two variables entered in the first step of the hierarchical regression analysis, sex and self-reported social class ($R = .27, F(2,139) = 5.43, p = .005$). Sex significantly contributed to the prediction of the Rational style, and the direction of the beta weight indicates that being female led to less reported use of this style than did being male. The

Table 8.1
Summary of Means (M) and Standard Deviations (SD) of Decision-Making
Styles and Demographic Variables

Variables	Rational		Dependent		Intuitive	
Class	M	SD	M	SD	M	SD
Freshmen (n=30)	7.37	3.51	2.53	2.36	3.73	7.26
Sophomore n=29)	6.72	3.48	1.38	1.42	3.31	2.19
Junior (n=43)	6.86	2.89	2.81	2.03	3.20	2.16
Senior (n=40)	7.18	3.44	2.32	2.38	3.20	2.16
Region						
Midwest 1 (n=54)	6.78	3.55	2.20	2.11	3.67	2.42
Midwest 2 (n=37)	8.03	2.55	2.46	2.36	3.40	2.03
South (n=23)	5.96	3.76	2.39	1.71	2.83	2.17
West (n=28)	7.07	2.97	2.30	2.44	4.14	2.43
Racial Designation[a]						
Afro-American						
(n=23)	7.43	3.44	2.30	2.44	3.48	2.33
Negro (n=14)	6.07	3.24	1.86	1.29	4.07	2.70
Black (n=99)	7.07	3.28	2.45	2.20	3.49	2.25
Sex						
Female (n=91)	7.20	3.09	2.39	2.21	3.75	2.24
Male (n=45)	7.49	3.03	2.24	1.78	3.47	2.28
Total	7.30	3.06	2.34	2.08	3.65	2.25

Note: Total N = 142
[a]Subjects who labeled themselves "colored" (n = 2) or "other" (n = 4) and subjects who did not report their sex (n = 6) were not included in the two relevant ANOVAs.

racial identity attitudes that were entered on the second step also significantly predicted the Rational style ($R = .40$, $F(6,135) = 4.37$, $p = .001$). By using the racial identity attitudes, the percentage of variance explained was increased from 7% to 16%. However, examination of the individual beta weights indicated that only Internalization attitudes uniquely contributed to the prediction of the Rational style; as shown in Table 8.2, the higher the person's Internalization attitudes, the more likely he or she was to report using a Rational decision-making style.

The Dependent decision-making style was not predicted by social class and sex ($R = .04$, $F(2,139) = .09$, $p = .91$) nor by racial identity attitudes ($R = .11$, $F(6,135) = .28$, $p = .94$). Nor was Intuitive decision-making predicted by social class, or sex ($R = .09$, $F(2,139) = .55$, $p = .58$), or racial identity attitudes ($R = .14$, $F(6,135) = .45$, $p = .84$).

If one wished to replicate the results of the present study using a different sample, one would, of course, estimate racial identity by form-

Table 8.2
Summary of Regression Analyses Predicting Decision-Making Styles from Sex, Social Class, and Racial Identity Attitudes

Predictor Variables	r	Beta	T	P	R^2	R^2 Adj
		Rational Style				
Social Class	-.05	-.02	.37	.79		
Sex	-.27	-.27	3.23	.002		
Step 1 Model					.07*	.06
Encounter	-.12	-.16	1.36	.18		
Preencounter	-.20	-.09	1.36	.26		
Internalization	.22	.27	2.91	.004		
Immersion/ Emersion	-.13	-.10	.84	.04		
Overall model					.16***	.12
		Dependent Style				
Social Class	.03	.03	.38	.71		
Sex	-.02	-.02	.25	.81		
Step 1 Model					.00	.00
Encounter	-.06	-.03	.26	.79		
Preencounter	-.01	.01	.14	.88		
Internalization	.03	.08	.83	.41		
Immersion/ Emersion	-.08	-.09	-.72	.47		
Overall model					.01	.00
Social Class	.00	.01	.16	.87		
Sex	-.09	-.09	1.05	.30		
Overall model					.01	.00
Encounter	-.01	.00	.03	.97		
Preenconter	-.08	-.04	.49	.62		
Internalization	.08	.09	.91	.36		
Immersion/ Emersion	-.04	-.07	.59	.56		
Overall model					.02	.00

Note: R^2 adj = percent of variance explained after adjustment for shrinkage.

Table 8.3
Summary of Means (M) and Standard Deviations (SD) for Racial Identity
Clusters

Cluster Names	n	Decision Making Styles						Racial Identity Attitudes								
		Rational		Intuitive		Dependent		Pre		Enc		Im		Int	
		M	SD	M	SD	M	SD	M	SD	M	SD	M	SD	M	SD
Encounter (I)	25	5.20	4.30	2.96	2.60	2.40	2.30	3.02	.46	3.85	.65	3.37	.46	3.55	.58
Internalization (II)	-54	7.50	2.73	3.76	2.21	2.17	1.90	1.93	.50	2.59	.54	2.53	.39	3.80	.43
Preencounter (III)	15	7.33	3.22	3.67	2.44	2.60	1.70	2.83	1.06	1.67	.41	1.77	.26	2.61	.98
Internalization/ Encounter (IV)	-46	7.52	3.01	3.52	2.05	2.50	2.38	1.60	.41	3.76	.55	3.21	.36	4.31	.41

Note: Pre = Preencounter; Enc = Encounter; Im = Immersion/Emersion; Int = Internalization.

ing a prediction equation in which the racial identity attitude scale scores were each weighted by their respective beta weights (see Table 8.2), and added to a regression constant (8.30 in the case of the Rational decision-making style). Such an approach assumes that each racial identity attitude contributes to the person's personality profile. However, because Cross (1971) had originally proposed that people could be classified into discrete groups on the basis of racial identity attitudes, we decided to determine whether such classification would shed further light on our results.

For this investigation, BMDP K- means cluster analysis was used (Engelman & Hartigan, 1981) to group subjects on the basis of their pattern of racial identity attitudes. Four clusters were extracted because Cross's theory had proposed four distinctive types of attitudes, although Helms (1986) has pointed out that the attitudes may not be mutually exclusive. Using this procedure, all but 2 of the 142 subjects were assigned to a cluster. As can be seen in Table 8.3, the pattern of racial identity attitudes characterizing the clusters was somewhat different. In Cluster 1, which accounted for 25 people, Encounter attitudes were strongest; in Cluster 2 (n = 54), Internalization attitudes were strongest; in Cluster 3 (n = 15), Preencounter attitudes were strongest; in Cluster 4 (n = 46), Internalization attitudes were strongest, but were supplemented by a relatively high level of Encounter attitudes.

In order to determine whether these four clusters were differentially related to the three decision-making styles, a 4 X 3 treatment by subjects analysis of variance (ANOVA) was performed. This analysis revealed a significant main effect due to cluster membership ($F(3,136)$ = 3.38, p = .05). Cluster 1, the Encounter attitude group, used all of the decision-making styles less than did the other three groups. There was also a significant main effect due to decision-making style ($F(2,272)$ = 151.19, p = .000). The Rational style was used more than the other two styles. A significant cluster X decision-making style interaction was also found ($F(6,272)$ = 2.85, p = .025). Figure 8.1 illustrates the significant interactions. Encounter (Cluster 1) subjects used decision-making styles less than the other two groups and did not show as strong a preference for the Rational style over the Dependent and Intuitive styles as did the other three clusters. Thus, the results of the ANOVA indicated that the present sample used a Rational decision-making style, primarily with Internalization and perhaps Preencounter racial identity attitudes being most indicative of such usage, and Encounter attitudes being least indicative of usage of decision-making styles as operationalized in the present study.

DISCUSSION

Contrary to what one would have anticipated on the basis of most theoretical descriptions of Black people's cognitive styles (e.g., Norman & Atlas, 1978; Shade, 1982), the primary cognitive style used by subjects in this study was Rational, as measured by Harren's (1979b) academic decision making scale (ACDM). Not only were the Rational scale scores highest when compared to the other two scale scores within this sample, but when one compares the mean Rational scores of this sample to those obtained by other authors (e.g., Harren, Kass, Tinsley, & Moreland, 1978), then one finds that the mean scores of the Black subjects used in the present study tended to be approximately twice as high as those of their (presumably) White counterparts.

It appears that under some circumstances Blacks may use rational rather than group-centered or emotional cognitive styles. Nevertheless, it can be argued that university students are an elite group that has been educated to use rational strategies more so than have their less educated cohorts, or that a natural selection process occurs such that those students who attend college are likely to be the ones who use planful decision-making strategies; attending college may be merely one step in their overall plan. It can also be argued that, given that some of the students' decision-making scale scores indicated that they used none of the styles (7%) and some indicated the three styles were used equally (18%), then it is possible that Harren's (1979b) scale does not adequately measure the full range of decision-making styles exhibited by Black people. Even so, it appears that further empirical investigations of Black people's

Figure 8.1
Decision-Making Styles as a Function of Racial Identity Cluster Membership

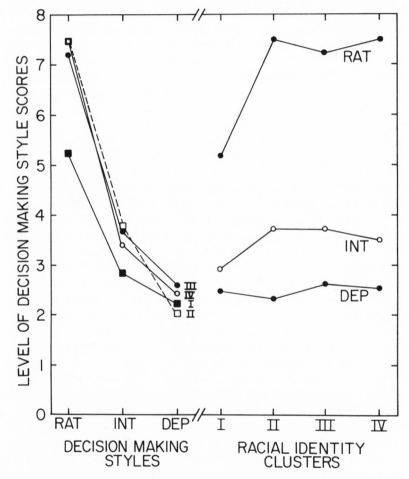

Note: Pre = Preencounter; Enc = Encounter; Im = Immersion/Emersion; Int = Internalization.

cognitive styles, involving samples of a variety of age groups, from a variety of settings, via measures permitting different operationalizations of cognitive styles, are warranted.

Of the three decision-making styles measured in the present study, only the Rational style was predicted by demographic factors and/or racial identity attitudes. Males were more likely to use the Rational style than were females; higher Internalization attitudes contributed to greater use of the Rational style. In Cross's (1971) Nigrescence model, the Internalization stage and, consequently, Internalization attitudes are postulated to represent a transcendent stage in which the person no longer defines her or his identity merely in response to race and racism. He describes this stage as one in which the person's intellect rather than emotions controls her or his world view and information-processing strategies. The significant linear relationship between Internalization attitudes and the Rational style provides some support for Cross's postulations. It is not clear why the Intuitive and Dependent styles were not linearly related to racial identity attitudes. One possibility is that because these styles were used so infrequently by subjects, there was not enough heterogeneity among scores to detect significant relationships. It is also possible that if the various types of racial identity attitudes develop at different rates, with Internalization attitudes being the last to develop, then the level of Internalization attitudes may reflect the person's level of identity crystallization. That is, prior to the development of a significant proportion of Internalization attitudes, perhaps the person's world view with respect to racial identity is still too diffuse to permit it to shape other stable personality characteristics such as cognitive styles. Thus, Preencounter, Encounter, and Immersion/Emersion attitudes may not have predicted Intuitive or Dependent decision-making styles because these attitudes reflect that portion of a person's racial identity that is reactive or transitional rather than proactive and stabilized.

Nevertheless, it is interesting that when subjects were assigned to groups on the basis of their configuration of racial identity attitudes, then some promising theoretical issues were raised. It appears, for instance, that although a preponderance of Internalization attitudes was still the best predictor of usage of a Rational decision-making style, Preencounter attitudes may also lead to usage of a Rational style. This finding suggests that both transcendence over the effects of race and racism and denial of such effects may be typical of individuals who are able to "rationalize" their life experiences, though the former manner of rationalization is presumably healthier than the latter. Examination of the relationship between racial identity attitudes and use of defense mechanisms might be a useful step in the effort to tease out the effects of cultural/racial identification on cognitive styles.

The finding that people who reported a predominance of Encounter attitudes were less likely to use or favor any decision-making styles than were the other groups is consistent with Cross's (1978) and Parham and Helms's (1985b) characterization of these attitudes as affect governed. Thus, people whose racial identity rests primarily on Encounter attitudes may use their emotions rather than structured information-processing strategies to make their decisions. It is possible that Harren's (1979b) decision-making scale does not adequately assess those decision-making styles that are dynamic and emotional rather than logical and stable.

Perhaps the most useful result of the present study is that it did not confirm previous theoretical formulations concerning Black people for the most part. That is, the subjects used in the present study were not found to be apathetic, emotional, or group dependent rather than logical analytic, and individualistic (Harrel 1979; Shade, 1982). One way that this study differs from previous empirical studies is that it focuses on a young adult sample rather than a sample of elementary school children. It seems reasonable to assume that cognitive styles may become more systematic as the person matures. The present study also seems to be the first to use a measure devised from Black personality theory to study cognitive styles. Possibly the absence of measures for categorizing within-group differences among Blacks may have resulted in biased perceptions of Black people's cognitive styles. Whichever is the case, it seems reasonable to conclude that more studies are needed that investigate the cognitive styles of Black subjects of various ages and occupational statuses via a variety of measures. One hopes that some of these measures will be decendants of Black personality theory.

PART III

PRACTICAL APPLICATIONS OF RACIAL IDENTITY THEORY

9

Counseling Attitudinal and Behavioral Predispositions: The Black/White Interaction Model[1]

JANET E. HELMS

INTRODUCTION

Individuals at different stages of racial consciousness probably enter counseling relationships with different attitudinal and behavioral predispositions. The manner in which these predispositions are actually expressed may depend upon a variety of factors including the race, the racial attitudes, and the perceived racial attitudes of the other person(s) with whom a counseling relationship is sought. In this chapter, counselor and client predispositions associated with the various stages of racial consciousness will be described. For the sake of simplicity, only counseling dynamics as they might occur within counseling dyads of the same race are outlined in detail. In a subsequent section, procedures for using the stages to explain cross-racial dyads will be explored. In chapter 12, the feasibility of using the dyad model to analyze noncounseling dyadic relationships will be explored.

Black Dyads

Various authors (G. G. Jackson, 1977; Milliones, 1980; Parham & Helms, 1981, 1985a) have recommended that the Cross (1971) model

[1]This chapter is an excerpt from "Toward a theoretical explanation of the effects of race on counseling: A Black and White model" by J. E. Helms, 1984, *The Counseling Psychologist*, 12(4) 153–165. Reproduced with permission of Sage Publications.

be used to interpret counseling dynamics involving Black clients. In counseling dyads in which both the counselor and client are Black, both must be at some stage of racial consciousness, though not necessarily the same one. Thus, it seems important to speculate about how the attitudes of each might contribute to the counseling process.

Preencounter. A Preencounter client, because he or she feels negatively about Black people, feels insulted when he or she is assigned to a Black counselor. Present literature suggests that there are at least two ways in which a client might express Preencounter attitudes when assigned to a Black counselor. Gardner (1971) hypothesized that clients who reject Blackness will project "their own self-hatred, and manifest intense, overt hostility toward their Black therapist" (p. 85). Vontress (1971b) implied that those Black clients whom he classified as "colored" might approach the Black counselor with condescending attitudes and/or feelings of embarrassment (see Tounsel & A. C. Jones, 1980, for a description of such a client). Whether the denigration of Blacks is expressed overtly via hostility or covertly via embarrassment, it seems likely that the Preencounter client will spare no effort in apprising the counselor of the counselor's inferior status and he or she will have no intention of revealing significant aspects of herself or himself to the counselor.

A Preencounter counselor is likely to share the dominant society's racial stereotypes of Blacks and to behave in a manner toward the client that confirms these stereotypes. Due to his or her professional training, the Preencounter counselor might attempt unsuccessfully to empathize with his or her Black client. In support of the position that some therapists can be biased against members of their own race, Brown (1950) found that Black social workers tended to be more punitive toward clients of their own race than toward White clients, whereas Clanek (1970) reported that Black therapists working with Blacks seemed to avoid acknowledging that the client was Black.

Encounter. The Encounter client possibly assumes that any Black counselor can help him or her resolve his or her problem no matter what. At the same time, he or she feels self-conscious about not being "Black enough" and is likely to spend a great deal of time and effort apologizing for not fitting what he or she erroneously perceives to be the Black lifestyle. Because he or she wants the counselor, a Black person, to approve of him or her, he or she may avoid discussing issues about which he or she thinks members of the Black culture are likely to disapprove.

The Encounter counselor probably approaches a Black client with a mixture of fear and anticipation. Fear, because the counselor wants to be approved of by other Black people but is not sure he or she can measure up to their expectations; anticipation, because the opportunity to become close to another Black person is compelling. Thus, he or she might avoid using techniques in the counseling interaction (e.g., confrontation) that he or she thinks will antagonize the client.

Immersion. The Immersion client is likely to be pulled in two directions. On the one hand, he or she wants to feel positive toward the counselor because he or she is Black, but on the other hand he or she feels compelled to test the counselor to ensure that the counselor has not been co-opted by the White world. The client's predominant demeanor will be tinged with anger and hostility; counselors will probably have to pass covert and overt tests before they are permitted any psychological closeness. The Immersion client most closely corresponds to Vontress's (1971b) "militant" Black client.

The Immersion counselor possibly will feel duty-bound to reeducate the Black client who is being and behaving in ways that the counselor feels are inconsistent with being a Black person or with advancing the Black culture. Possibly the reeducation attempts will be tinged with covert hostility expressed via nonaccepting attitudes if the client refuses to be reeducated. Likewise, it might be difficult for such a counselor to aid the client in separating issues of actual abuse from obsessions about hypothesized or potential abuse.

Internalizing. Racial identification issues per se are not likely to be the primary concerns of the Internalizing client. Although racial issues will not automatically disappear from her or his life, she or he is not afraid to tackle them when they occur. Moreover, her or his life issues are now centered around becoming the best person he or she can become rather than the best Black person because such dichotomies no longer have meaning for her or him. In seeking a counselor, the Internalizing client may prefer a Black counselor, but he or she will judge the counselor regardless of his or her race on the basis of the quality of her or his demonstrated skills.

Likewise, the Internalizing counselor no longer regards the client's race as either a major asset or deficit. It just is. Therefore, he or she attempts to help the client resolve presenting problems and/or become self-actualized, but recognizes that acceptance of one's race is an important part of the actualization process.

Research on Black stages of racial consciousness and counseling. Empirical investigations of how Black people's racial attitudes influence the counseling process are rare. As a consequence, empirical support for the proposed counselor/client predispositions is virtually nonexistent. Nevertheless, Parham and Helms (1981) did find that Preencounter attitudes were associated with Black students' greater preference for White rather than Black counselors; Immersion attitudes tended to be associated with a stronger preference for Black rather than White counselors. These findings offer some confirmation for the proposed model, though additional investigation is needed to determine the manner in which attitudes associated with specific stages actually are expressed in counseling relationships.

White Dyads

To the author's knowledge, no study exists in which the racial attitudes of Whites toward other Whites have been investigated for their effect on counseling process or outcome. Maybe concern about personal racial adjustment is not an issue that occupies much time or space in the average White person's life, particularly since it has been defined exclusively in terms of how he or she relates to other racial groups. Surveys of college students' concerns, for instance, show that racial issues are less likely to be reported as a problem area by White students than by minority students (e.g., Webster, Sedlacek, & Miyares, 1979). The few counseling and psychology preference studies in which investigators have attempted to determine White students' preference for race of counselor have revealed no clear-cut same-race preference (see Sattler, 1977). Although it is possible that Whites have no actual racial preferences, a more likely explanation for such findings is that racial preference for counselors is not an issue that has meaning for White potential clients because Black counselors are so rare that such matches seldom occur. It is also possible that, for many potential clients, greater experience is attributed to being a Black professional in a primarily White occupation. In either case, it seems unlikely that race will occur as a central theme between White/White counseling dyads unless the client finds herself or himself in an environmental cross-racial interaction from which extrication is not easy (e.g., living or working with a roommate or colleague of another race). Although it is conceivable that feelings such as guilt, anger, and anxiety may be associated with being at a particular stage of White racial consciousness, it is unlikely that these affective issues will occur in therapy in the absence of external race-related stimuli. Therefore, discussion of the White racial consciousness stages in counseling will proceed using possible interracial dilemmas occurring outside the counseling session.

Contact. The client in the Contact stage of development probably seeks counseling because naive attempts to satisfy curiosity about another racial group have led to unanticipated psychological repercussions. For instance, Whites (usually females) who date interracially often have no intention of marrying the person whom they are dating, whereas Blacks (usually males) whom they date consider marriage a serious possibility (Pope, 1978). Perhaps the White interracial dater is trying to satisfy her curiosity or exert her independence from familial constraints. However, if she begins to feel some pressures from her partner to make the relationship more permanent, then she may begin to feel some guilt about having misled him, though not necessarily at a conscious level. D. W. Sue's (1981) vignette of a cross-racial couple seems to be an example of this dynamic. The client in such a predicament may enter the counseling relationship with the latent goals of trying to figure out what she should do about this particular relationship as well as understanding her own confusing feelings that others' reactions to the relationship may have elicited.

The counselor in the Contact stage has probably learned very little about other cultures in his or her formal professional training (Arredondo-Dowd & Gonsalves, 1980). What he or she knows is what can be inferred from traditional programs, that is (a) although some White people are biased against Blacks, (b) therapists should not be, and (c) the particular therapy skills taught by the program should be applicable to all clients regardless of race. Therefore, the Contact therapist enters the relationship with the expectation that people in general should be treated equally. Thus, the counselor minimizes or ignores racial issues that have an impact upon the White client.

Disintegration. The Disintegration client may be the person whose ostensibly benevolent actions and attitudes toward Blacks have not resulted in positive consequences. For instance, White civil rights workers who were ostracized from the movement by Black militants during the sixties might be expected to have had feelings of Disintegration (P. Moore, 1982). Because they may feel that they have been abused and their sacrifices are unappreciated, these clients might enter counseling for some guidance about how they should react and behave with Blacks.

Perhaps the Disintegrated counselor is a person who has been exposed informally (e.g., via minority peers and clients or incidental readings) to information suggesting that typical counseling techniques do not work with Black clients; believing such supposition to be fact, he or she may approach cross-racial problems with the expectation that there is no way that Whites and Blacks can interact effectively, a viewpoint that is likely to be communicated to the White client dealing with racial issues outside of counseling.

Reintegration. The Reintegration client often feels very negatively about Black people. He or she is likely to magnify racial differences and to harbor feelings of unexpressed (in most cases) anger. This person may enter counseling if environmental situations (e.g., job demands) force the person into a supposedly harmonious relationship with Blacks. The Reintegrated person might seek help in integrating internal feelings with external expectations.

The Reintegration counselor may believe that he or she should not be biased against Blacks, perhaps because of the equalitarian philosophy implicit in most training programs. Therefore, he or she attempts to camouflage negative feelings toward Blacks, but these feelings may be expressed in more-or-less subtle means such as "double-binding" the client who insists upon resolving racial issues. For instance, the counselor's verbal behavior may indicate that bias is wrong but her or his nonverbal behavior may reinforce the bias. In addition, the counselor may be unable to see obvious negative implications of specific behaviors when they occur in cross-racial situations.

Pseudo-Independent. The Pseudo-Independent client may have a tendency to intellectualize about racial issues and/or to believe that he or she is more knowledgeable about Blacks and Whites than is actually the case. Therefore, this client may enter the counseling relationship with no clear idea of how to integrate general knowledge about cultural issues with feelings associated with specific issues. A person, for instance, may understand intellectually why affirmative action policies are necessary, but may still feel upset if he or she anticipates that his or her own employment opportunities will be limited by such policies.

The Pseudo-Independent counselor can provide the client with information and guidance necessary to help the client understand racial issues that impact the client. Yet because the counselor's knowledge at this stage may be more intellectually diverse than it is affectively diverse, he or she may have difficulty in empathizing with the emotional dimensions of clients' concerns.

Autonomy. The Autonomous client is not likely to bring racial issues per se into the counseling relationship. Such issues as do occur perhaps will concern helping her or his racial peers to understand Black/White issues and eliminating oppressive environmental circumstances. The Autonomous client is sensitive to the possibility that social problems involving a Black person may, in fact, be fueled by covert interracial dynamics and is willing to explore such possibilities.

The Autonomous counselor, for her or his part, is willing to tackle racial issues when they occur and to actively search for them when he or she feels that such exploration will be beneficial to therapy. Because he or she feels comfortable about her or his racial identity, the Autonomous counselor is able to empathize with the client's frustration and anger, even when it is directed toward members of his or her own race and to help the client in her or his search for a more tolerant world.

Analyzing Counseling Process and Predicting Outcome

When both counselor and client stages of racial consciousness are assessed and used to predict the counseling process, four types of relationships are possible: parallel, crossed, progressive, and regressive. When counselors and clients are of the same race, a parallel relationship is one in which the counselor and client belong to the same stage of racial consciousness and necessarily share the same attitudes about Blacks *and* Whites (e.g., Preencounter/Preencounter or Contact/Contact); a crossed relationship is one in which counselor and client belong to opposite stages of racial consciousness, defined as having opposing attitudes about both Blacks and Whites (e.g., Preencounter/Immersion or Reintegration/Autonomy); a progressive relationship is one in which the counselor's stage of racial consciousness is at least one stage more advanced than the client's (e.g., Disintegration/Contact or Immersion/Preencounter); a regressive relationship is one in which the client's stage of development is at least one stage more advanced than the counselor's.

When the counselor's and client's races are different, parallel dyads are defined as those combinations of stages in which counselors and clients share similar racial attitudes about Blacks *and* Whites (e.g., Internalization/Autonomy), whereas crossed dyads involve those combinations of stages that are characterized by opposing attitudes toward Blacks and Whites (e.g., Immersion/Reintegration). Each dyad involves two types of attitudes per person (i.e., a general attitude toward Blacks and a general attitude toward Whites). In those instances in which only one type of attitude is similar (or dissimilar) the counseling process will include a blend of the characteristics of each of the stages that are involved.

Ideally, in a progressive relationship, the counselor will be able to gradually move the client toward a healthier stage. Yet if the counselor remains at the same stage, then the relationship becomes parallel, a condition likely to result in a counseling impasse. The counselor cannot move the client further than the counselor has come. To the extent that racial issues are an important concern in the counseling process, regressive relationships are likely to end in termination because the counselor is unable to enter the client's frame of reference. The specific implications of parallel and crossed relationships will probably differ depending upon whether the counselor and/or client is Black or White and whether the counseling is intra- or cross-racial; but by identifying the counselor and client's racial consciousness stages, it should be possible to make predictions about the quality of their counseling relationship as well as possible counseling outcomes.

In Table 9.1, examples of each of the types of racial consciousness relationships, within and between races, are presented as a means of illustrating how the proposed model might be used. Given a general conceptualization of likely dimensions and characteristics, one needs to operationalize them in a manner that permits empirical verification.

Table 9.1
Examples of the Four Types of Counseling Relationships Based on Racial Identity Stages

| Stages of Identity[1] | | Type of Relation-ship | Common Affective Issues | Counseling Process | |
Counselor's	Client's			Counselor/ Strategies	Counseling Outcome
			Black Dyads		
1. Preencounter	Preencounter	Parallel	Anger about being assigned to a Black person. Guilt about negative feelings.	Both will use strategies de-signed to deny and avoid issues to reinterpret whatever happens in a manner consistent with perceived negative stereotypes.	Client termi-nates with little symptom remission. Counselor "pushes" client out of counseling.
2. Immersion	Preencounter	Crossed (Progres-sive)	Counselor may feel angry and rejecting; client feels fearful and intimidated.	General non-acceptance of one another; counselor may be low in em-pathy, use much advice giving; client is passive and tries not to become involved in the process.	If counselor can act as positive role model, client may develop positive feelings about Blackness; self-esteem is enhanced.
3. Preencounter	Immersion	Regressive (Crossed)	Counselor shares White society's fear, weariness and anxiety; client dis-places anger.	Client attempts to reform coun-selor; counselor attempts to avoid issues.	Short relationships; client's anger may be enhanced, counselor's anxiety may be increased.
4. Encounter	Preencounter	Progressive	Counselor feels excited and appre-hensive about working with Black client; client feels angry and apprehensive and distrusting.	Social discussion in which counselor tries to prove he/she is Black; client tries to prove he/she isn't.	long relationships if counselor uses enthusiasm to engage client; limited symptom remission if counselor avoids doing therapy.
			White Dyads		
1. Contact	Contact	Parallel	Counselor and client exhibit curiosity and naivete about racial issues.	Information sharing, avoid-ance of negative affect related to racial matters.	Discussion of racial issues is aborted because neither knows how to resolve them.

142

Table 9.1 (continued)

	Counselor's	Client's	Type of Relation-ship	Common Affective Issues	Counseling Process Counselor/ Strategies	Counseling Outcome
				Black Dyads		
2.	Contact	Reintegration	Crossd (Regression)	Mutual dislike because they don't empathize with one another's racial attitudes.	Argumentative attempts to re-educate each other.	Premature termi-nation; client's symptoms may be aggravated because he/she doesn't respect counselor.
3.	Autonomous	Disintegration	Progressive	Counselor may be empathic and accepting; client needs to deal with self-concept issues and confused feelings.	Counselor attempts to encourage self-awareness and understanding of racial dynamics.	Potential for client insight and knowledge acquisition is good.
4.	Disintegration	Autonomous	Regressive	Friction; low levels of empathy and under-standing.	Counselor attempts to protect and nur-ture client inap-propriately.	Premature termination; client perceives counselor as in-expert.
				Mixed Dyads		
1.	Preencounter	Reintegration	Parallel	Mutual anxiety; coun-selor wants to prove competence; client dis-places anger previously denied.	Abusive relation-ship; client tests and manipulates; counselor is unas-sertive and task oriented.	Relationship may be long-lasting because it re-inforces stereo-types; little symptom remission.
2.	Immersion	Reintegration	Crossed	Direct overt expression of hostility and anger by both.	Debates; refusal to become involved with one another.	Short-lived; leaves both feeling frustrated about original beliefs.
3.	Internal-ization	Disintegration	Progressive	Client's self-concept issues, feelings of confusion, and help-lessness are the focus.	Counselor attempts to model positive adjustment and to elicit denied feelings.	Potential for client cross-racial skill development and improved self-confidence is good.
4.	Disintegration	Internali-zation	Regressive	Counselor experiences pain and/or anxiety about cross-racial issues.	Counselor inter-acts with undue reserve, uneasi-ness, and incon-gruence; client senses counselor's discomfort.	Premature termination; client will seek counselor more in tune with her/his needs.

[1]*Note*: Individual stages are described in chapters 2 and 4.

10

Does Race or Racial Identity Attitudes Influence the Counseling Process in Black and White Dyads?

ROBERT T. CARTER

The racial identity perspective in counseling and psychotherapy was developed as an alternative to what might be called "the race perspective." The race perspective advocated one or more of the following assumptions: (a) the client's and perhaps the counselor's race influence their manner of interacting with one another (e.g., Orlinsky & Howard, 1978); (b) racial stereotypes and cultural biases present in American society are also expressed in cross-racial therapy relationships (e.g., Adams, 1970; Gardner, 1971; A. Jones & Seagull, 1977); and (c) potential conflict between the Black client and White counselor is of primary concern (e.g., Vontress, 1970; Griffith, 1977) if effective cross-racial services are to be delivered.

The racial identity perspective (Butler, 1975; Helms, 1984b) assumes that one's stage of racial identity, regardless of whether one is Black or White, counselor or client, may have a stronger impact on the therapy process than race per se. That is, products (e.g., cognitions) resulting from one's racial world view may influence how counseling participants perceive and interact with each other. Different combinations of stages should result in different styles of interactions.

Thus, the two positions differ in the amount of importance they give to racial category membership per se as opposed to psychological characteristics resulting from such membership. If the race perspective is correct, one would expect that race alone, without consideration of racial identity attitudes, would influence the counseling process. However, if the racial identity development theorists are correct, one would expect to find that counselor and client racial identity attitudes would be related to the counseling process in same and cross-race counseling dyads. Therefore, the present study (a) explored whether there were differences in counseling process variables when racially homogeneous and cross-racial dyads were compared, and (b) examined how clients' and counselors' racial identity attitudes were related to the counseling process. In both instances, counseling process was operationalized as counselor intentions and client reactions.

METHOD

Subjects

The subjects in the study were drawn from participants who attended cross-cultural training conferences for mental health workers held in New York, California, and Maryland. However, the focus of the present study was the workshop attendees who participated in simulated counseling sessions. The racial compositions of the dyads were as follows: 19 had White counselors/White clients; 8 had White counselors/Black clients; and 4 had Black counselors/White clients. The mean ages for clients and counselors were 34.59 (SD = 14.02) and 33.06 (SD = 9.38), respectively. Self-reported socioeconomic status was middle class. The average years of education was 17.16 (SD = 1.93) for clients and 17.79 (SD = 1.50) for counselors.

Instruments

The instruments used in this study consisted of the Black and White racial identity attitudinal measures (described in chapters 3 and 5, respectively), two counseling process measures, and a personal data sheet.

Counseling Process Measures

Therapist's intentions (Hill & O'Grady, 1985). In a recent paper by Hill and O'Grady (1985), a therapy process measure consisting of 19 intentions was described. According to the authors, a counselor intention is defined as a "therapist's rationale for selecting a specific behavior, response mode, technique or intervention to use with a client at any given moment within the process of the session" (p.3). Thus, "counselor intentions" seems to refer to the reason why a therapist chooses a particular intervention or response. Counselor intentions seemingly guide the choice of interventions according to Hill and O'Grady.

The 19 intentions proposed by the authors are: Get Information, Give Information, Support, Focus, Cognitions, Feelings, Insight, Change,

Challenge, Therapist Needs, Set Limits, Clarify, Hope, Cathart, Behavior, Self-Control, Reinforce Change, Resistance, and Relationship. The results of two studies reported by Hill and O'Grady (1985) suggested that the therapist's intentions system could be used to assess differential counselor intentions as proposed by Helms's (1984b) model. Basically, Helms proposed that counselors with different types of racial identity attitudes use different counseling strategies, which here is operationalized according to intentions.

Client reactions. Hill, Helms, Spiegel, and Tichenor (1988) have developed a client reactions system that consists of 19 positive, negative, and neutral client reactions. The measure consists of 19 reactions: Supported, Understood, Hopeful, Relief, More Clear, Feelings, Negative Thoughts or Behaviors, Better Self-Understanding, Responsibility, Challenged, Got Unstuck, New Perspective, Educated, Learned New Ways to Behave, Miscommunicated, Felt Worse, Lack Direction, Ineffective, and No Reaction. In their paper, a series of studies attesting to the validity of the systems were reported. Their studies suggest that the client reaction system is (a) sensitive to differing types of client therapeutic experiences, (b) capable of discriminating between experienced and inexperienced counselors, and (c) appears to have content validity in that the clients felt the system was representative of their experiences in therapy.

Personal data sheet. The personal data sheet, designed for this study, was used to investigate professional characteristics (e.g., years of counseling experience, level of training, and prior training in cross-cultural counseling) of participants. Also, participants were asked to indicate their age, socioeconomic status, race/ethnicity, educational level, and their country of origin. In this study, only the information pertaining to race was used for descriptive purposes. Summaries of the remainder can be found in Carter (1987).

Procedure

As mentioned in the Subjects section, data were collected in day-long training workshops for mental health workers. The advertised purpose of the workshop was to develop counseling skills in cross-racial therapy (see Carter, 1987, for a description of the workshop). During one part of the workshop, volunteers from small groups simulated counselor/client interviews that were audio- or video-taped depending on what kind of equipment was available at the site. The participants who chose to be clients were given a list of potential racial topics and were asked to choose a topic that resembled a personal racial experience to discuss during the simulation. The counselors were simply instructed to counsel the clients using their customary counseling/therapy skills. A 15-minute session was conducted while the members of the small groups not in the simulation acted as observers.

After completion of the simulated interview, the client and counselor reviewed the taped interview. During the review process, the client recorded his or her reactions using the Hill et al. (1988) client reactions system and the counselor indicated his or her intentions underlying each counselor statement using the Counselor Intention List (Hill & O'Grady, 1985). Group members then offered participants verbal feedback about the interactions. A second simulation was then conducted following the same format.

RESULTS

Race Perspective

To determine whether counselor and client usage of intentions and reactions, respectively, differed according to the racial compositions of the dyads, 38 separate analyses of variance were used to examine the effects of race on these process variables. Independent variables in these analyses were the three dyadic racial combinations (White counselors/White clients, White counselors/Black clients, Black counselors/White clients) as previously described, and the dependent variables were proportions of usage of each of the 19 counselor intentions and 19 client reactions. Tukey post hoc tests were used to determine differences between dyads when the omnibus F test was significant. Note that use of so many analyses slants the results in the direction of finding relationships in support of the race perspective and, consequently, against the racial identity perspective.

These analyses revealed that the counselor intention of Relationship ($F(2,28) = 3.25$, $p <.05$) differed significantly according to dyad racial composition. Counselors in White counselor/Black client dyads (M = .008, SD = .008) and Black counselor/White client dyads (M = .001, SD = .012) used the counselor intention of Relationship significantly more often than counselors in the White counselor/White client dyads (M = .002, SD = .002).

When client reactions among dyads of different racial combinations were examined, only the comparison involving the client reaction of Hopeful ($F(2,28) = 4.25$, $p = .05$) showed a significant difference. Clients in White counselor/Black client relationships (M = .007, SD = .004) and White counselor/White client (M = .008, SD = .003) tended to report the reaction of Hopeful more often than did clients in Black counselor/White client dyads (M = .02, SD = .015).

Given the number of analyses conducted, two between-group comparisons would be expected to be significant by chance. Therefore, one significant reaction and one significant intention do not exceed chance expectations.

Relationships of Racial Identity Attitudes to Counseling Process

To investigate the hypothesis that counselors' usage of certain intentions and clients' reactions to counselors within dyads of each racial combination would be related to counselors' and clients' racial identity attitudes, Pearson correlations were computed. For each of the dyadic racial combinations, correlations among counselor racial identity attitudes and counselor intentions and client reactions; and client racial identity attitudes and counselor intentions and client reactions were computed. All significant correlations reported were at or beyond the .05 level of significance. In Black/White dyads, a total of approximately 9 correlations of attitudes with reactions and intentions can be expected to be significant by chance; in White/White dyads a total of approximately 10 correlations can be expected to be significant by chance. No Black/Black dyads were included in these analyses.

Counselor intentions in White counselor/Black client dyads. When the correlations of counselor intentions with counselor racial identity attitudes within White counselor/Black client dyads were examined, White counselor racial identity attitudes were correlated with three counselor intentions: (a) Set Limits, (b) Support, and (c) Resistance. White counselor Disintegration attitudes were positively related to the counselor intention of Set Limits ($r(6) = .74$), and Set Limits was negatively related to White counselor Pseudo-Independent attitudes ($r(6) = -.79$). White counselor Pseudo-Independent attitudes were also negatively related to the counselor intentions of Support ($r(6) = -.78$) and Resistance ($r(6) = -.81$).

The analyses to examine the relationships among counselor intentions and Black client racial identity attitudes showed that two client racial identity attitudes were related to four counselor intentions: Black client Preencounter attitudes were positively related to the counselor intentions of Set Limits ($r(6) = .71$), Hope ($r(6) = .75$), and Behaviors ($r(6) = .76$); Black client Encounter attitudes were significantly positively related to the counselor intention of Cathart ($r(6) = .74$).

Client reactions in White counselor/Black client dyads. With four significant relationships, Black client Immersion/Emersion racial identity attitudes were most often correlated with their reactions during the counseling process. Black client Immersion/Emersion attitudes were significantly positively related to the client reaction Understood ($r(6) = .75$), and significantly negatively related to Relief ($r(6) = -.72$) and Got Unstuck ($r(6) = -.71$). Black client Encounter attitudes were significantly negatively related to the client reaction of Relief ($r(6) = -.80$). Black client

Internalization attitudes were significantly negatively related to the client reaction of Hopeful ($r(6) = -.78$).

Six of the correlations concerning Black client reactions and White counselor racial identity attitudes were significant. Black clients' reactions of Supported were significantly positively related to White counselors' Contact attitudes ($r(6) = .71$), whereas the Black client reactions of More Clear ($r(6) = -.72$) and Negative Thoughts and Behaviors ($r(6) = -.81$) were significantly negatively related to White counselor Contact attitudes. White counselors' Disintegration attitudes were significantly positively related to the client reaction of Lack Direction ($r(6) = .72$). White counselor Pseudo-Independent attitudes were significantly negatively related to the client reactions of Learn New Behavior ($r(6) = -.76$) and Ineffective ($r(6) = -.74$).

Counselor intentions in Black counselor/White client dyads. The significant correlations pertaining to counselor intentions and Black counselor racial identity attitudes involved the Preencounter and Encounter attitudes. Preencounter attitudes were significantly negatively related to the counselor intention of Hope ($r(2) = -.97$), and counselor Encounter attitudes were significantly positively related to the counselor intention of Feelings ($r(2) = .96$).

Only one significant relationship was found when Black counselors' intentions were correlated with White clients' racial identity attitudes. The significant positive correlation involved client Pseudo-Independent attitudes and the counselor intention of Hope ($r(2) = .96$).

Clients' reactions in Black counselor/White client dyads. Overall, two client reactions were related to White client racial identity attitudes in Black counselor/White client dyads. White client Disintegration attitudes were significantly positively related to their reactions of Lack Direction ($r(2) = .97$) and Ineffective ($r(2) = .97$). Reintegration attitudes were also significantly positively related to the client reaction of Lack Direction ($r(2) = .98$) and Ineffective ($r(2) = .98$).

Two of the correlations were significant for the analyses correlating White client reactions and Black counselor racial identity attitudes. The client reaction of Better Self-Understanding was significantly positively related to counselor Encounter attitudes ($r(2) = .96$). Counselor Internalization attitudes were found to be significantly positively related to the client reaction of No Reaction ($r(2) = .96$).

Counselor intentions in White counselor/White client dyads. Summaries of significant correlations among the counselor intentions and racial identity attitudes for White Counselor/White Client dyads show that White counselor Contact attitudes were significantly negatively related to the counselor intentions of Set Limits ($r(17) = -.61$), Clarify ($r(17) = -.56$), and Hope ($r(17) = -.64$). White counselor Disintegration attitudes were significantly positively related to the counselor intentions of Hope ($r(17)$

= .74) and Behaviors ($r(17)$ = .65). White counselor Reintegration attitudes were significantly positively related to the counselor intentions of Set Limits ($r(17)$ = .48), Hope ($r(17)$ = .65), and Behaviors ($r(17)$ =.55), and were significantly negatively related to Feelings ($r(17)$ = −.50). White counselor Pseudo-Independent attitudes were significantly positively related to the counselor intentions of Get Information ($r(17)$ = .48) and Self-Control ($r(17)$ = .48). White counselor Autonomy attitudes were significantly negatively related to the counselor intentions of Hope ($r(17)$ = −.61) and Behaviors ($r(17)$ = −.52).

When the relationships between White client racial identity attitudes and White counselor intentions were considered, it was found that White client Contact attitudes were significantly positively related to the counselor intentions of Support ($r(17)$ = .61), Feelings ($r(17)$ = .48), and Reinforce Change ($r(17)$ = .58). White client Disintegration attitudes were negatively related to Set Limits ($r(17)$ = −.53). The counselor intention of Cathart ($r(17)$ = −.51) was found to be significantly negatively related to White client Reintegration attitudes. White client Pseudo-Independent attitudes were significantly negatively related to the counselor intentions of Give Information ($r(17)$ = −.49) and Cognitions ($r(17)$ = −.50). White client Autonomy attitudes were significantly negatively related to the counselor intentions of Get Information ($r(17)$ = −.48), Change ($r(17)$ = −.50), Relationship ($r(17)$ = −.48), and Therapist Needs ($r(17)$ = −.52).

Client reactions in White counselor/White client dyads. The correlations for White client racial identity attitudes in White counselor/White client dyads revealed that six reactions were significantly correlated with clients' racial identity attitudes. Client Contact attitudes were significantly positively related to the client reactions of Support ($r(17)$ = .50) and Understood ($r(17)$ = .53). Client Disintegration attitudes were significantly positively related to the client reaction of Ineffective ($r(17)$ = .45). Client Pseudo-Independent attitudes were significantly positively related to the client reaction of New Perspective ($r(17)$ = .45). Also, client Autonomy attitudes were significantly negatively related to the client reactions of Responsibility ($r(17)$ = −.46) and Lack Direction ($r(17)$ = −.46).

Seven significant correlations were found between counselor racial identity attitudes and client reactions in White counselor/White client dyads. Counselor Contact attitudes were significantly positively related to the client reactions of Better Understanding ($r(17)$ = .45), and significantly negatively related to the client reactions of Relief ($r(17)$ = −.47) and No Reaction ($r(17)$ = −.53). Counselor Disintegration attitudes were significantly positively related to the client reactions of Relief ($r(17)$ = .45), Got Unstuck ($r(17)$ = .57), and Ineffective ($r(17)$ = .52). Counselor Reintegration attitudes were significantly positively related to the client reaction of Lack Direction ($r(17)$ = .45).

DISCUSSION

Helms's (1984b) interaction model proposed that racial identity development rather than racial group membership per se determines the quality of the counseling process. On the other hand, what is here being called the race perspective assumes that different racial combinations of counselors and clients should reveal a qualitatively different counseling process. Specific issues investigated in the present study, which address these contrasting assumptions, were: (a) whether there were substantial qualitative differences in counseling process due to race in same and cross-racial dyads, and (b) whether racial identity attitudes were related to counselor intentions and/or client reactions within same and cross-racial (i.e., White counselor/White client, Black counselor/White client, and White counselor/Black client) counseling dyads.

Analyses of variance were used to determine whether race alone differentiated dyads with regard to usage of 19 counselor intentions and 19 client reactions. Only one significant relationship involving race was found for each set of variables. Consequently, it is highly likely that these findings were simply due to chance. However, the possible meaning of these two relationships will be discussed because this study was exploratory.

Racial Differences

The counselor intention of Relationship was used significantly more often in Black counselor/White client and White counselor/Black client dyads than in White counselor/White client dyads. The Relationship intention concerns the counselor's desire to improve the quality of the relationship (cf. Hill & O'Grady, 1985). In other words, Black and White counselors in mixed-race dyads intended their interventions to resolve problems in the relationships, possibly so that they could maintain a strong working relationship. Perhaps this finding indicates that in biracial dyads, counselors believe that additional attention to relationship building is needed when the counseling dyads involve Blacks and Whites in either the counselor or client roles.

The client reaction of Hopeful also differed significantly by dyad type. Clients in Black counselor/White client dyads reported feeling hopeful more often than clients in White counselor/White client or White counselor/Black client dyads. It seems that White clients felt more confident and encouraged to change when their counselors were Black. Perhaps White clients felt that their Black counselors were better able to understand the racial issues that they raised during the simulated counseling. It may also be that Black counselors' interventions were such that they were able to communicate effectively to the client that their situation was not hopeless.

In confirmation of one of Helms's (1984b) assertions and contrary to most contemporary racial theorizing, it appears that race alone (i.e., without considering psychological variables such as racial identity development), at least as operationalized in the present study, may not have a particularly strong effect on the counseling process.

Racial Identity Attitudes and the Counseling Process

Implicit in the interaction model is the idea that what the counselor does as a result of his or her racial identity attitudes influences clients' reactions, and also that client racial identity attitudes might influence counselors' behaviors (inferred here from counselor intentions). Such a sequence would occur if counselors' or clients' racial identity attitudes influenced their overt behavior in a manner that was discernable to the other party. Although counselor and client behaviors were not investigated directly in the present study, it seems reasonable to speculate that the counselors' intentions were influenced by some things the clients were doing and that the clients' reactions were influenced by some things the counselors were doing. Therefore, if these speculations are warranted, it seems reasonable to discuss the findings in the present study interactively. That is, for each racial dyad combination, the counseling process variables associated with racial identity attitudes will be presented and discussed in terms of how the counselor's and client's racial identity attitudes seemed to influence the counselor's intentions as well as the client's reactions. For example, the counselor intentions and client reactions associated with counselors' Contact attitudes will be discussed as will be the counselor intentions and client reactions associated with clients' Contact attitudes, and so forth.

White counselor/Black client dyads. Helms's (1984b) other assumption concerns the extent to which racial identity attitudes, which presumably interact with race, are better predictors of the counseling process than racial group membership itself. Figure 10.1 shows that in White counselor/Black client dyads, both White counselor racial identity attitudes and Black client racial identity attitudes were related to counselor intentions and client reactions, but no more of the intentions were related than would have been expected by chance. However, two more than chance expectations were found with respect to reactions.

White counselor Contact attitudes were not associated with counselor intentions, but were related to three Black client reactions. The client reaction of Supported, which reflects the client's belief that the counselor accepts the client and believes that change is possible, was positively related to counselor Contact attitudes, whereas the client reactions of More Clear and Negative Thoughts and Behaviors were negatively related to counselor Contact attitudes. The client reaction of More Clear

Figure 10.1
Relationships among Counselor Intentions, Client Reactions, and Counselor
and Client Racial Identity Attitudes for White Counselor/Black Client Dyad
Types

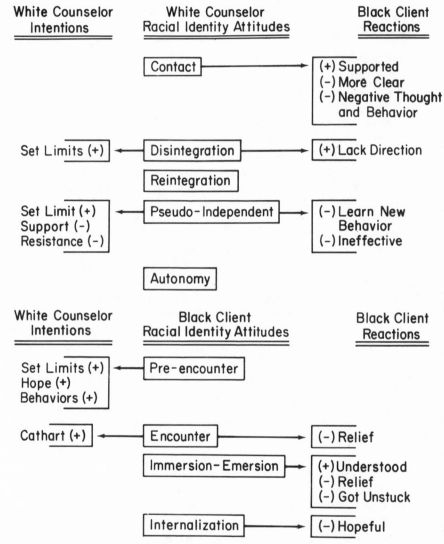

Arrows show intentions and reactions correlated with racial identity attitudes; (+) indicates
positive relationship; (−) indicates negative relationship.

reflects the client's feeling that he or she was able to become more focused about the presenting problem; the client reaction of Negative Thoughts and Behavior reflects the feeling that the client was able to become aware of specific thoughts and behaviors that caused problems. It seems that Black clients were more likely to feel supported when the White counselor's Contact attitudes were high, but were less likely to feel focused about their problem or able to identify specific cognitive or behavioral issues. Since Contact attitudes involve the belief that racial issues are not important, the counselor with a predominance of these attitudes may be unable to focus the Black client's attention on racial issues.

The counselor intention of Set Limits was positively related to White counselors' Disintegration attitudes, and their Disintegration attitudes were also positively related to the Black client reaction of Lack Direction. Disintegration attitudes are believed to reflect confusion about racial issues. It appears that counselors high in Disintegration attitudes may misperceive the Black client's needs. The counselor may assume that Black clients need structure, whereas the Black client may react to the structuring by not recognizing it as such.

The last White counselor racial identity attitude that was related to counselor intentions and client reactions was Pseudo-Independent attitudes. Counselors' Pseudo-Independent attitudes seemed to be associated with intentions to establish goals, but not to provide a supportive environment, or deal with the clients' obstacles to change or progress. The Black client reactions of Ineffective and Learn New Behaviors were negatively related to White counselor Pseudo-Independent attitudes. Pseudo-Independent attitudes have been hypothesized to reflect primarily intellectual investments in understanding racial similarities and differences. In this regard, it may be that when a White counselor high in Pseudo-Independent attitudes works with a Black client, the counselor is able to structure the session, but is less able to provide emotional support or deal with the Black client's resistance to the counseling, which may manifest itself in emotional terms. Thus, to the extent that the client is seeking emotional support from the counselor, the client may feel that the White counselor is not very effective when the counselor's Pseudo-Independent attitudes are strong.

The findings with respect to counselors' Disintegration and Pseudo-Independent attitudes seem to be consistent with Helms's (1984b) notion that Disintegration attitudes result from a person's loss of a reliable racial structure on which to base one's interactions, and Pseudo-Independent attitudes are associated with a distancing, "White liberal" attitudinal orientation. Consequently, the counselor with high levels of Disintegration attitudes might have her or his ability to structure the process reduced because of his or her own uncertainty; Pseudo-Independent attitudes may have contributed to counselors' inability to perceive accurately what goals and obstacles needed attention.

In examining the Black clients' racial identity attitudes and their influence in the counseling process with a White counselor, it appears that Preencounter and Encounter attitudes may have influenced counselor intentions, whereas Encounter, Immersion/Emersion, and Internalization attitudes may have had the most influence on client reactions. Black clients' Preencounter attitudes seem to have influenced White counselors to provide structure, convey expectations that change is possible, and provide feedback about the client's inappropriate behavior when racial issues were the topic of the counseling. Since Preencounter attitudes are related to Anti-Black/Pro-White attitudes, counselors may perceive that clients with high levels of these attitudes require structure and direction as well as specific information about how to change when discussing racial issues.

Black client Encounter attitudes were associated with the White counselors' intention to help the client relieve tension and unhappy feelings. At the same time, Encounter attitudes were negatively related to the client reaction of Relief. Therefore, although counselors apparently perceived that when Black clients' Encounter attitudes were high, usage of relief-giving interventions was in order, clients apparently did not perceive counselors' interventions in that way.

Black client Immersion/Emersion and Internalization attitudes were not related to counselor intentions, but were related to client reactions in White counselor/Black client dyads. Immersion/Emersion attitudes contributed to Black clients' feelings that the White counselor understood what they were saying, but did not appear to contribute to feelings of release from tension or anxiety, or better self-awareness. Internalization attitudes were less likely to be associated with feeling that change was possible or expected.

In summary, White counselor/Black client dyads are the racial combination about which there is most speculation in the counseling/psychotherapy literature. Though the tendency has been to assume that Whites cannot counsel Blacks, these results suggest that their counseling effectiveness may depend on which racial identity attitudes they bring to the counseling process and which racial identity attitudes their clients bring to the process. Interestingly, in the case of White counselors, Disintegration and Pseudo-Independent attitudes generate the most counselor activity, but Contact and Pseudo-Independent attitudes seem to affect client reactions most. In the case of Black clients, Preencounter and Encounter attitudes seem to contribute to the most cognitive "work" on the White therapist's part, but Immersion/Emersion attitudes contributed to the most varied client reactions.

Black counselor/White client dyads. The characteristics of therapy dyads involving Black counselors and White clients have received some, albeit minimal, attention in the therapy literature (e.g., E. E. Jones, 1974). In general, speculation regarding this particular combination has focused on the negative reactions White clients are likely to have toward Black counselors and how these reactions might be used therapeutically. In the present study, nine correlations involving racial identity and intentions and reactions were significant, which is the number expected by chance. Nevertheless, the relationships tended to be very strong since correlations had to be in the .90s to be significant for these dyads (n = 4).

The best evidence of what Black counselors *think* they are supposed to do in Black counselor/White client dyads is the correlations of Black counselor racial identity attitudes with counselor intentions. Two significant correlations were found (see Figure 10.2). Black counselor Preencounter attitudes were related to the counselor's not intending to convey expectations for change. It may be that when the Black counselor's Preencounter attitudes are high, he or she feels that the White client does not need to change his or her manner of handling racial issues.

High levels of counselor Encounter attitudes were related to Black counselor's intending to deepen the White client's awareness of his or her feelings regarding the racial issues being discussed. The counselor's intention of focusing on Feelings may reflect the Black counselor's willingness to confront difficult feelings the client is experiencing, feelings that the counselor may also be struggling to understand.

The relationship between White client reactions and Black counselor racial identity attitudes pertains to clients' perceptions of Black counselors who (presumably) exhibited different levels of the various Black racial identity attitudes. High levels of Black counselor Encounter attitudes were associated with White clients' feeling deeper self-understanding and self-acceptance, and high levels of Internalization attitudes were associated with a neutral reaction. Perhaps the emotional turmoil associated with their own Encounter attitudes facilitates counselors' abilities to encourage White clients to be more accepting of themselves when racial issues are the topic of counseling. The relationship between Internalization attitudes and the No Reaction on the part of the client may reflect the White client's misunderstanding of the Black Internalized counselors' interventions or possibly the Black counselors' tendency to intellectualize racial issues when their Internalization attitudes are high.

Only one significant correlation was found between White client racial identity attitudes and Black counselor intentions in Black counselor/White client dyads. High levels of White client Pseudo-Independent attitudes were related to Black counselors' intention to convey expectations that change is possible. It seems that Black counselors may per-

Figure 10.2
Relationships among Counselor Intentions, Client Reactions, and Counselor
and Client Racial Identity Attitudes for Black Counselor/White Client Dyad
Types

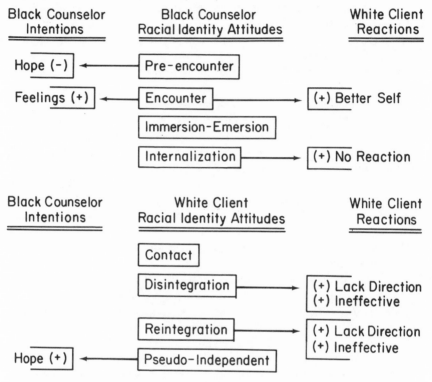

Black Counselor Intentions	Black Counselor Racial Identity Attitudes	White Client Reactions
Hope (-)	Pre-encounter	
Feelings (+)	Encounter	(+) Better Self
	Immersion-Emersion	
	Internalization	(+) No Reaction

Black Counselor Intentions	White Client Racial Identity Attitudes	White Client Reactions
	Contact	
	Disintegration	(+) Lack Direction (+) Ineffective
	Reintegration	(+) Lack Direction (+) Ineffective
Hope (+)	Pseudo-Independent	

Arrows show intentions and reactions correlated with racial identity attitudes; (+) indicates
positive relationship; (-) indicates negative relationship.

ceive that the White client who is intellectually accepting of racial
similarities and differences, in a counseling situation with a Black counselor, needs reassurance that he or she can work through possible emotional issues regarding racial issues. Perhaps the Black counselors
recognize the presence of intellectualization as a defense in such clients.

Information concerning White clients' reactions to Black counselors
is provided by the relationships between White clients' reactions and
their racial identity attitudes. Both Disintegration and Reintegration attitudes were positively related to the client reaction of Lack Direction
and Ineffective. Helms (1984b) suggests that the Disintegration client
enters counseling in a state of confusion or disorientation with respect
to racial matters. Therefore, any intervention by a Black counselor that
increases such confusion may be perceived as unfocused or unhelpful.

Reintegration attitudes are described as involving negative feelings toward Blacks. Thus, Reintegration attitudes may serve a protective function in that they contribute to the White clients' resistance to exploring racial issues that they may have been avoiding and may leave the White client feeling that the Black counselor is ineffective and cannot "direct" the counseling process.

In summary, the counseling process involving Black counselors/White clients is potentially influenced by the counselor's and client's racial identity attitude development. However, the White clients' reactions were more often related to racial identity attitudes than were the counselors' intentions. Moreover, White client reactions were more often related to their own racial identity attitudes than was true of Black counselors and their intentions.

White/White dyads. With the exception of Helms's (1984b) interaction model, theorists have been unlikely to speculate about whether race matters in dyads in which both counselor and client are White. When the relationships between racial identity attitudes and counselor intentions for White counselor/White client dyads were addressed, seven different counselor intentions were predicted by White counselor racial identity attitudes. Each type of White counselors' racial identity attitudes was related to a minimum of two counselor intentions (see Figure 10.3).

Counselors with high levels of Contact attitudes were willing to allow the client to establish the agenda (Set Limits) and neither intended to encourage the client to be clear and complete in the problem presentation (Clarify) nor to provide the client with a sense that change was likely or possible (Hope). When White counselors were (presumably) expressing Contact attitudes, White clients felt that they were able to become more aware of themselves, but were not able to experience release of anxiety or tension; additionally, White clients did not feel neutral about their counselors' interventions when the counselors' Contact attitudes were high. Contact attitudes seemed to be associated with avoidance of dealing with racial issues when race was the topic of counseling. The clients seem to have developed some self-knowledge that may or may not have been related to their presenting problem, but they did not seem to experience emotional relief.

Counselor Disintegration attitudes seem to have influenced White counselors to convey the expectation that change was possible and to identify or give feedback about the White clients' inappropriate behavior. Counselor Disintegration attitudes were related to clients' feeling able to release tension and anxiety and overcome barriers. Yet counselors' high Disintegration attitudes also contributed to clients' perceptions that counselors were ineffective. These findings may reflect the ambivalence regarding racial issues associated with the counselors' Disintegration attitudes.

Figure 10.3
Relationships among Counselor Intentions, Client Reactions, and Counselor and Client Racial Identity Attitudes for White Counselor/White Client Dyad Types

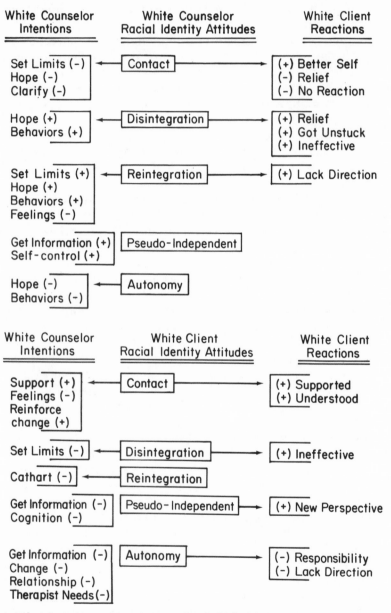

Arrows show intentions and reactions correlated with racial identity attitudes; (+) indicates positive relationship; (−) indicates negative relationship.

Counselor Reintegration attitudes seem to have influenced the counselors to provide structure for the session, convey an expectation for change, identify problematic behaviors for the client, and discourage clients' awareness of deep feelings. Thus, these attitudes seem to have inspired the White counselor to take control of the situation when race was an issue for the White clients. Counselor Reintegration attitudes were related to the client feeling that the White counselor lacked direction.

It appears that counselors with high levels of Reintegration attitudes were able to confront racial issues—however, these attitudes were also associated with unwillingness to deal with clients' feelings about these issues. The clients' reactions may indicate that they sensed the counselors' reticence. Perhaps counselors with high levels of Reintegration attitudes are caught between their racial attitudes and their humanistic counselor training.

Counselor Pseudo-Independent attitudes were associated with the counselor's intending to acquire specific facts and information about the client's history and functioning and encourage the client to own or gain a sense of mastery or control over his or her feelings, thoughts, and behaviors. It appears that Pseudo-Independent attitudes influence the White counselor to focus on the cognitive aspects of the White client's situation. Interestingly, counselor Pseudo-Independent attitudes were not related to clients' reactions.

Finally, counselors high in Autonomous attitudes were less likely to convey an expectation for change or to identify inappropriate behaviors. Counselor Autonomy attitudes seem to lessen the counselor's need to influence the counseling process, and if the absence of correlated reactions are an indicator, then clients did not seem to feel any distinct influence of Autonomy attitudes.

Just as counselor racial characteristics in White/White dyads have been overlooked, so too have client racial characteristics in such dyads. When clients' Contact attitudes were high, counselors perceived that the clients needed feedback regarding their efforts to change and a warm, supportive environment. Clients' Contact attitudes were also related to counselors' beliefs that clients' emotional experiences should not be intensified. High levels of Contact attitudes were related to the White clients' feelings that the White counselor liked, understood, and supported them. White clients with high levels of Contact attitudes may have experienced their White counselors as supportive and understanding because they had little or no alternative experiences by which to evaluate them, or because they were receptive to members of their own race in response to their social conditioning.

Clients' Disintegration attitudes influenced counselors to avoid providing structure or establishing goals for counseling with these clients.

Disintegration attitudes were related to clients' feeling that the counselors' interventions were ineffective. It is possible that any intervention by a White counselor that increased the White clients' confusion regarding racial issues may have been perceived as ineffective.

White counselors seem to have thought that White clients with a predominance of Reintegration attitudes did not need help in letting go or talking through feelings or problems. Clients' expression of Reintegration attitudes seemed to have led counselors to feel that they should protect clients (or themselves) from a full expression of feelings.

The client reaction of New Perspective was positively related to White clients' Pseudo-Independent attitudes, but the counselor intentions of Get Information and Cognition were negatively related. Perhaps these findings reflect Pseudo-Independent clients' cognitive perspective and high valuing of experiences that provide them with a new way of intellectualizing about racial matters. This cognitive orientation may convince the counselor that the client is in control of her or his thoughts about racial issues.

Clients' Autonomy attitudes influenced the White counselor to avoid seeking information about the White client's history and functioning, building new coping mechanisms, analyzing relationships, and/or focusing on the counselor's anxiety or needs. High levels of client Autonomy attitudes contributed to clients' feeling less responsible for the racial problem they were presenting as well as believing that the process did not lack direction. Thus, the clients' Autonomy attitudes appear to have influenced counselors and clients to accept the situation as it was. The client did not feel responsible for causing it and the counselor did not appear to be motivated to change it.

SUMMARY

In summary, the strongest, supportive evidence for a relationship between racial identity attitudes and the counseling process occurred in dyads involving White counselors and White clients. With a total of 37 significant correlations, it is unlikely that the findings were due to chance. In general, more counselor intentions than reactions were related to counselor and client racial identity attitudes, a finding similar to those reported by Carter (1987). That is, in White/White dyads counselor intentions may be more influenced by racial attitudes during the process than client reactions.

Of the other racial combinations investigated, those involving White counselors and Black clients yielded more than twice the number of significant relationships than would be expected by chance. However, in this case Black clients' reactions were more often related to the counselors' and clients' racial identity attitudes than were the counselors' intentions. Since most of the reactions were negative, it is possible that Black clients felt that the counseling was not very beneficial when the counselors' Disintegration or Pseudo-Independent attitudes were high or their own Encounter, Immersion/Emersion, or Internalization attitudes were high.

Be that as it may, it seems that levels of White racial identity attitudes were related to counseling process variables in accord with Helms's (1984b) interactive counseling model. Furthermore, use of race to classify dyads in the absence of measures of within-racial-group variability, in this case, racial identity attitudes, was not particularly useful for describing the counseling process. In every racial combination, racial identity attitudes led to more significant relationships than race alone. Contrary to what one might anticipate from the literature, racial identity attitudes were most often related to counselor intentions in White counselor/White client dyads, to client reactions in Black counselor/White client dyads, and client reactions in White counselor/Black client dyads. Although it is conceivable that differences in sample sizes across dyads of different racial combinations accounted for the differing numbers of significant correlations, the results still seem to support further consideration of the contribution of racial identity attitudes to "real-life" counseling situations. In addition, the results of the present study seem to provide some support for the racial identity attitudes perspective and little if any support for the race-alone view.

11

Black Racial Identity Attitudes and White Therapist Cultural Sensitivity in Cross-Racial Therapy Dyads: An Exploratory Study

DEEJON BRADBY AND JANET E. HELMS

For some time now, theorists have discussed the proposition that Black people will not be receptive to counseling and/or psychotherapy when it is offered by White mental health personnel. On one side of the discussion are those authors (e.g., W. M. Banks, 1972; Barnes, 1980; Hayes & W. M. Banks, 1972; Kleiner, Tuckman, & Lovell, 1960; Vontress, 1970) who have charged that because White therapists have failed to understand and appreciate the unique culture, history, and life experiences of Black people, they are unable to empathize with Black clients. Consequently, virtually *all* Black clients are hypothesized to be unwilling to trust their mental health to White therapists.

On the other side of the discussion concerning the desirability of matching therapists and clients according to race are those who advocate what Steele and Davis (1983) have called the "integretivistic" position. Advocates of this position with respect to counseling and psychotherapy essentially contend that whether and how race is important in the therapy process depends upon the individual racial attitudes of the participants who are involved, especially the Black clients. Proponents of this position argue that since Black clients may develop any of a variety of types of racial identity (Butler, 1975; Helms, 1984b; Milliones, 1980; Parham & Helms, 1981; Parham & Helms, 1985b), they can also display a variety of reactions to White therapists. Some version of Cross's (1971, 1978) "Negro-to-Black" conversion model typically has been used by these theorists to describe the racial identity development process (see chapter 2).

So far, neither the therapist insensitivity nor the racial identity perspective has generated much research involving actual therapy. One can find four studies in the literature in which the insensitivity assumption is at least implicit and none in which the racial identity assumption is either implicit or explicit (cf. E. E. Jones, 1978b, 1982; Terrell & Terrell, 1984; Turner & Armstrong, 1981). Nevertheless, Terrell and Terrell (1984) did find that Black clients' premature termination rate with Black relative to White therapists varied according to the clients' levels of cultural mistrust. Their results appear to indirectly support the assumption that Black clients' race-related attitudes influence their perceptions of cross-racial therapy. However, the purpose of this study was to examine the racial identity assumption directly.

Specifically, we used four types of racial identity attitudes derived from Cross's (1971) model and investigated their relationship to Black clients' satisfaction with the early phase of therapy when the therapists were White. The four attitudes investigated were Preencounter (idealistic White/denigrating Black), Encounter (confused White/euphoric Black), Immersion/Emersion (denigrating White/idealistic Black), and Internalization (racially self-actualized). Although no prior studies of actual therapy relationships involving Black clients' racial identity attitudes existed, two analogue studies (Pomales, Claiborn, & La Fromboise, 1986; Richardson, 1987) found some evidence that different racial identity attitudes might be associated with different perceptions of counselors' behaviors. In Pomales et al.'s videotape study, observers with high Encounter attitudes preferred a culturally sensitive over a culturally oblivious therapist; observers with high Internalization attitudes evaluated the two conditions similarly. Preencounter and Encounter attitudes were not measured in the study. In an audiotape study, Richardson (1987) found that Encounter attitudes were related to negative perceptions of counseling simulations involving White therapists, whereas none of the other attitudes was significantly related to Black listeners' perceptions.

One might infer from the Pomales et al. (1986) and Richardson (1987) studies that in actual therapy situations, Black clients are likely to be less satisfied with White therapists to the extent that the clients' Encounter attitudes are high, though the relationship of racial identity attitudes to satisfaction with therapists in actual therapy never has been examined directly. In this study, satisfaction measures, number of sessions attended, and number of sessions desired were used to operationalize Black clients' satisfaction.

In addition, we attempted to determine whether therapists' cultural sensitivity might be related to client perceptions and/or characteristics. In an analogue study, Mitchell (1974) used R. L. Williams's (1972) Black Intelligence Test of Cultural Homogeneity (BITCH) to measure counselors' sensitivity to the Black cultural experience. Even though he found no association between cultural sensitivity so measured and therapy effectiveness, we also used the BITCH to operationalize therapist sensitivity because other measures of this construct were not available when we originally designed the study.

Thus, as conceived, the study was intended to provide some information about whether the counselor insensitivity or the racial identity assumption best explains Black clients' reactions to the first four or five sessions of brief therapy, since this phase of therapy has been hypothesized to be problematic for Black clients (e.g., S. Sue, McKinney, Allen, & Hall, 1974). The specific research questions posed in the present study were: (a) What are the relationships between White therapists' cultural sensitivity to Black clients and the number of sessions Black clients attend and clients' satisfaction with therapy? (b) Do Black clients' racial identity attitudes relate to the number of therapy sessions they attend and their satisfaction with therapy? (c) What is the relationship of the interaction between therapist sensitivity and racial identity attitudes to client satisfaction and the number of sessions attended? In exploring these questions, racial identity attitudes derived from Cross's (1971, 1978) Nigrescence model were used to operationalize clients' racial identity attitudes. Following Helms (1986) and Parham and Helms's (1981, 1985b) recommendations, correlational analyses were used to analyze the data.

METHOD

Subject

Subjects were 20 bi-racial dyads involving 20 Black clients and 17 White therapists participating in short-term, time-limited therapy at a counseling center in a predominantly White (less than 8% Black) university located in the east. At the counseling center, clients were assigned to therapists on the basis of (a) mutual availability of therapist and client hours, (b) the client's request for a particular therapist and/or type of therapist (e.g., sex or race), and (c) the intake therapist's judgments concerning urgency of the presenting problem, level of therapist experience required, and potential client/therapist goodness-of-fit.

Clients. The dyads consisted of 14 female and 6 male Black students who were involved in therapy during the fall, 1983 and the spring, 1984, semesters. Ages of the sample ranged from 19 to 40 years, with the mean age being 22.05 (SD = 4.75). Of the 20 subjects who participated, 15 indicated that they were born in the the United States, and 5 indicated that they were born in Africa, Spain, Canada, or the West Indies. Racial self-designations indicated by the clients were "Black" (n = 17) and

"Afro-American" or "other" (n = 3). Statistical comparisons between clients born in the United States and those who were not were conducted; since they differed significantly on only one variable, age (non-United States born Blacks tended to be older), which could have been due to chance given the large number of variables on which they were compared, the two groups were combined for subsequent analyses.

Therapists. Therapists were 10 females and 7 males ranging in age from 23 to 55 years (M = 31.50; SD = 8.72). All but three therapists saw a single client. Twelve therapists were at pre-doctoral levels ranging from pre-masters to intern, and five had from 2 to 29 years of post-doctoral experience. To examine differences between the pre- and post-doctoral therapists, t tests or chi squares were performed as appropriate on the variety of predictor and demographic variables used in this study. Not surprisingly, there were significant differences between the two groups in age, total number of Black clients they had treated, and the highest level of education attained. Relative to the post-doctoral group, the pre-doctoral group was younger, had treated fewer Black clients, and had attained a lower level of education. However, there were no significant differences between the two groups on sex or scores on the therapist sensitivity measure; none of the therapists in either group had previously taken the measure. Therefore, to increase the generalizability of the results, pre- and post-doctoral therapists were combined for all of the subsequent analyses.

Measures

The measures used in the present study to assess therapist cultural sensitivity and client racial identity attitudes were the Black Intelligence Test of Cultural Homogeneity–100 (R. L. Williams, 1972) and the Racial Identity Attitude Scale (Helms & Parham, in press), respectively. The Counseling Evaluation Inventory (Linden, Stone, & Shertzer, 1965), a therapist post-initial session questionnaire, and number of sessions of therapy were used to assess reactions to therapy. In addition, client and therapist demographic data sheets were used.

Black Intelligence Test of Cultural Homogeneity–100 (BITCH–100). R. L. Williams (1972) originally designed the BITCH–100 to be a culture-specific intelligence measure with items drawn from Black people's cultural experiences in the United States. Since then, it has been used by Mitchell (1974) to assess knowledge of and/or sensitivity to Black cultural experiences and was used for that purpose in the present study. The 100-item measure consists of words, terms, and expressions, each of which is followed by four possible response alternatives. The examinee selects a "correct" answer by placing a checkmark beside the alternative that most accurately reflects the manner in which Black people would and/or generally do use the terminology. A total score is obtained by subtracting the number of omitted and incorrect responses from 100, with higher scores indicating greater knowledge of and/or sensitivity to Black cultural language usage.

Williams (1972) reported a split-half reliability of .86 and a one-month test-retest reliability of .84 for a White sample of respondents. In assessing the validity of the measure, researchers have reported that Southern rural White students scored higher than their Northern urban counterparts (R. L. Williams, 1972), and younger respondents obtained higher BITCH scores than older respondents (Mullen, 1972, cited by Bradby, 1986). Results such as these can be taken to mean that the more opportunities Whites have had to associate with Blacks, the higher will be their BITCH scores and presumably their cultural sensitivity.

Racial Identity Attitude Scale. To measure Black clients' racial identity attitudes in the present study, the Black Racial Identity Attitude Scale (Helms & Parham, in press) was used. The Black Racial Identity Attitude Scale, intended to be used exclusively with Black populations, was designed to measure attitudes consistent with the first four stages of Cross's (1971) model of psychological Nigrescence (i.e., Preencounter, Encounter, Immersion/Emersion, and Internalization). Respondents obtain a score on each of four subscales by using a five-point Likert scale (1 = Strongly Disagree; 5 = Strongly Agree) to indicate the extent to which each item is descriptive of her or him; the sum of appropriately keyed items is divided by the total number of items comprising the subscale. The higher the scores on the subscales the more descriptive of the respondents' racial identity attitudes are the subscales.

Helms and Parham (in press) reported coefficient alpha reliabilities of .69, .50, .67, and .72 for the Preencounter, Encounter, Immersion/Emersion and Internalization subscales, respectively. The reliability estimates compare favorably with the median of .54 for personality measures reported by Anastasi (1982). As evidence of the validity of the scale, subscales have been found to be differentially related to respondents' therapist preference (Parham & Helms, 1981), affective states (Parham & Helms, 1985a), and self-esteem (Parham & Helms, 1985b) in a manner mostly consistent with theoretical speculation.

Counseling Evaluation Inventory. The Counseling Evaluation Inventory (Linden et al., 1965) is a client self-report measure that is used to describe clients' perceptions of therapist and therapy effectiveness. As designed, the scale consists of 21 items that are clustered into three subscales: therapy climate, therapist comfort, and client satisfaction. In the present study, only the client satisfaction subscale was used. Subjects responded to the five items comprising the satisfaction scale via five-point scales (1 = never; 5 = always). Thus scores could range from 5 to 25, with higher scores indicating greater satisfaction. The subscales were originally constructed via factor analysis and thus no internal consistency reliability coefficients were reported. However, test-retest reliability coefficients ranged from .62 to .83. A variety of studies exist that attest to the validity of the Counseling Evaluation Inventory. For example, Linden et al. found that therapists-in-training who received grades of A, B, or C were rated significantly differently on the subscales in directions consistent with expectations, for example, "A" students received the highest client satisfaction ratings.

Number of sessions. Number of therapy sessions was measured in three ways. At the close of the 1983/1984 academic year, records of the counseling center were checked and the total number of sessions attended by each client in this study was tallied. Secondly, because the counseling center in which this study was conducted regularly imposes a 12-session limit on the number of sessions available to subjects during a school year, subjects were asked how many sessions they would ideally like to have as a means of compensating for a potential ceiling effect due to agency restrictions. Finally, following their first session with the client, therapists were asked to estimate the number of sessions the clients should have if there were no counseling center constraints.

Demographic data sheets. Individual therapist or client demographic data sheets were included in their separate respective data packets. The therapists' sheet was designed to collect information for descriptive purposes such as experience level, age, gender, and so on. The clients' sheet allowed the client to report demographic descriptive information (e.g., age, sex, class) as well as racial self-designation and information about the client's previous therapy history.

Procedure

Bi-racial (Black client/White therapist) dyads were identified in weekly consultation with the counseling center staff person who was responsible for case assignments and by examining the active case files at the center. The agency's receptionist gave numbered data packets to identifiably Black clients along with other regular intake forms prior to their intake session. The packets contained a letter explaining that the purpose of the study was to examine the effectiveness of therapy services for Black clients. Subjects' voluntary participation was also solicited via this letter. If they were willing to participate, clients were asked to complete the accompanying measures at the counseling center and return them to the receptionist. Ideally, the Counseling Evaluation Inventory (Linden et al., 1965) was administered by one of the researchers within the first five weeks (potentially four sessions) after the client had been assigned to a therapist. However, due to the relatively small number of Black clients available during the time period in which we were permitted to collect data, one client was included in the study after only one session and one (who had terminated after four sessions) was included two weeks after termination. Since the purpose of the study was to investigate reactions to actual therapy relationships, clients who did not attend any sessions other than intakes were not included in the sample.

Participating therapists were identified via personal contacts and consultation with the staff member responsible for the approval of research projects conducted at the counseling center. Therapists were given data packets within one week after they had been assigned a Black client, but before they actually saw the client. Following their initial session with the client and review of intake materials, therapists were asked to estimate the ideal number of sessions the client should have via a post-initial session form and to return this information to one of the researchers prior to the second session.

With the two exceptions previously noted, during the fifth week of therapy the administrative staff and/or a researcher administered a second packet of measures to the clients. The second packet contained a letter again seeking voluntary participation and the satisfaction measure. If a client did not attend her or his session during the fifth week, then the administrative staff or a researcher gave them the packets when they returned for their next appointment. The client contacted after termination completed all of the measures at that time.

RESULTS

Partial correlations were used to investigate those research questions concerning the relationships between racial identity attitudes and the therapy reactions measures, including actual number of sessions attended, client satisfaction with therapy, and client and therapist ideal number of sessions. Use of partial correlations removes the variance that two attitudes have in common, leaving the remainder to be correlated with subsequent variables. For these analyses, each of the racial identity attitudes subscales was controlled in succession. The partial correlations for the four therapy reactions measures with each of the four racial identity attitudes successively controlled are shown in Table 11.1.

Client Satisfaction

Examination of the significant correlations indicates that when Preencounter (idealized White/denigrating Black) attitudes were controlled, Internalization ($r(17) = .49, p = .03$) attitudes were significantly related to clients' satisfaction with therapy during the early phase of therapy, and Encounter ($r(17) = .45, p = .06$) attitudes tended to be related. Similar relationships between client satisfaction and Encounter ($r(17) = .48, p = .04$) attitudes were found when Immersion/Emersion attitudes

Table 11.1
Summary of Partial Correlations between Racial Identity Attitudes and Client Reactions Measures

Client Satisfaction Measures

Sessions

Controlled Attitudes	Satisfaction				Actual				Ideal			
	Pre	Enc	Im	Int	Pre	Enc	Im	Int	Pre	Enc	Im	Int
Preencounter (Pre)		45	16	49*		01	00	17		-30	-20	10
Encounter (Enc)	-03		-20	32	31		16	14	-08		09	31
Immersion/ Emersion (Im)	13	48*		48*	34	21		33	-20	-30		36
Internalization (Int)	07	25	-04		32	05	-26		-20	-45	-40	

*$p < .05$
Note: Decimal points omitted to conserve space.

were controlled. The direction of the correlations in both instances indicated that the higher were clients' Encounter or Internalization attitudes, the more satisfied were they with the therapy as reflected in their ratings on the Counseling Evaluation Inventory (Linden et al., 1965). None of the other correlations was significant when Preencounter or Immersion/Emersion attitudes were controlled.

When Encounter attitudes were controlled, none of the correlations was statistically significant. Controlling Internalization attitudes revealed that none of the correlations was significant, but clients' ideal number of sessions and Encounter attitudes ($r(17) = -.45, p = .06$) and Immersion/Emersion attitudes ($r(17) = -.40, p = .09$) tended to be related in a manner suggesting that higher levels of these attitudes were related to clients' desire for fewer numbers of sessions.

Thus, when either the Encounter or Internalization attitudes were controlled, none of the relationships between racial identity attitudes and therapy reactions was statistically significant, suggesting that these may have been important contributors to Black clients' attitudes toward White therapists.

Therapists' Sensitivity

Pearson product moment correlations were used to study the relationship between therapist cultural sensitivity (BITCH) scores, the interaction between sensitivity and racial identity attitudes (i.e., the product of BITCH and RIAS-B scores), and the reactions to therapy measures. None of the correlations between therapist sensitivity scores and therapy reactions measures was significant. Correlations (with 18 degrees of freedom) between sensitivity scores and client satisfaction, number of sessions attended, therapists' ideal number of sessions, and clients' ideal number of sessions were .14 ($p = .28$), $-.02$ ($p = .46$), .00 ($p = .49$), and .06 ($p = .40$), respectively.

Interestingly, the strongest correlation where therapist sensitivity was concerned occurred when it was correlated with Black clients' Preencounter attitudes ($r(18) = -.61, p = .002$), an incidental analysis. This correlation suggests that the stronger clients' Preencounter attitudes were, the higher was the cultural insensitivity of their assigned therapist. None of the other client racial identity attitudes was significantly related to therapist sensitivity.

The correlations pertaining to the interactions between therapists' cultural sensitivity and racial identity attitudes indicated that the interactions involving the product of BITCH scores and Encounter attitudes and satisfaction ($r(18) = .48, p = .03$), and BITCH scores and Internalization attitudes and client satisfaction ($r(18) = .50, p = .03$) were statistically significant. If their Encounter or Internalization attitudes were high, clients were more satisfied with culturally sensitive therapists.

DISCUSSION

For Black clients who consented to be treated by White therapists, it appears that racial identity attitudes, derived from Cross's (1971) Negro-to-Black conversion model, were more clearly related to their experience of the process than was therapists' cultural sensitivity. In discussing the differential meaning of the four kinds of racial identity attitudes, Parham and Helms (1985b) distinguished between attitudes that appear to be primarily reactions to racism—Preencounter (adaptive racism) and Immersion/Emersion (angry racism)—and those that represent emotional (Encounter) and rational (Internalization) acceptance of one's Blackness and tolerance of Whiteness. In the present study, these two types of client attitudes were related to different aspects of the therapy process where clients' satisfaction, as variously defined, was concerned.

Encounter and Internalization attitudes were both positively related to satisfaction when the variance shared with Preencounter or Immersion/Emersion attitudes was removed. If it is accurate to conceptualize these attitudes as representing different forms of bi-racial acceptance, then it appears that Black clients' satisfaction and, possibly, receptivity to White therapists may be greater when their Encounter and/or Internalization attitudes, that is, attitudes of bi-racial acceptance, are high. When Internalization attitudes were controlled, Encounter and Immersion attitudes tended to be related to a desire for fewer numbers of sessions, though not to the actual number of sessions attended. Perhaps Encounter and Immersion attitudes have in common emotionality about one's Blackness. Internalization attitudes may moderate the Black person's feelings about race. Thus, to the extent that the person's Internalization attitudes are high, he or she may be likely to remain in therapy even though the Encounter and Immersion attitudes elicit opposite feelings. The findings that different attitudes are (or are not) related to the same aspects of the therapy relationship seem to support Helms's (1986) recommendation that some sort of profile analysis be used to interpret the effects of racial identity attitudes on therapy process variables.

In the case of therapists, there were no statistically significant relationships between therapists' cultural sensitivity and the various measures of satisfaction and/or reactions to therapy, but at least one interesting finding suggests why significant correlations may not have been found. There was a significant negative relationship between client Preencounter attitudes and therapist sensitivity. According to racial identity theory, Preencounter attitudes represent, in part, the Black person's lack of awareness of or insensitivity to Black culture. Thus, various authors (e.g., Butler, 1975) have suggested that to the extent that these attitudes are high, the client is especially in need of a therapist who is sensitive to Black culture and related issues. However, it seems that in the agency in which this study was conducted, when the Black clients' Preencounter attitudes were high, their White therapists' cultural sensitivity was low. Thus, perhaps some subtle matching on the basis of racial attitudes was occurring in the agency such that Black clients were being paired with therapists according to some evidence of clients' racial identity attitudes that might have been apparent during the intake interview and/or the intake therapist's familiarity with her or his colleagues' manner of expressing their racial identity development. If such attitudinal matching did occur, then therapists and clients may have been engaged in what Helms (1984b) calls parallel dyads, that is, dyads involving therapists and clients who share similar racial identity attitudes. In such cases, one would expect Black clients to remain in therapy and evaluate it positively regardless of whether it was beneficial to them (e.g., solved therapy issues). The virtual absence of outcome measures in this study makes it impossible to examine this hypothesis.

Further study is needed of the intake process as it involves racial identity. Toward this end, it would be useful to include routinely some sort of racial identity measure (e.g., Helms & Parham, in press; Milliones, 1980) in the intake process. In the present study, it was necessary to secure clients' permission to participate in a "special" study of agency services. Yet if racial identity theory is accurate, it should be the case that clients who volunteer to participate in a study conducted by a Black researcher will have a predominance of certain types of racial identity attitudes (i.e., Immersion/Emersion, Encounter, and/or Internalization), and clients who agree to treatment by a White therapist may have a predominance of certain other types of racial identity attitudes (i.e., Preencounter, Internalization). Taking some of the "voluntariness" out of the assessment process might expand the range of attitudes clients exhibit in research projects of this sort and give a better sense of how attitudes are differentially related to other factors.

Another possible reason for the lack of significant relationships between therapist sensitivity and therapy reactions concerns the use of R. L. Williams's (1972) BITCH scores to operationalize sensitivity to Black culture. Although BITCH scores had been used in this manner in one previous study (Mitchell, 1974), it is possible that the language comprising this measure no longer reflects contemporary Black culture. In informal discussions with Black students following the study, we found that some terms were unfamiliar to them and some (e.g., "cock") were associated with White rather than Black culture in their minds. Other methods for assessing therapist cultural sensitivity, including a White racial identity inventory (see chapter 5) and a cultural competence measure (La Fromboise, cited in Pomales et al., 1986), have become available, and it might be useful to investigate some of these measurement approaches in subsequent studies.

Finally, this study does seem to provide some information that is germane to the question of whether the therapist insensitivity or the racial identity explanations of the dynamics of cross-racial therapy involving Black clients and White therapists is more useful. At least, as these variables were operationalized in the present study, it appears that the racial identity assumption may offer more avenues for understanding when and how the process works.

12

Applying the Interaction
Model to Social Dyads

JANET E. HELMS

It is conceivable that the factors hypothesized to characterize counseling dyads may generalize to other types of dyadic interactions in which the participants differ in social power and/or status due to role expectations (e.g., parent-child; teacher-student; husband-wife). Table 9.1 can be modified slightly to show how this generalization might work. The modifications require that one substitute the more powerful person or authority figure for "counselor" and the less powerful or perhaps more dependent person for "client." Thus, using teacher-student dyads as an example, "teacher" would be substituted for "counselor," and "client" would be replaced by "student" wherever these terms occur. In addition, "relationship dynamics" should be substituted for "counseling process" issues. When relationships are described in this manner, then "termination" refers to the various strategies that individuals may use to end or disrupt relatively permanent associations (e.g., divorce, running away, dropping out of school).

GENERALIZING FROM COUNSELING RELATIONSHIPS

The same types of interactions (i.e., parallel, crossed, progressive, regressive) should occur in social dyads as occur in counseling relationships. Table 12.1 shows which combinations of authority-partner racial identity attitudes lead to which of the four types of interactions. Since each of the racial identity attitudes implies different cognitive, affective, and behavioral issues, it is likely that the various combinations of attitudes

Table 12.1

Summary of Relationship Types Defined by Various Combinations of Racial Identity

Dyad's race	Participants' Stages of Identity		General Theme
	Authority	Partner	
	Parallel Dyads		
Black/Black	1. Preencounter	1. Preencounter	Stable, placid and
	2. Encounter	2. Encounter	harmonious dyads.
	3. Immersion	3. Immersion	Participants feel supported and
	4. Internalization	4. Internalization	understood. Racial attitudes are not apt to change.
White/White	1. Contact	1. Contact	
	2. Disintegration	2. Disintegration	
	3. Reintegration,	3. Reintegration	
	4. Pseudo-Independent	4. Pseudo-Independent	
	5. Autonomy		
White/Black	1. Contact	1. Preencounter	
	2. Reintegration	2. Preencounter	
	3. Autonomy	3. Internalization	
	Progressive Dyads		
White/White	1. Disintegration, Reintegration Pseudo-Independent, Autonomy	1. Contact	Some tension in relationship due to racial issues. The greater the distance between stages, the greater the tension. Greatest growth occurs because
	2. Reintegration, Pseudo-Independent, Autonomy	2. Disintegration	participants' role expectations are not violated.
	3. Pseudo-Independent, Autonomy	3. Reintegration	
	4. Autonomy	4. Pseudo-Independent	
Black/Black	1. Encounter, Immersion, Internalization	1. Preencounter	
	2. Immersion, Interalization	2. Encounter	
	3. Internalization	3. Immersion	
White/Black	1. Disintegration, Reintegration, Pseudo-Independent, Autonomy	1. Preencounter	
	2. Reintegration, Pseudo-Independent Autonomy	2. Encounter	

178

Table 12.1 (continued)

Dyad's race	Participants' Stages of Identity		General Theme
	Authority	Partner	

Parallel Dyads

	3.	Pseudo-Independent Autonomy	3.	Immersion

Regressive Dyads

		Authority		Partner	General Theme
White/Black	1.	Contact	1.	Encounter, Immersion, Internalization	Conflicted relationships marked by covert and overt fights about racial issues. The greater the disparity in participants' identity, the greater the conflict. Usually these are dysfunctional relationships in which participants' growth is stifled.
	2.	Disintegration	2.	Encounter, Immersion, Internalization	
	3.	Reintegration, Pseudo-Independent, Autonomy	3.	Interalization	
Black/Black	1.	Preencounter	1.	Encounter, Immersion, Internalization	
	2.	Encounter	2.	Immersion, Internalization	
	3.	Immersion	3.	Internalization	
White/White	1.	Contact	1.	Disintegration, Reintegration, Autonomy, Pseudo-Independent	
	2.	Disintegration	2.	Reintegration, Pseudo-Independent, Autonomy	
	3.	Reintegration	3.	Pseudo-Independent, Autonomy	
	4.	Pseudo-Independent	4.	Autonomy	

Crossed Dyads

					General Theme
Black/Black	1.	Preencounter	1.	Immersion	Most conflicted relationship type. Characterized by disharmony mutual fear, covert and overt warfare. Least likely to promote individuals' growth
White/White	1.	Reintegration	1.	Contact	
White/Black	1.	Reintegration	1.	Immersion	

within a relationship type will result in different ways of coping with the diverse racial issues. For instance, participants in parallel Preencounter or Contact dyads might coexist by denying the significance of race in their daily interactions, whereas participants in parallel Immersion/ Emersion or Reintegration dyads might exaggerate the salience of race. Thus, what the sets of attitudes that are of the same relationship type have in common is the general style or manner of handling racial issues. As one example, Table 12.1 shows that parallel dyads, regardless of the actual attitudes involved, affectively are rather placid. More generally, the combined content of the participants' core racial issues, that is, their respective stages of racial identity, determines whether their interaction is placid, contested, or conflictual. If the stages are in harmony, then the relationship is likely to be placid; if they are somewhat similar, then the relationship may be contested; if the participants' stages are conceptual opposites, then the interaction probably will be conflict ridden.

Relationship Types in Social Interactions

It might be useful to highlight some of the themes potentially inherent in the various relationship types using parent-child interactions as the exemplars.

Parallel. Parallel relationships are perhaps the least contentious of dyadic interactions because parent and child (or other participants) share a racial world view. Problems in these types of relationships, to the extent that they occur, are in response to one member's (usually the least powerful) communications being perceived by the other member as challenges to her or his world view. In parallel relationships, the impetus for such communications would almost have to come from outside the parent-child relationship. Peers, other authority figures, and so forth, might be the agents who supply racial viewpoints that are potentially disruptive of the parallel interaction. In such cases, the parent attempts to maintain the relationship as is by reshaping the child's interpretation of racial events to be consistent with the parent's world view. Since the parent's view and the child's are not very far from one another and since most new information that either brings to the relationship is generally perceived and therefore presented in a manner that is acceptable to both, then the reshaping process in parallel relationships will not require a major expenditure of energy.

Regressive. The affective style of regressive relationships can vary from testy to conflictual, depending upon how much more advanced (i.e., how many stages beyond) the child's racial identity development is than the parent's. Recognize that a regressive relationship in the case of parents and children is one in which the child's identity development is at least one stage more advanced than the parent's. When the stages involved are adjacent to each other in the racial identity developmental model (e.g., Preencounter parent/Encounter child; Contact parent/Disintegration child), then there should be some tension in the relationship around racial issues, but not a great deal. In other words, because the two still have some overlap in their manner of viewing the world, they do not disagree about everything racial. However, if the child advances more than one stage beyond the parent, then one can expect increasing levels of tension as the participants' world views become more disparate.

Progressive. In progressive parent-child relationships, the parent's stage of identity is at least one stage more advanced than the child's. These relationships provide the best opportunity for growth on the child's part since the parent is in her or his customary role of teaching the child that which the parent knows better. Consequently, although the child may resist or appear to resist the parent's instructional efforts as is often the case in parent-child interactions, the resistance is unlikely to be acrimonious as long as the parent is not dictatorial, allows the child to progress at her or his own pace and to express his or her genuine thoughts and feelings, and the relationship is sound otherwise. Again, because some commonality in world views probably works better than total disparity, progressive parent-child interactions are apt to be most growthful and harmonious when the parent's stage of racial identity does not exceed the child's stage by more than one stage.

Crossed. In crossed relationships, parent and child world views are complete opposites. Therefore, they have difficulty communicating with each other because they do not share any part of a common frame of reference where the racial parts of themselves are concerned. That this kind of relationship has evolved in the first place possibly indicates that communication barriers in the parent-child relationship have reached a point where the child no longer wishes to please or model herself or himself after the parent. Thus, crossed relationships are at greatest risk for long-lasting conflict.

Relationship Dynamics

One does have to use some imagination in defining the affective issues, participant strategies, and relationship outcome or quality of social dyads in a manner that makes sense within the context of the particular social interaction under consideration. Table 12.2 shows examples of how Black, White, and mixed regressive relationships involving various authority-figure/partner combinations might appear. Notice that it is proposed that the themes present in each dyad tend to be similar. What varies is the participants' manner of expressing their affective issues. In general, the more dependent the partner is on the authority figure for

Table 12.2
Examples of Regressive Relationship Types Using Various Partner Interactions

Participants' Role and Stage	Affective Issues	Relationship Authority/Partner Strategies	Dynamics Relationship Quality/Outcome
		Black Dyads	
Authority Partner			
1. Preencounter Parent	Immersion Child	Parent shares society's denial, devaluation of and consequent fear of Blackness; child recognizes own Blackness and feels rejected, angry, unloved by parent.	Parent attempts to protect child by teaching her/him to be "White". Praises White qualities in child, punishes Black qualities. Child fights for parental acceptance of Blackness; does things to force parent to accept Blackness.	Both are hypersensitive to the other's racial references and reactions but indifferent directions. Tumultous relationship. Child's anger of non-acceptance are solidified. Parent's fear and anxiety are enhanced.
2. Preencounter Teacher	Immersion Student	Teacher devalues Blackness, feels threatened by the student's embracing a Black culture. Child feels devalued and incompetent.	Teacher dichotomizes behaviors according to race. Criticizes child for "Black" behaviors. Out of anger student resists learning. "White" material. May act stereotypically Black.	Covert and overt suppression of student's Blackness and student's passive and active rebellion makes this a tenuous relationship.
3. Preencounter Spouse 1	Immersion Spouse 2	Spouse 1 feels threatened by spouse's racialism; Spouse 2 feels unloved.	Spouce 1 discounts or distorts feelings and thoughts. Spouse 2 tries to force partner to accept a Black perspective.	Each invalidates the other's reality. Feelings of non-acceptance and misunderstanding due to race are displaced into non-racial fights.
		White Dyads	
1. Contact Parent	Reintegration Child	Mutual misunderstanding and lack of confidence.	Parent distances self and wants child to outgrow phase. Child tries to force parent to deal with racial issues and set guidelines.	Parent ignores issues as long as possible. child may join groups or engage in activities with White superiority emphasis to gain parental attention.
2. Contact Teacher	Reintegration Student	Teacher feels anxious and helpless. Student feels angry and powerful.	Teacher ignores race-related behavior. Student controls interactions by defining appropriate behavior.	Neither person respects the other. Social roles are reversed, so each feels inadequate.
3. Contact Spouse 1	Reintegration Spouse 2	Spouse 1 lacks confidence in self. Spouse 2 is overly self-confident.	Spouse 1 avoids confrontation for fear of exposing naivete. Spouse 2 uses confrontation to to squelch contrary views.	Spouse with least social power controls race-related issues in relationship. Spouse 1 retaliates by exercising power in other aspects of relationship.

Table 12.2 (continued)

Participants' Role and Stage		Affective Issues	Relationship Authority/Partner Strategies	Dynamics Relationship Quality/Outcome
			White/Black Dyads	
1.	Contact Parent	Encounter Child	Both are curious and naive about Blackness and ambivalent about Whiteness.	Parent attempts to teach child to be a "human being"; denies race has differential meaning. Child brings racial events to parent for interpretation.	Parent teaches child a White view of Blackness. Child "chooses" to internalize White identity though parent supports self-initiated attempts to become Black as long as they're not perceived as deviant.
2.	Contact Teacher	Encounter Student	Teacher feels curious about students' racial group, but is unaware of own racial issues. Student enjoys attention for being Black, feels confused about Whiteness and lacks knowledge about Blackness.	Teacher encourages student to teach her/ him about Blackness; student role-plays Black to gain approval.	Superficial relationship that appear to be amiable, but is based on racial facades.
3.'	Contact Spouse 1	Encounter Spouse 2	Spouse 1 attempts to avoid personal and intra-personal racial conflict by becoming Black. Spouse 2 oscillates between being Black and pretending that race is irrelevant.	Together the couple develops a definition of Blackness around which they structure their behaviors. Whiteness is ignored.	Although roles are reversed, neither one recognizes it. Relationship is fairly harmonious as long as being Black is a shared goal.

survival, the more active the latter is in attempting to shape the partner's world view.

Notice also that the affective issues and strategies tend to be similar when the attitudes involved are the same, though the types of participants involved may differ. What varies most in the various authority/ partner dyads are the means available to the less powerful member for resolving relationship conflict. For instance, a child might "fight" with her or his parents by bringing home a person who represents all of the racial characteristics that the parent values least; a student might "fight" with her or his teacher by refusing to learn anything that he or she associates with the disfavored racial group; a spouse might "fight" with a spouse by discounting the spouse's feelings or thoughts about race. Authority figures are likely to become even more entrenched in their viewpoint when attacked by a partner if such attack heightens personal feelings of inadequacy, and thus the two may be engaged in a virtual tug of war for a long time.

Nevertheless, relationships are not necessarily static. In fact, one can find a number of case studies in which participants' racial identity appears to change over the course of the relationship (cf. Gibbs, 1974, 1987; Ladner, 1977; McRoy & Zurcher, 1983). Most of these involve mixed-race (Black/White) or all-Black participants. Still there is ample

impressionistic literature to support the observation that White participants do engage in socializing one another around racial identity issues
(cf. Bowser & Hunt, 1981).

Gibbs (1974, 1987) presents a number of case vignettes that can be
used to examine the role of parent-child dynamics in shaping the child's
racial identity as well as how that identity might evolve over the course
of time as the child's social horizons expand. The case of "Ruth D" offers
a good example of the evolution of a regressive Black parent-child dyad.
As a child, Ruth D had few contacts with Blacks other than her parents,
and they did not permit her to have friends who were "ghetto types."
Thus, during her childhood, Ruth D's parent-child interaction could be
characterized as parallel Preencounter. Her contact with Blacks in her
college dorm when she was a freshman triggered reactive but naive
attempts (e.g., using Black slang, wearing an Afro) to "be Black." At this
point, she was engaging in Immersion identification. When she returned
home for summer vacation, she found that her parents criticized her
new-found Blackness. Thus, the parent-child relationship shifted from
parallel to regressive.

Counseling Implications

In her presentation, Gibbs (1974) discusses the kinds of intrapsychic
symptoms that can occur when the adolescent is in conflict with her or
his environment over racial identity issues. These include depression,
suicidal thoughts and behavior, anxiety, and delusions. While these are
undoubtedly the most extreme reactions to identity conflicts, it is possible
that less extreme reactions, such as refusing to participate in classroom
activities, go unnoticed until they become problematic to someone else.
Adolescence, the phase in life when one is most concerned with a variety
of identity issues, also seems to be the time at which one's racial identity
issues are most salient. Nevertheless, Spaights and Dixon's (1984) discussion of pathological mixed-race romantic alliances implies that racial
identity issues may persist into adulthood. Clearly individuals who select
a mate in order to "Whiten" themselves, expiate the sins of their race,
or obtain revenge against the abusing racial group, are dealing with
unresolved racial identity conflicts.

By extrapolation from the body of literature on mixed-race alliances,
it seems possible to anticipate the kinds of situations that might contribute
to problematic racial identity issues regardless of the race of participants.
They include the person's (a) existence in racially isolated environments;
(b) consistent exposure to stereotyped parental or educator racial attitudes—especially those concerning intellectual development and
achievement; (c) being the recipient of either unusually positive (e.g.,
being singled out for special attention) or negative (e.g., avoidance) treat-

ment based on skin color and/or race; (d) being subjected to stigmatization due to racial characteristics, particularly those that are virtually unchangeable such as physical attributes; (e) need to coexist with authority figures who prohibit the discussion of racial issues or distort the significance of race in contemporary society.

Not surprisingly, it appears that parents and educators exert a significant influence on the individual's racial identity development from childhood through adulthood. Therefore, it behooves such authority figures to monitor their own racial identity development if they intend to produce adults who can function optimally in a multi-racial society.

Research Implications

Presently, the supposition that the Black/White interaction model is applicable to social as well as therapy dyads is merely an idea. Unfortunately, empirical investigations of dyadic relationships rarely focus on racial adjustment as a significant aspect of the relationship. Additionally, with the exceptions of studies by Pomales et al. (1986), Richardson (1987), and Carter (1987; see chapter 10), little attention has been devoted to analyzing the import of racial content to the quality of relationships from any theoretical perspective.

Even so, conceptualizing dyadic interactions via the dyadic model opens a myriad of possible research questions. Here are a few: Do particular combinations of racial identity attitudes contribute to differentially functional dyads? How do race, social power or role, and racial identity interact to influence the adjustment of individuals within dyads? How is racial identity communicated within dyads?

Until data concerning these and similar questions can be obtained, it seems reasonable to conclude this chapter as Helms (1984b) concluded her original formulation of the Black/White interaction model. That is, much is to be gained by understanding how race operates in social interactions if practitioners as well as researchers will exhibit more adventurousness in studying issues of racial identity development.

13

Generalizing Racial Identity Interaction Theory to Groups

JANET E. HELMS

Many of society's racial interactions occur on a group level. In fact, individuals do not develop a sense of racial identity independently of group interactions, but rather it evolves in response to various group-level socialization experiences from which the person makes inferences about herself or himself. Moreover, one has only to read daily news-papers to obtain a running digest of how groups seemingly acting as one personality express their issues of racial conflict (cf. *Frontline*, 1988). Yet, though issues of intergroup conflict have been studied extensively, with the possible exception of psychoanalytic theory, theoretical discus-sions of how individual characteristics combine to form a particular group climate when race is a potential issue are relatively rare. However, if it is true that a group's climate is determined by the accumulation of the intrapersonal and interpersonal characteristics of its members, then it ought to be possible to use racial identity theory with some elaboration to explain group dynamics as well as those of individuals and dyads.

In presenting the case for generalization of racial identity theory to group processes, the dyadic interaction model will be elaborated to apply to larger groups. However, some dimensions of interaction may be more apparent in groups (defined as more than two people) than in dyadic interactions. These dimensions include: structural factors, racial climate, and leader characteristics. Each of these dimensions may have some implications for interventions and research as well as theory. Although all three dimensions will be discussed in subsequent sections, the reader should be forewarned that empirical investigations of the influence of racial issues on the evolution of groups are extremely rare.

The global studies of intergroup contact (see Amir, 1976, and Riordan, 1978, for reviews) and the "minority status" social influence studies (e.g., Chaiken & Stangor, 1987; Maass & R. D. Clark, 1984) provide the best empirical information concerning groups, though these two bodies of empirical literature are of limited usefulness in explaining the workings of naturally occurring groups. The contact studies, which typically have examined the role of intergroup contact in reducing racism, seem to be most pertinent to issues of group structure, but are of limited utility for explaining group intra- and inter-communication because they have favored examination of group outcome (e.g., What are the end results of contact?) over group process issues (e.g., How do group members communicate their attitudes?). For their part, the minority influence studies, in spite of their appellation, have rarely investigated the operation of racial groups and/or political "minorities" (e.g., Blacks) in the influence process. Instead, these studies typically have defined minority as the person(s) who deviates from the group norm with respect to some perceptual task. Additionally, the minority status studies have relied on "minimal" groups (i.e., groups that only exist to satisfy the conditions of a single session experiment). These two omissions make generalization regarding group structure to naturally occurring groups somewhat problematic.

For information on group process or climate issues, one must depend primarily on the infrequent descriptions of racial issues in group therapy. However, these group process expositions typically have addressed conflict in interracial groups, treated the Black or other "minority" person as the source of the conflict, and have not used racial identity theory to analyze group dynamics. Consequently, the racial information available for analyzing group process cannot be assumed to be objective.

Given these considerations, although the literature in these three topic areas (i.e., intergroup contact, minority status influence, and group therapy) save the succeeding discourse from being entirely speculative, as is true of the dyadic model of racial identity interaction, the group model is intended to be a tentative framework by which practitioners and researchers can begin to systematically attend to racial issues as they occur during the functionings of groups.

Also, as was the case with counseling and social dyads, a basic assumption concerning group interaction is that the combinations of group members' stages of racial identity rather than race per se influence the quality of the group process. An additional assumption is that one's role as a majority or minority group member (as subsequently defined) acts interactively with racial identity stages to influence the group communication process. It also may be assumed that the same types of relationships (i.e., crossed, parallel, regressive, progressive) characterize the group process. However, it is likely that the process is more complex than that of dyads because of the multiplicity of ways in which the structure of the group and the collectives of individuals within the group can influence the climate of the group. Climate or cohesiveness determines whether or not group participants will experience the group as attractive and, therefore, permit their attitudes and behaviors to be shaped by it (cf. Yalom, 1970).

Group Structure

As used here, group structure refers to the objective or measurable qualities of a group that give it a particular character. These elements, which are not assumed to operate independently of climatic or process factors, include format or kind of group, proportions of different racial group representation, as well as varieties of racial identity stages evident.

Group format. Groups may be created to serve specific functions or they may evolve more or less spontaneously from the collection of people within a particular environment. Examples of the former kind of group include formal counseling or therapy groups, supervised work teams, families, classes, military squadrons, and so on; examples of the latter include informal discussion groups, recreational teams, neighborhoods, free play situations, and so on. Racial identity issues may be undercurrents in either kind of group, which, if left untreated, can contribute to the group's demise or dysfunctionality. Groups constructed for the purpose of considering racial identity matters (e.g., J. Katz, 1977) seem to survive better than groups in which such issues are camouflaged by other considerations within the group. Groups in which the exploration of racial identity is guided and purposive may serve to modify racial attitudes better than groups in which the exploration is haphazard (e.g., Burke, 1984).

Also, racially homogeneous groups may have an easier time managing racial identity issues than racially mixed groups. Effective Black groups have been described by Boyd-Franklin (1987); effective White groups have been described by J. Katz (1977) and Terry (1977). It is clear, however, that these successes did not occur without much directive intervention by group leaders in which group members were encouraged to confront racial issues. Thus, it is a strong possibility that even when a group is entirely of one race, its climate may be affected by the racial identity issues of its members, including its leader(s). Therefore, establishing a cohesive climate may require a group leader who can either move the group members toward the same direction or help them to maintain momentum in the direction in which the group is already moving. The perpetuation of virulent groups built around racial issues (e.g., the Ku Klux Klan) suggests that effective leaders may be capable of maintaining group cohesiveness even when that cohesiveness is not necessarily beneficial to individual members' racial identity development.

Nevertheless, when groups with racial undercurrents survive, then they too seem to have the capacity to progress along a developmental continuum analogous to those of the respective racial identity models. That is, Black groups do seem to move through the Black identity stages and White groups seem to move through the White identity stages. When groups are racially mixed, the climate conceivably reflects some combination of the stages. It also appears that the same sorts of adaptive and defensive strategies as occur with individuals (e.g., denial, minimization, withdrawal) can occur on a group level as well. Consequently, whether a group moves toward the higher levels of identity development often depends on the group leader's skillfulness in encouraging it to so move.

Racial proportions. The number of Blacks relative to Whites and vice versa may influence the character of the group. As discussed in greater detail subsequently, existing evidence indicates that Whites are likely to prefer heteroracial groups in which they are numerically dominant, whereas Blacks are likely to prefer groups in which there are equal numbers of Blacks and Whites. However, aside from systemic studies (e.g., housing and school desegregation), empirical studies of the influence of differing Black/White proportions on the process or outcome of small groups are extremely rare. Giles, Cataldo, and Gatlin (1975), and Stinchcombe, McDill, and Walker (1969) did find in naturalistic neighborhood groups and school settings behavior suggestive of reactivity in response to a rapidly changing Black/White racial ratio. That is, as the numbers of Blacks entering these environments increased, the numbers of Whites leaving also increased. A possible interpretation of Stinchcombe et al. and Giles et al.'s findings for other groups is that when the entry of new group members or the exit of old members changes the Black/White racial ratio, then racial identity conflict in some form might best be anticipated.

Proportions of racial identity stages. Although some controversy exists concerning how best to assess individuals' stages of racial identity (cf. Cross et al., in press; Helms, 1986), it ought to be possible to perform such an assessment. In group situations, perhaps individuals of similar identity stages band together and are affected by the group in similar manners. Thus, the numbers of individuals within each stage of identity may determine the direction of the group. Logically, one would expect that the larger the number of people within a particular stage, the stronger that stage's influence on the quality of the group. According to this expectation, for instance, if most people are in the Preencounter stage, then the issues typical of individuals in this stage should also dominate the group. On the other hand, particular stages that are only minimally represented might exert greater influence than other stages that are more abundantly represented if the members of the smaller group are more forceful. For instance, those stages in which racism is actively confronted (i.e., Black and White Immersion/Emersion) often seem to contribute to greater group tension than their proportion within the group would warrant.

If the observation that some stages of identity can result in disproportionate influence is supportable, then it is possible that some clusters of group members may become "minorities" by virtue of their mutual stages of identity. That is, they may *feel* powerless in spite of their greater numbers. In such cases, majority and minority interactions whose purpose is to consolidate or obtain power within the group might be expected to proliferate. It should follow that stages of identity that are evident in the group shape the tone and direction of these power negotiations.

Group Racial Climate

Racial climate refers to the conduciveness of the group's atmosphere to resolving intra- and inter-racial conflict and encouraging the development of positive racial identity development of group members regardless of their racial categorization. In addition to the structural factors previously discussed, climate is influenced by (a) perceptions of power, (b) group racial norms, and (c) racial identity coalitions.

Perceptions of power. Psychological power within a group refers to individuals' perceptions that they can control the resources of the group in a manner that is beneficial to themselves. Power can result from the numerical representation of one's racial or attitudinal kinspeople in the group. It can also result from one's perceived ability to influence the norms of the group. Where numerical representation is concerned, a fairly common finding is that Whites tend to be most comfortable in racially heterogeneous groups when the proportion of Whites to Blacks is around 70% to 30%, whereas Blacks are most comfortable when the proportion is around 50% to 50% (cf. Farley, Schuman, Bianchi, Colasanto, & Hatchett, 1978; L. Davis, 1979). If these figures are translated to commonly occurring group situations, then on average in a therapy group or discussion group of eight people, Whites would feel comfortable if six or more of the participants were White, whereas Blacks on average would feel comfortable if at least four were Black; in a classroom of 25 students, Whites would feel comfortable if 18 or more of the students were White, whereas Blacks would feel comfortable if half were of each race.

L. E. Davis (1980) uses the concepts of "psychological minority" and "psychological majority" to explain why Whites, the numerical majority in this society, require greater numbers of their racial compeers to feel safe in the presence of Blacks than Blacks, the numerical minority in this society, require to feel safe in the presence of Whites. Accordingly, psychological minority refers to a group or member of a group that, though an actual numerical majority, feels itself to be in the minority, whereas a psychological majority is the converse.

L. E. Davis (1980) suggests that Blacks and Whites operate from two different adaption levels, and since most Whites are accustomed to interacting with Blacks only in minimal numbers, they become distressed when the number of Blacks in any setting exceeds Whites' relatively low racial diversity adaptation levels. That is, Whites view themselves as a "minority" and consequently perceive that they have less "psychological power" in bi-racial interactions, where power is equivalent to feelings of security and/or control of the situation. Conversely, since Blacks are accustomed to functioning at a numerical disadvantage, then according to L. E. Davis, it takes relatively few other Blacks to increase their sense of power in a given situation. Said a different way, racial numerical equality hypothetically contributes to a Black person's feelings of power, whereas racial numerical superiority contributes to that of Whites.

A racial identity interpretation of psychological "minorityness" requires the assumptions that (a) given that Whites have greater choice as to how or whether their racial identity will develop, they most often choose to remain at stages that involve the least immediate psychological discomfort for themselves; (b) since Blacks are more often forced to grapple with issues of racial identity, larger proportions are likely to have evolved to successively higher stages of Black identity development; and (c) one's stage of racial identity influences how one stereotypes one's own as well as other racial groups.

The White stereotypes of Blacks congruent with the abandonment of racism stages portray a consistently frightening and distasteful picture of Blacks (cf. Shipp, 1983; Gardner, 1971). Not one of the stages of any of the NRID models portrays consistently negative stereotypes of Whites. Nor do empirical data usually confirm that Blacks' attitudes toward Whites are as negative as Whites' attitudes toward Blacks. One suspects that Whites at early stages of identity expend considerable energy defending themselves against their own stereotypes of Blacks (i.e., paratactic distortions) rather than the actuality of Blacks, and in interracial groups they may seek to fortify their defenses with like-minded individuals.

Nevertheless, according to the "minority" explanation of power and depending somewhat upon their stages of identity, one might expect Whites at lower stages of identity to experience racial identity induced conflict when the percentage of Blacks relative to Whites surpasses 30%, and Blacks at higher stages to experience their conflict when the percentage of Whites relative to Blacks exceeds 50%. According to the "identity" explanation, conflict should occur when the group members' stages of identity are incompatible. Moreover, Kibel's (1972) and Brayboy's (1971) description of their experiences as group leaders suggests that Whites' expression of anti-Black attitudes and Blacks' expressions of anti-White attitudes may depend not only on having the correct Black-to-White or White-to-Black proportions in a group, but also on how powerful those present are perceived to be.

For instance, in Kibel's (1972) therapy group, consisting of eight group members (six White women and one or two Black men) and one (presumably) White male psychiatrist, during the early sessions, when only one Black male had joined the group, the group members did not react to the man in a manner apparently indicative of racial consciousness. Kibel described the man as "rather light skinned" and as consciously identifying with "White society" (possibly Preencounter). Thus the group acted as though it were in the Contact and Preencounter stages. That is, they merely pretended that racial differences did not exist and treated the Black member as though he had no power.

However, when a Black male who visibly elicited the group's (including the therapist's) stereotypes (e.g., he was dark-skinned and ethnically dressed) joined the group, the group, including the therapist, interacted with him as though he confirmed their racial stereotypes even though his demeanor was not aggressive or violent. Subsequently, group members generally continued to ignore racial issues when the men were present except when the arousal of other group issues made it safer to deal with both men in an anti-Black confrontative manner than to deal with other issues. Thus, the Black members' lack of conformity to stereotypes, coupled with their numerical underrepresentation permitted them little power to shape the norms of the group. However, the White members' shared stages of identity combined with unbalanced numerical representation gave them power to shape the group norms in a manner that was comfortable to themselves.

Considered in tandem, Kibel's (1972) and Brayboy's (1971) case reports support the assumption that an important compositional element in the life of a group is the racial identity development of its group members. Yet one can also infer from their discussions that it is not so much the identity development of each individual that structures the climate of a group, but the stages of racial identity as exhibited by subgroups or coalitions within the larger group.

Group racial norms. Each group member brings to any particular group the racial norms prevalent in the more influential group(s) to which he or she belongs. When a number of group members bring a common norm into the new group, then this norm has a strong potential to become the attitudinal set around which the group dynamics evolve. That is, if left to its own devices, a group will probably adapt the norms or viewpoints that feel most comfortable to the largest proportion of its members. Minorities, that is, those who do not come to the group with the same norm, must either try to influence the majority to modify its norm, shift in the direction of the majority, or leave the group. For its own part, the majority will attempt to influence the minority toward the group norm, thereby demonstrating the "rightness" of the norm. Social influence research appears to indicate that the majority needs to exert very little active influence on a minority in order to induce conformity. In fact, the mere presence of a numerical majority espousing similar viewpoints is a powerful influence (cf. Tanford & Penrod, 1984; Chaiken & Stangor, 1987). What a minority must do to influence the majority to modify its stance is much more complex.

Paicheler (1977) uses the term "zeitgeist" to mean the direction in which the norm trend of a particular group (e.g., therapy groups, classes, political parties, etc.) tends to evolve. It seems possible that there exist "meta-zeigeists," that is, internalized normative trends adopted from other more powerful groups to which the potential group member belongs, which he or she carries to new group experiences.

In this society, since the advent of slavery, the societal (i.e., group) meta-zeitgeist has been White superiority/Black inferiority, that is, White racism. So crystallized has been the racism meta-zeitgeist that White people originally wrote it into the country's Constitution. Though successive efforts have been made to alter the country's racism meta-zeitgeist by repairing the Constitution via various amendments, in fact, very little has been done to change the attitudes that contributed to this meta-zeitgeist in the first place. Thus, the racism meta-zeitgeist, which conceivably has been passed on from generational group to generational group, potentially shapes many group interactions to some extent.

Up to this point it has also been argued, more implicitly than explicitly, that the various stages of racial identity occupy different positions vis-a-vis the racism meta-zeitgeist. The Contact, Disintegration, Reintegration, and Preencounter stages are in varying levels of agreement with the meta-zeitgeist, whereas the Pseudo-Independent, Immersion/Emersion, Internalization, and Autonomy stages reflect varying levels of disagreement with it. Membership in any of the stages that oppose the meta-zeitgeist also places one in a minority status group on a societal level, regardless of whether one is Black or White.

Support for this definition of minority status can be surmised from the interracial contact literature. The basic premise of this literature is that individual racism can best be eliminated by causing Blacks and Whites of equal status to interact. However, several reviews (e.g., Riordan, 1978; Triandis, 1977) of the resulting literature have noted the inconsistent effects on racial attitudes of "equal status" interventions. In his analysis of some of the major contributions to this literature, Riordan (1978) noted the virtual impossibility of constituting equal status cross-racial groups unless some interventions (e.g., S. W. Cook, 1978; E. G. Cohen & Roper, 1972) are used to alter the racial attitudes of group members prior to the "equal status" manipulation. Therefore, perhaps unknowingly, Riordan appears to be arguing the pervasiveness of a societal racism meta-zeitgeist; and if it functions so consistently in cross-racial interactions, chances are it is also operative in homoracial inter-actions as well.

Though it is not presently possible to empirically demonstrate the role of the societal racism meta-zeitgeist on small group interactions with any conclusiveness, various authors (Ganter, 1977; Harris, 1977; and Quayt-man, 1977) have noted its operation among White (and Black) mental health professionals and clients. Clinical portrayals of group process also offer some ways in which the societal racism meta-zeitgeist operates in small group settings and suggest that it might shape institutional meta-zeitgeists as well (e.g., M. Davis, Sharfstein, & Owens, 1974; O. S. Smith & Gundlach, 1974).

M. Davis et al.'s (1974) presentation supports the hypothesis that in-dividuals may operate according to several meta-zeitgeists, societal and institutional, a conjunction that might go unnoticed if the meta-zeitgeists are of similar content. On the occasion of the formation of a six-member Black therapy group in a predominantly White (75 patients) community mental health center, Davis et al. noted several types of staff and patient fear and apprehension reactions that may, in fact, be illustrative of the racism meta-zeitgeist in operation at both institutional and small group levels. Among Whites, these reactions included: (a) fear that the group would become a political force, (b) concern for their own physical safety, (c) oversolicitousness, and (d) indifference. Among Blacks, reactions in-cluded (a) concerns about the therapist's competence and (b) fear of promoting segregation. Underlying most of the reactions run anti-Black stereotypes and fear of the racial group not one's own, rather than objective analyses of the situation (e.g., How could six or seven Black patients run roughshod over 75 or more Whites?).

Not every person within a group necessarily will adhere to the racism meta-zeitgeist, regardless of its origins. In fact, racial identity theory speculates about how or why one might hold alternative viewpoints. Those persons in a group who are not in agreement with the societal racism meta-zeitgeist or the particular group's zeitgeist (whether it is racial or not) become part of a minority coalition of one or more.

Minority-influence research (see Maass & R. D. Clark, 1984, for a review) suggests that there may be some conditions under which the group minority can influence the majority in the direction of the mi-nority's interests. Maass and R. D. Clark (1984) summarized the con-ditions of potential minority influence over the majority in group situations. Accordingly, they proposed that the majority will be influenced by a credible minority if the latter is consistent in its behavioral style, which then allows the majority to infer that the minority really believes in the position it is advocating. However, minority credibility can be diminished by any of several conditions, which Maass and R. D. Clark list as follows: "(a) a rigid style of negotiation in situations in which the minority's behavior can easily be ascribed to its idiosyncratic psychological characteristics, (b) discordance of the minority's position, (c) a zeitgeist that is unfavorable to the minority's point of view, and (d) double minority status" (p. 432). Maass and R. D. Clark define minority status according to group members' positions relative to the group zeitgeist and/or ascribed category membership or social categorization (e.g., Black).

Let us add two further conditions that might contribute to minority status and loss of credibility in naturally occurring groups. These include (a) stage of racial identity as expressed in the group, and (b) group member's position relative to the operative meta-zeitgeist(s). Thus, as one example, in a group in which the group zeitgeist is also the societal racism meta-zeitgeist expressed via denial of racial import, then a White person who insisted upon discussing the significance of race in this situation would become a single minority for having opposed the group zeitgeists; if her or his discussion also advocated the fallaciousness of the societal premise of White superiority as might be expected of a person in the Immersion/Emersion and Autonomy stages of development, then the person would become a double minority; if, additionally, the White person did not present his or her viewpoint in a flexible manner (Maass & R. D. Clark's, 1984, first criterion), then he or she would become a triple minority and so on. If the positions of double minorities are typically discounted by majorities, then one can only suppose that the more minority characteristics one exhibits, the more likely one is to be discounted. Terry's (1977) discussion of the ostracism by Whites of "New Whites" and Brayboy's (1971) description of a similar process in his interracial group demonstrate the principle that racial similarity does not necessarily ensure one's place among the majority.

Visibly Black group members in predominantly White groups automatically begin with one dimension of minority status (physical appearance). However, it is not clear from existing literature whether or how this factor contributes to "minorityness" in exclusively or predominantly Black groups. Interestingly, in White-majority/Black-minority groups, inference from the minority-influence literature (e.g., Maass, R. D. Clark, & Haberkorn, 1982) would lead to the observation that if Black persons wish to avoid further minority attributions, and consequently, rejection, as well as influence the direction of the group, then they should at least appear to agree with the societal racism meta-zeitgeist (i.e., pro-White/anti-Black) and the group zeitgeist if the two coincide. If this speculation

is accurate, then clearly the Black person, who ought to be more influential in a majority White group, is usually going to be the one who acts
in a manner consistent with the Preencounter stage. In such instances,
the direction of group influence will be toward the racism meta-zeitgeist.
Consequently, neither the Black multiple minority nor the White multiple majority will be influenced toward healthy identity development.
Be that as it may, there appear to be few circumstances of interracial
interaction that would automatically promote healthy racial identity development given the prevailing societal racism meta-zeitgeist. Moreover,
some combinations can only serve to strengthen non-healthy attitudes.

    Racial identity coalitions. Coalitions are alliances held together by shared
racial identity world views. Remember that shared world views imply
shared attitudes, beliefs, and perceptions, which include paratactic distortions or stereotypes to which the perceiver reacts as though they were
real. To the casual observer, coalitions appear to be based on racial
similarity, that is, Whites unite with other White group members as do
Blacks with Black group members. Yet appearances might be misleading,
since under some circumstances (e.g., single minority status), Black
group members are permitted to join White coalitions. An example of
this type of coalition involved the light-skinned Black man in Kibel's
(1972) study previously discussed. Relatedly, not all Blacks within the
same group necessarily form unions with each other; nor do Whites (cf.
Brayboy, 1971).

    If racial identity coalitions are structured around stages of racial iden-
tity development in interaction with psychological power and minority/
majority status, then White coalitions should accept Black members as
long as their numbers do not exceed the White numerical level of psychological comfort and the Blacks' expression of their own racial identity
does not lead to their being relegated to multiple minority status. Brayboy's (1971) observations suggest, for instance, that presumably Disintegration and Reintegration Whites discounted Immersion Blacks and
ostracized Pseudo-Independent Whites when the first two types of White
coalitions were in the majority.

    Theoretically it seems that White individuals in the Contact, Pseudo-
Independent, and Autonomy stages should be more receptive to Black
potential coalition members than individuals in the remaining stages of
White identity. Of course, the increased or decreased receptivity may be
attributed to different motivational factors. On the one hand, Contact
members may be amenable to Black group membership when they are
able to minimize racial differences; Pseudo-Independent coalition members may accept Black members who do not force them to question their
own liberalism too deeply; Autonomous group members may accept
them because of mutual respect. On the other hand, Disintegration and
Reintegration coalitions conceivably consider Blacks too threatening to
be admitted into a coalition, whereas Immersion/Emersion Whites might

exclude Blacks from White coalitions until the Whites have learned how to resolve their racism without using Blacks for verification.

Where Black entry into White coalitions is a possibility, Blacks at the Preencounter, Encounter, and Internalization stages should be able to enter White coalitions, if permitted. Individuals in these stages should also be tolerant of White entry into Black coalitions. Again, however, the quality of the coalitions may differ depending upon which particular stage of racial identity is predominant. A Preencounter coalition may be one in which race is denied or minimized, an Encounter coalition could be one in which race is idealized, and an Internalization coalition may be one in which race is integrated into the work of the coalition. Immersion/Emersion coalitions should be least receptive to cross-racial coalition formation.

It follows that coalitions can be in harmony or conflict with one another, which in turn strongly influences group cohesiveness. Coalitions can also be of numerical as well as psychological majority or minority status. For instance, a coalition based on the Autonomy or Internalization stages would likely be a minority status coalition, both numerically and psychologically, when the societal racism meta-zeitgeist is operative. The same characteristics that have been used in prior sections to analyze the dynamics of individuals of minority status may also be used to examine the communication strategies of coalitions.

Usually majority status coalitions will have the most power in a group regardless of the actual number of members in the group. In such instances, minority status members of the other coalitions must decide whether they can influence the zeitgeist. If the decision is affirmative, they may remain and participate in the group's functions; otherwise, they may attempt to disrupt the activities of the group or they may leave. Which decision is made probably depends on which stages of racial identity are represented within the various coalitions, and how large or psychologically powerful the various coalitions are perceived to be by their members. For example, a small or less psychologically powerful coalition of Disintegration Whites might abandon a group if the remaining group members belonged to Immersion/Emersion coalitions. On the other hand, if coalitions are equal in size and/or power, then, again depending somewhat on the nature of the stages represented, the group is likely to dissolve. One can find a few descriptions of the latter outcome in existing group therapy literature (e.g., Burke, 1984).

Role of the group leader. In large part, the viability of a group experiencing racial identity conflict depends on the facility of the group leader in managing such conflict. The combinations of types of racial identity coalitions present in a group as well as the racial identity characteristics of the group leader(s) influence the process and outcome of the group.

The dynamics of purposeful groups generally are managed by a group leader(s) whose qualifications for the role are determined by outside forces (e.g., license boards, management, superintendents, etc.) prior to the group's inception. In spontaneous groups, leaders generally evolve from the consensus of group members, and are typically the persons who are perceived to be capable of minimizing the discomfort level of group members.

In both predetermined and spontaneous groups, the main task of the group leader is to increase group harmony by uniting the coalitions. However, the group leader's own level of racial identity development determines how successfully he or she can manage this task. In order to reduce the conflict, role playing, and scapegoating that can occur within and among coalitions as well as between coalitions and group leaders, the group leader must be sensitive to the racial identity issues inherent in each coalition and be able to select interventions appropriate for each coalition so as to defuse the discomfort inherent in such situations.

Faulkner (1983) provides an example of constructive coalition management. In her interracial groups, she pointed out to the White coalition that they were interacting with Black group members in a way that confirmed the societal racism meta-zeitgeist that Blacks should take care of Whites; to the Black coalition, she pointed out that they were resentfully succumbing to the societal expectation. Due to her observations, she was able to offer alternative strategies to reduce the dysfunctionality of the coalitions and successfully avoid joining any of the coalitions herself.

Compare Faulkner's (1983) strategy to Kibel's (1972) unsuccessful attempt to defuse coalitions in which he seemingly used a non-specific probe to urge group members to discuss racial issues. The Faulkner and Kibel papers considered together seem to confirm the idea that the successful group leader not only is capable of recognizing racial identity related issues while in the midst of the group process, but is also able to take explicit action toward resolving the issues while avoiding the appearance or reality of having joined either coalition. The leader's level of adeptness in performing these functions may depend upon her or his own stage of racial identity development as well.

Judging from the published group process literature, most group leaders are not very successful in negotiating conflict around racial issues (Brayboy, 1971; Kibel, 1972). What typically seems to happen in groups, particularly if they are mixed-race groups, is that either racial issues are denied, avoided, debated, or minimized, and/or the group leader either consciously or accidentally joins one of the coalitions. When the group leader joins a coalition, the balance of group power is shifted in the direction of that coalition, making it a majority status coalition. In such instances, majority and minority coalition members will engage in strategies appropriate to their stage of identity to secure personal power in the group.

Thus, it appears that coalitions can be in harmony or conflict individually or collectively with the group leader as well as with one another. Although the combinations of interrelationships among coalitions and group leaders determine the climate or cohesiveness of the group, the relationship of the coalitions to the group leader and her or his ability to negotiate the resulting conflicts may be crucial to the group's survival. Here it is being argued that the group leader's stage of racial identity influences her or his capacity to navigate the group through its stages of racial identity development. Therefore, it might be useful to consider some possible group relationship types involving the leader and single coalitions. Recognize, however, that when more than one type of coalition is present in the group, then the leader can anticipate having to manage more than one type of relationship.

Relationship Types

Four "pure" types of leader-coalition types will be considered: parallel, regressive, crossed, and progressive. By substituting "leader" for "counselor," "coalition" for "client," and "group" for "dyad" in Table 9.1 (see chapter 9), one can obtain a global picture of the leader-coalition process and outcome issues for each type of relationship. However, because each stage may have unique expressive aspects, specific dynamics of group leaders and their coalitions based on their racial identity stages are proposed in Table 13.1 for parallel relationships. In groups as well as dyads, the more powerful person (which in this case should be the group leader) and the less powerful (i.e., coalitions) are likely to express similar racial identity stages differently because of different role expectations. The group leader in every instance operates under the expectation that he or she will act to ensure the group's survival for as long as it is necessary for it to serve its purpose.

Parallel relationships. In group situations, parallel relationships are defined as those wherein the group leader and a coalition share the same or analogous stages of racial identity. In a completely parallel group, all group members share the same or analogous stages of identity. Thus, in White groups, parallel relationships involve leaders and coalitions that are both Contact or Disintegration, and so forth. Of course, Black parallel relationships involve leaders and coalitions who share common Black stages of identity. When the leader and group are racially heterogeneous, then parallel relationships involve Preencounter/Reintegration, Internalization/Autonomy, and perhaps Encounter/Disintegration stages.

The common theme in parallel relationships is inertia. That is, neither group leaders nor coalitions can function beyond their respective world views. Consequently, they cannot stimulate one another to move beyond their common world view. Yet this inertia is less problematic the more developmentally advanced the participants' stages of identity are. Whereas one might expect a relationship in which consideration of racial issues is short-circuited in some manner in the early stages (e.g., Contact or Preencounter), one might find their examination ad nauseam in parallel Autonomy and/or Internalization relationships. Thus, although the particulars of parallel relationships probably differ according to which stage the participants are in, there may be some commonalities. The commonalities have more to do with style or process than content. Table 13.1 illustrates some of the process issues in parallel group leader-coalition relationships involving the various stages of identity.

Regressive relationships. Regressive relationships in groups are characterized by a coalition whose stage of racial identity is more advanced than that of its group leader. The major theme of regressive relationships is regression. That is, group leaders view and attempt to influence coalitions to view racial matters in a way that is no longer functional for the coalition, though it may have been at some time during their development. The coalition resists such influence attempts and tries to force the group leader to perceive the world in a manner that is beyond the group leader's knowledge. Some tension exists in regressive relationships due to the leader's efforts to pull the coalition back to a place where the leader feels comfortable and the coalition's efforts to resist. The tension increases as the discrepancy between the group leader's and a coalition's stages of identity increases. By referring to Tables 9.1 (see chapter 9) and 12.2 (see chapter 12), the reader can obtain a more precise idea of the differential dynamics of regressive relationships based on various racial identity stages.

Crossed relationships. When the leader's and coalition's stages of identity represent conceptually opposite world views, then the resulting relationships are said to be crossed. Crossed relationships tend to be contentious and combative. Table 12.1 lists the potential crossed relationships for Blacks and/or Whites. Of course in this table, the group leader is in the role of authority and the coalition(s) is in the role of partner or follower. One can also acquire a sense of the climatic issues in groups involving crossed relationships by matching the appropriate stage descriptions from Table 13.1. For instance, the Internalization/Disintegration crossed relationship, based on the information in Table 13.1, might be one in which the leader (or coalition) is attempting to avoid discomfort by ignoring racial issues or turning them into something else, while the other party is attempting to accentuate discomfort for the purpose of better self-understanding. As a result of these antithetical efforts, the counseling climate will involve participants who are consistently operating at

Table 13.1
Dimensions of Group Leader and Coalition Parallel Same-Race Relationships

Climate	Stage	Leader	Coalition
		Blacks	
Denial	Pre	Avoids racial issues when possible. Otherwise attempts to stress racial similarities from a White perspective.	Supports racism meta-zeitgeist. Challenges contrary viewpoints and blames others for its discomfort.
Confusion	Enc	Superficial information-seeking rather than provision. Does not confront or structure interactions.	Can be either euphoric and optimistic or confused and self-protective.
Transcendence	In	Overt and objective focusing on racial impasses. Attempts to integrate racial issues into group process.	Interested in self-exploration and examination. Is willing to consider racial issues overtly and actively initiates such explorations.
		Whites	
Denial	Con	Avoids setting a direction for the group. Does not set limits or attempt to modify group's view of the world.	Discounts significance of racial issues; seeks support for naive view of world. Rejects information that change is required.
Avoid Pain	Dis	Interventions grow out of own need to feel better. Structures interactions to protect self. Focuses on behaviors and cognitions that lessen internal conflict. Detaches self from group.	Defends self against acknowledgment of racial issues. Feels challenged and threatened by such topics. Resorts to inertia and withdrawal as a means of self-protection.
Self-Rightousness	Re	Minimizes the uniqueness of racial/cultural perspectives other than his/her own. Translates group process to fit a White Superiority world view.	Encases self in White Superiority/ Black Inferiority. Engages in active and angry catharsis. Is immune to contrary viewpoints.
Tolerant	PI	Focuses on helping members achieve a cognitive understanding of racial issues and self-control. Avoids activities that might arouse emotions.	Wants to be taught about racial differences. Values information, but does not want to be emotionally aroused.
Exploration	Im	Leader emphasizes self-awareness and understanding. Engages members in cognitive and emotional examination of Whites' contribution to racism.	Values new cognitive and emotional perspective on racial issues. Actively engages in self- and other-exploration.
Transcendence	Aut	Encourages pluralism. Challenges defenses and tries to help coalitions become relativistic in their thoughts and feelings about racial groups.	Values in-depth self-exploration. Devalues superficial treatment of racial issues and inauthenticity. Is open to risk-taking.

Note: Pre = Preencounter; Enc = Encounter; Im = Immersion/Emersion; In = Internalization; Con = Contact; Dis = Disintegration; Re = Reintegration; PI = Pseudo-Independent; Aut = Autonomy.

cross-purposes. In such relationships, it would be quite reasonable to expect considerable anger and hostility due to what may be perceived as the other's recalcitrance.

Progressive relationships. In progressive relationships, the group leader's stage of racial identity is more developmentally advanced than that of the coalition. Any of the stages beyond the first has the potential to become a part of a progressive relationship. Again, Table 12.1 can be used to define the various types of leader-coalition progressive relationships for the different combinations of races. The general theme of progressive relationships is movement and energy. That is, the leader attempts to encourage the coalition to move beyond its present level of development. Such movement is not necessarily always experienced as pleasant by coalition members. Yet they are often willing to subject themselves to the experience if the leader is skillful in showing them why it is to their benefit to do so and protects their sense of power.

In many ways, progressive relationships are more energized than parallel relationships and are the antithesis of crossed and regressive relationships. With perhaps the exceptions of these parallel relationships based on the most advanced stages of identity, progressive relationships should work best in promoting the longevity and functionality of groups.

Counseling Implications

In using the group model to improve the racial identity of group members and thereby the functionality of the group, it seems important that the group leader be skilled in two diagnostic areas. The first concerns the group leader's familiarity with the societal racism meta-zeitgeist and how it typically is expressed by Blacks and Whites. Since by definition it cannot be expressed in ways that are healthful to group members, the group leader needs to be able to use this awareness to detect the operation of the societal meta-zeitgeist in small groups. The group leader's goal in such instances is to replace the racism meta-zeitgeist with a group norm that acknowledges and accepts racial similarities and differences and recognizes and eschews racism.

However, perhaps the more difficult diagnostic endeavor for the group leader concerns identifying the various types of coalitions within the group so that the group leader can provide purposeful interventions matched to the coalitions' levels of receptivity. Since there are currently no commonly accepted devices for performing these two aspects of diagnosis, the group leader likely will have to depend upon her or his ability to observe coalitions and group-coalition interactions within naturally occurring groups. If one is starting at the most basic level in developing such observational skills, then television talk shows offer excellent primers. At some time, major network talk shows offer what might be called "racial topics." Generally these are discussions involving Black and White panelists who present contrary views on some topic pertaining to interracial group interactions. Ordinarily, the Black panelist defines the tenets of one coalition by presenting a perspective in opposition to the societal racism meta-zeitgeist and the White panelist defines another by presenting a perspective in favor of it. Hosts (i.e., group leaders) and their audience (i.e., group members) then speak in support of one position or another. A coalition consists of those people who overtly or covertly align themselves with a position, though active and passive coalition members will not be equally apparent to the observer of television group interactions. The type of relationship can be roughly assessed by noting the various emotional climates that occur between coalitions and between coalitions and group leaders. For instance, what appear to be crossed relationships are frequently characterized by much shouting and other indications of agitation.

By noticing how individuals talk about and react to racial issues, the observer can begin to form approximate "guesstimates" about which of the stages are represented and in what quantity. By attending to structural characteristics of the situation such as Black/White ratio and percentages of the group committed to each coalition, one can get an idea about whether or not these characteristics favor constructive communications. Finally, by observing the hosts' maneuvers to maintain control, one can begin to figure out which interventions move which coalitions in which directions.

Assuming that one can tolerate this self-imposed training activity for a while, one eventually becomes attuned diagnostically to racial identity issues when they appear in more subtle forms in other kinds of groups. Once the potential group leader becomes adept diagnostically, then he or she needs to learn how to intervene to move the group in the healthiest identity direction. Chapter 14 describes racial identity promoting interventions. Naturally, successful use of these strategies requires that the group leader attend to the quality of her or his own racial identity development as well.

14

Interventions for Promoting Better Racial Identity Development

JANET E. HELMS

Although the notion that something needs to be done to improve interracial interactions in the United States has been around since the zenith of the Civil Rights Movement of the 1960s, interventions designed to improve racial relations have generally been atheoretical, sparce, and superficial at best. Initial attempts to modify racial attitudes seem to have been based on the assumption that if groups of Blacks and Whites could be encouraged to converse with each other in a structured environment, then interracial communication would occur on a broader societal level as well (cf. Wittmer, Lanier, & Parker, 1976). Interventions based on this assumption, which still predominates in educational institutions today, generally treat individual racism as the most significant barrier to interracial communication, do not consider the etiology and significance of racism in its various manifestations, assume personal racism results from racial isolation for both groups, and regard racial identity as a core element only of Black personalities.

In the mid–1970s, virtually simultaneously, mental health professionals began to attempt to devise strategies that would assist American nationals in communicating with people of other countries and Blacks and Whites in this country to communicate with each other. What made these strategies differ from their predecessors was that a few theorists began to design their interventions around theories of how cultural competence develops. Implicit in these approaches was an explicit statement of how people come to be as they are with respect to identity as well as what needs to be done to encourage them to grow in more positive directions. For the first time, it became possible to conceive of interventions matched specifically to each individual's particular developmental needs.

Two types of theory-based interventions, based specifically on stage models of identity development, can be found in contemporary literature. The first approach, called here the "environmental congruence perspective," proposes that when miscommunication between racial/cultural groups occurs, it is because the ethnocentric group (usually White Americans) has unwittingly trod upon the cultural norms of the other group. This approach is typically used to educate individuals anticipating cross-national interactions, but sometimes with little or no modification can be used to educate individuals anticipating cross-racial interactions as well. The second approach, which will be called the "racial identity perspective," specifically assumes that interracial conflict has personal racial identity developmental issues as its source, and therefore, if interracial communication is to be encouraged, then the individual must first come to understand her or his own racial identity issues. The second approach often shares some of the basic premises of environmental congruence models. However, in such instances it is generally assumed that racial identity stages are the dimensions to which interventions should be matched. In this chapter, each of these training approaches will be described and implications for research and training will be presented.

ENVIRONMENTAL CONGRUENCE MODELS

The common theme of environmental congruence models is that trainees can be helped to develop healthy identities by matching interventions to trainees' stages of identity development. When an intervention is appropriately matched, that is, is congruent, then the trainee does not feel threatened by new information and is willing to let it into his or her belief system. Environmental congruence models also assume that the ideal goal of training is to help the individual reach the highest stage of development, though the amount of time required for this to occur is rarely specified.

Bennett's (1986) Intercultural Sensitivity Approach

Bennett's (1986) model was developed as a strategy for reducing intercultural rather than interracial conflict, but can be easily adapted for racial identity training. In fact, basically all one would have to do to use it in this manner is to substitute "race" (or derivatives thereof) where Bennett uses "culture."

The basic goal of Bennett's (1986) model is to move trainees from ethnocentrism or denial of group differences to ethnorelativism or constructive marginality. This movement hypothetically involves six developmental stages of intercultural sensitivity. Briefly, these stages in sequential order are: (a) Denial or parochialism, during which the person refuses to acknowledge the existence of cultural differences; (b) Defense, during which the trainee engages in denigration of groups other than her or his own and/or assumes that one's own group is superior to all others that have existed; (c) Minimization, that is, the trivialization of overtly acknowledged cultural differences; (d) Acceptance, defined as acknowledgment and respect for behavioral and cultural value differences; (e) Adaptation or empathic understanding of the other person's cultural world view; and (f) Integration, which involves "constructive relativism" or the absence of any absolute cultural identification as well as "contextual relativism" or the ability to judge the worth of an action according to the culture in which it occurs.

Bennett (1986) proposes that specific interventions be matched to each stage. Thus, individuals in the Denial stage should be exposed to cultural awareness activities such as music, dance, travelogues, and so on. Discussions for building the trainee's cultural self-esteem are recommended for the Defense stage. For the Minimization stage, he recommends "protected" cross-cultural interactions in which the trainee is exposed to individuals from another culture who themselves are developmentally advanced. Interventions for persons at the Acceptance stage are supposed to emphasize the usefulness of this perspective in facilitating intercultural communication. When the trainee reaches the Adaptation stage, Bennett advises using face-to-face interactions with partners from other cultures (e.g., multicultural group discussions and dyads), which are increasingly under the control of the trainee rather than the trainer. At the Integration stage, the trainee should be competent to select experiences that promote her or his own intercultural sensitivity.

As previously mentioned, Bennett's (1986) model could probably be used for teaching trainees to be interracially sensitive. However, the model does seem to assume that the trainee's cultural group and those to which the trainee does not belong have equivalent sociopolitical power, an assumption that makes more sense when one is talking about interactions among visitors to another country and their hosts than it does when talking about Black and White interactions in the United States. Therefore, the proposed sequence of development and recommended matching interventions of the model might be most descriptive of the manner in which Whites develop a racially/culturally pluralistic or transcendent identity. However, it might not be as appropriate for describing Blacks' identity development process.

Counselor Development Model

Carney and Kahn (1984) proposed a model for matching the training environment of White counselor trainees to their level of cultural (read racial) development. In terms of structure, their model differs from Bennett's in that it specifically postulates developmental stages of (presumably White) American counselor trainees rather than of potential sojourners to another country or culture. Additionally, Carney and Kahn speculate about cultural conflicts assumed to characterize trainees as they move toward the development of intergroup sensitivity.

The stages of Carney and Kahn's (1984) model are summarized in Table 4.1 (see chapter 4). Here it might be useful to summarize the stage-related conflicts. In Stage 1, the trainee's conflict concerns the disparity between the trainee's ethnocentric world view and the egalitarian values of the counseling profession. The Stage 2 conflict centers around the trainee's certainty that her or his basic counseling skills and knowledge are sufficient for helping clients from other groups in spite of her or his awareness of contrary viewpoints. In Stage 3, the conflict is defined as finding a strategy for managing one's feelings of guilt and responsibility for one's own ethnocentricism. The trainee's conflict in Stage 4 pertains to choosing interventions that are most appropriate for the client. The counseling conflict for Stage 5 trainees regards how and to what extent one should become personally involved in cross-cultural counseling situations.

Thus, in Carney and Kahn's (1984) developmental model, counselor trainee characteristics, including their conflicts, are hypothesized to move from a mono-world view in which the trainee attempts to impose her or his views on the client, to an expansive world view in which the trainee attempts to determine how best to fit with other cultures. In a like manner, the training strategies, which Carney and Kahn call "learning environments," vary from trainer initiated and structured to trainee initiated and increasingly spontaneous. Accordingly, in Stage 1, the trainer should provide information about the various cultural/racial groups via readings, lectures, and so on. The appropriate learning environment for Stage 2 involves trainer-provided information about trainee ethnocentricism and how it functions as a barrier to effective cross-cultural communication in the mental health professions. In Stage 3, the matching learning environment is one in which the trainer helps the trainee to self-explore the impact of his or her attitudes and behaviors on culturally different individuals. A congruent Stage 4 learning environment involves a trainer who offers supervision aimed at encouraging the trainee to select a personal program of development. For Stage 5, the congruent learning environment is one wherein the trainer becomes a peer consultant in helping the trainee define and pursue future developmental goals and directions.

Carney and Kahn (1984) assert that resistance to change, that is, retarded advancement toward higher levels of development, occurs when the challenges and supports of the learning environment do not match the trainee's knowledge, attitudes, and/or competencies. As appears to be true of Bennett's (1986) model, Carney and Kahn's approach, as is, seems to be most appropriate for White trainees. Some of their recommended interventions might also be useful for Black trainees, but not necessarily in the sequence they propose.

Summary

The White environmental congruence models have in common the assumption that racial/ethnic or cultural identity progresses most expeditiously when the interventions are matched to the trainee's level of identity development. Also, although the stages proposed by the models vary somewhat in content and/or sequence, they are in surprising agreement as to what kinds of interventions promote development as well as where in the process particular kinds of interventions ought to be implemented. Early in the person's development, "safe" cognitive information is generally recommended. Somewhere in the middle of the process the trainee's emotions concerning racial identity should be aroused. In later stages, the person should be encouraged to integrate abstract thinking and emotional learning to form a new, more inclusive racial world view.

What is most problematic about the environmental congruence models is that, when used as a group intervention, they should work best when all members in an instructional group are at the same stage of development so that congruent interventions can be selected. Otherwise, the trainer risks selecting techniques that are either too advanced or primitive for some trainee's level of development or, in other words, incongruent.

Avoiding the problem of incongruence requires use of some manner of diagnosing trainees' levels of development prior to the group's inception and preselection of participants according to fit. However, in most naturally occurring groups (e.g., classes, organizations) neither use of diagnostic nor preselection procedures are feasible. Workshop versions of the environmental congruence model are one alternative that has been used when the trainer's control over the identity characteristics of instructional groups is constrained by the circumstances of the training environment.

RACIAL IDENTITY INTERVENTIONS

Interventions based on racial identity models examine the role of the trainee's own identity resolutions on the quality of her or his interracial or intercultural competence. The applicable training models use racial identity development theory per se as the foundation for matching interventions to the trainee's level of identity development. The explicit emphasis of the racial identity training models on the trainee's racial socialization experiences makes it possible to propose interventions that take into account differences in the racial experiences of Blacks and Whites. Consequently, training programs have been proposed that are intended for one or the other of the two groups.

Gay's (1984) Classroom Model for Black Development

Gay (1984) collapsed the racial or ethnic identity models of J. A. Banks (1981), Cross (1971), and Thomas (1971) to form a three-stage sequential paradigm that she uses as the basis for proposing classroom interventions for precollege youths. The particulars of her stages are summarized in Table 2.1 (see chapter 2). What is most pertinent here are the kinds of interventions that she views as being appropriate for each of the three stages (Preencounter, Encounter, and Postencounter) of development.

Gay (1984) bases her interventions on what she says are five generally accepted principles of developmental psychology, learning theory, curriculum development, and classroom instruction. The principles are:

(a) development in any one aspect of human growth (e.g., mental, emotional, physical, moral) affects all others; (b) maturation, learning, and experience interact to determine the rate and speed of human growth; (c) students learn best when they are psychologically receptive to and intellectually capable of responding to instructional stimuli, or when a comprehensive conception of the principle of readiness is being applied; (d) the potential for learning is highest when levels of student readiness, curriculum materials and instructional processes are congruent; and (e) self-concepts and academic achievement are interactive. (p.50)

One major implication of her principles for Black students' identity development, according to Gay (1984), is that how these students view themselves with respect to race influences how well they function in other aspects of their academic lives. She speculates that impaired ethnic identity development, if managed inappropriately, can contribute to disrupted intellectual performance as well as interpersonal and discipline problems. As is true of the other learning environmental models presented so far, appropriate "treatment" consists of diagnosing the student's stage of identity and exposing her or him to compatible learning activities.

However, in Gay's (1984) model, one assesses the student's racial identity level to infer what kind of cognitive and affective learning are within the student's capacity. Accordingly, in the cognitive domain, students in Stage 1 are most receptive to knowledge or facts about ethnicity; in Stage 2, students seek to understand how their ethnic group's history relates to present-day conditions; in Stage 3, students are capable of analyzing various ethnic groups' life experiences and synthesizing the information into principles for remediating personal and collective ethnic concerns.

The kinds of techniques Gay recommends vary from information provision and ethnic consciousness arousal in Stage 1, to self-involving experiences such as sociodramas in Stage 2, to activities requiring abstract thinking and the development of interethnic negotiation skills in Stage 3. Though Gay's model is ostensibly written for the benefit of teachers in educational institutions, it is straightforward enough to be useful to other "teachers," such as parents, as well. Moreover, though the sequence of the activities she proposes may not necessarily be appropriate for White children, some of the activities, if matched to their stages of identity, might indeed be appropriate.

J. Katz's (1976) White Awareness Workshop

Using a slightly different interpretation of environmental congruency, J. Katz (1976; J. Katz & Ivey, 1977) developed a workshop specifically for the purpose of promoting the White racial identity development of White trainees. In her model, the definition of White identity approximately corresponds to the first phase of Helms's White racial identity model, the abandonment of racism (see chapter 3). That is, the workshop is a systematic attempt to aid White people in recognizing their racist attitudes and behaviors. To accomplish this goal, J. Katz (1976) developed or collected a rich array of psychological exercises, experiences, and readings that can be used to assist trainees in acquiring cognitive understanding, identifying and articulating personal feelings associated with racism, and developing strategies to eliminate racism among Whites. These activities are collected into six stages of learning: (a) Stage 1 activities are basic definitions of racism and prejudice; (b) Stage 2 activities help the person recognize how racism has been ingrained in her or him since birth; (c) Stage 3 activities encourage the exploration of unconscious feelings, fears, and fantasies; (d) Stage 4 activities examine the operation of cultural racism; (e) Stage 5 activities elicit acknowledgment of one's Whiteness and personal racism; (f) Stage 6 activities encourage the development of action strategies to eliminate racism. The workshop was designed to be a "white-on-white" educational experience in which White group facilitators help White group members to abandon their racism while accepting their Whiteness.

Participants in the workshop as originally conceived were White undergraduate students (J. Katz, 1976; J. Katz & Ivey, 1977). J. Katz (1977) conducted an empirical study of the overall effects of the workshop on participants' subsequent racist attitudes and behaviors. She used a pretest-posttest design and found that following participation in the workshop, trainees were significantly more aware of racism as a White problem than they had been prior to participation and they were more likely to engage in activities to combat racism involving other Whites.

Patterson (1981) studied a modified version of the White awareness workshop. In his investigation, a Black group leader offered to White graduate-level counselors-in-training a workshop comprised of the first four stages of J. Katz's (1976) model and a fifth stage, "biracial counseling dyad," developed by Patterson. In addition to attempting to determine whether or not trainees' racist attitudes were changed due to participation in his day-long workshop, Patterson also investigated the effects of workshop participation on trainees' interviewing behavior as perceived by Black interviewees. Additionally, he examined the relationship of interviewees' Black racial identity attitudes to their perceptions of workshop participants and non-participants.

Considering trainees' racist attitudes, Patterson (1981) found that trainees' attitudes following the workshop agreed more with the learning objectives of the workshop than did those of White graduate students who had not participated in the workshop. However, he did not find differences in interviewees' reactions to trained versus untrained interviewers. There was tenuous evidence that Internalization attitudes were positively related to interviewees' attraction to untrained interviewers and Preencounter and Immersion attitudes were related in opposite directions to perceptions of the racial sensitivity of interviewers. Yet given the ambiguousness of Patterson's racial sensitivity measure, it is difficult to figure out what, if anything, the significant correlations involving this measure mean. One possibility is that Preencounter attitudes may have contributed to greater awareness of the interviewer's discussion of race, whereas Immersion attitudes may have contributed to greater obliviousness to such discussion by the White interviewers.

The White awareness workshop is unique in that investigators have attempted to validate its effectiveness empirically. Both the J. Katz (1976, 1977) and Patterson (1981) studies suggest that it is possible to modify White trainees' racist attitudes and these modifications may generalize to their post-workshop behaviors, though it is not clear in what manner behavior changes or how long changes in attitudes and/or behaviors last. Also, there is no way of ascertaining which interventions are most responsible for any ensuing changes. Therefore, based on the data available so far, successful implementation of the White awareness workshop seems to require administration of procedures matched to at least four of J. Katz's (1976) original stages of learning.

Helms's Interactive Counselor Training Workshop

Based on her 1984 analysis of the crucial components of environments conducive to stimulating healthy Black and/or White racial identity, Helms developed a multicomponent workshop for encouraging the racial identity development of Whites and Blacks in homoracial or heteroracial counselor training environments. The basic assumptions of her approach are: (a) that individuals can be helped to explore their own racial identity development via the appropriate racial identity models; (b) self-exploration is most effective when the process elicits trainees' personal attitudes and emotions; and (c) the trainee's level of racial identity is expressed in her or his interactions with others, particularly when racial issues are salient.

Typically a workshop consists of a cognitive component in which participants are introduced via mini-lectures and discussion to the two racial identity models presented in chapters 2 and 4 and the interaction model presented in chapter 9. They are then engaged in some experiential activity such as Freedman and Perlmitter's (1976) racial rebirth fantasy. The experiential activity is selected to encourage trainees to identify their own racial attitudes, those of their racial peers, as well as those of members of other racial groups. Of course this experience is processed with the intent of helping participants understand how their attitudes evolve, are reinforced, and express themselves in the participants' social interactions. Trainees then participate in counseling simulations concerning racial issues with a partner of the same or different race. The workshop customarily has been presented during an eight-hour period, though ideally it should be extended over as much time as it takes to permit each component of the workshop to be processed sufficiently.

The interactive workshop appears to be the only one that stresses the importance of systematically analyzing the counselor-client interaction during training. Helms uses counseling "simulations" for this purpose. Simulations are role-played counseling sessions involving "helpers" and "helpees" in a counseling session of 10 to 15 minutes duration. The stimuli for these interactions are brief counselor or client roles derived from racial identity theory and counseling practice, called "racial simulators" (see appendix I), which trainees role-play in dyads of any combination. The simulators essentially serve as projective experiences and seem to be most useful in groups where defensiveness about racial issues appears to be high, since they allow participants to act out their fantasies without necessarily having to accept responsibility for them immediately.

Carter (1987) developed a briefer form of the simulators, which is essentially a list of common racial conflicts generated from his own professional and personal experiences. The topic list seems to work best with groups whose members have some successful history of trying to work on racial issues in one another's presence.

Since Helms (1984b) believes that trainees become more adept at self-analysis of their interactions as their own racial identity development advances, she generally recommends that racial identity simulations initially occur in the presence of observers who can help the trainee recognize how her or his identity issues express themselves in interactions; the observers, in turn, can learn about themselves vicariously by helping the role-players identify their racial identity issues. Observers can provide feedback about the simulations either formally (e.g., via discussion of some evaluative measure) or informally (e.g., via discussion based on their own reactions).

Table 14.1 illustrates a dialogue resulting from use of the racial simulators and shows how a structured feedback system might be used to identify counseling impasses. In this interaction, the "counselor" was attempting to role-play Pseudo-Independent attitudes and the "client" was attempting to role-play Encounter attitudes.

One rather extensive study of the relationships of White and Black interviewers' racial identity attitudes to various attitudinal and affective variables (Carter, 1987; see chapter 10) does appear to demonstrate that participants' racial identity attitudes are expressed in verbal interactions. In Carter's study, the list of racial issues was used in counseling simulations of approximately 15 minutes each, involving professional mental health workers as well as graduate students in training. Consequently, his results may mean that professional experience as such does not necessarily camouflage the helper's underlying attitudes and feelings about racial issues.

Nevertheless, there is neither empirical evidence that the interactive workshop contributes to changes in racial identity development nor that participation in any component of it has any enduring effect. Trainees' immediate evaluations of the experience indicate that they find each of the components useful and provoking. So, for the moment, trainers interested in the interactive workshop approach may have to enter the training process with similarly modest goals.

Summary

The racial/ethnic identity workshops have in common their concentrated focus on changing how individuals perceive themselves with respect to race by engaging their thoughts, feelings, and behaviors in the process of self-exploration. They differ in the particulars of how this

Table 14.1
Sample Workshop Interaction with Observer Ratings

Speaker	Comment	Observer Ratings	Author's Comments
Counselor	Jay, how can I help you today?	11	
Client	Well, (sigh) (silence) right now I feel somewhat confused and frustrated by a lot of things.		
Counselor:	Can you tell me a few of those things that you're confused about?	11	Counselor is possibly demonstrating color-blindness.
Client:	Well, I have this girl friend and, uh, I don't know, we've been having problems, but we just broke off our relationship and, uh, there was this, I don't know, I really don't know what to make of it cause there are a lot of things that have happened to us and a lot of things that I'm feeling.		
Counselor	So you're frustrated how this relationship ended and you're not too sure how to understand what's going on, what you're going to do next?	11,4	He may be color-blind as he does not seem to consider that race might be an issue.
Client:	I guess I'm just pissed off because I feel like it's so many people involved in giving their input about our relationship, what should happen, what we should be doing, (pause) not really knowing what to do, you know, feeling one way, but also feeling that pull in another direction too.		
Counselor:	I remember being in a situation similar to that, confused about myself, not really sure what, what I wanted to do in relationships and that's a tough spot to be in. Umm, now that I've become aware of my identity -- mostly my racial identity -- I'm able to make those kinds of decisions.	10,4	Color-blindness can lead to misunderstanding the client.
Client:	But I don't think that -- it's the same thing you know. Uh, my girlfriend is White and --		
Counselor:	You date a White person?		
Client:	Yeah. And.		

Table 14.1 (continued)

Speaker	Comment	Observer Ratings	Author's Comments
Counselor:	I can just see that being a problem there too. I mean is that, now that'd	6, 10	Counselor begins to impose his own racial world view on the client.
Client:	Why should that be a problem?		
Counselor:	Just associating with a White person, how that'd interfere with you developing your own Black identity. How that'd be confusing for you and how that would - you have trouble understanding your own values.	9, 10	Seeing the problem according to counselor's world view can prevent hearing the issues.
Client:	But if I feel a certain way, why do I have to stifle the way I feel just because this person's White? And because other people say that that's not supposed to happen?		The counselor has created this counseling barrier.

Note: Observer rating categories are as follows: 1 = Counselor discourages any discussion of racial issues; 2 = Counselor suggests that discussion of racial issues is not important if client brings them up; 3 = Counselor gets defensive when racial issues are discussed; 4 = Counselor is oblivious or unaware of racial cues given by client; 5 = Counselor encourages discussion of racial issues, but does not integrate them into counseling process; 6 = Counselor brings up racial issues client may be ignoring or is unaware of; 7 = Counselor integrates racial issues into counseling process; 8 = Counselor educates or informs the client about relevant racial issues; 9 = Counselor reinforces or shares racial stereotypes; 10 = Counselor projects or assumes that client shares counselor's attitudes; 11 = Miscellaneous or not explicit racial content.

goal is accomplished. The White awareness model slants heavily in the direction of separating racial groups for training purposes; the classroom model leans in the direction of applying the same theory and experiences regardless of the race/ethnicity of trainees; whereas the interactive model assumes that either or both racial groups can be influenced by the same activities, though the cognitive explanation for their reactions may differ.

It is impossible to tell whether these workshop approaches, in part or in toto, have any long-term effects on participants' racial identity. One would suspect not, given that those for which information is available only last from 8 to 26 hours. It is difficult to believe that such brief interventions could lead to changes in a lifetime of thinking. Nevertheless, J. Katz (1976) did find that eight weeks after training Whites' changed attitudes and behaviors were maintained. Still, a variety of environmental forces in individuals' lives can conspire to maintain the societal racism meta-zeitgeist. The individual's stage of racial identity prior to participation in a training experience presumably governs how receptive he or she is to the message of the experience; her or his stage following participation determines her or his resistance to the countervailing environmental forces. For individuals judged to be at problematic stages of identity, some ongoing inoculative educational activities might have to occur if relapse or fixation is to be avoided.

RESEARCH IMPLICATIONS

Generally speaking, neither the environmental congruence nor the racial identity training model has been subjected to adequate empirical investigation. Additionally, with one exception (Carter, 1987), empirical investigations of models as opposed to interventions have attempted to evaluate the effectiveness of entire workshops rather than components within workshops or models. Furthermore, the existing empirical data are typically comprised of trainees' rather immediate reactions (i.e., attitudes and behaviors) in contexts in which the demand to appear changed must be quite high.

Therefore, a number of questions need to be answered before we can say which kinds of models and which aspects of the models are appropriate for guiding racial identity development and in which directions. Different questions may be germane for the environmental congruence approach as opposed to the racial identity approach. For the environmental congruence models, more evidence is needed concerning the validity of the assumptions that (a) matching particular stages or levels of identity development to particular interventions does result in greater immediate comfort and openness with racial concerns, and (b) exposure to congruent training at each level of development does result in prolonged improvement in racial identity attitudes, behaviors, and/or emotions. At a minimum for the racial identity training models, some empirical information is needed concerning (a) whether racial identity changes follow participation in such training experiences; (b) if so, which components of the training are necessary or sufficient for generating change; and (c) whether changes in development last.

Be that as it may, some empirical investigations of atheoretical interventions designed to modify racial attitudes do offer indirect support for using some overall theoretical model for deciding the appropriateness of interventions and the desirable direction of change. Additionally, this research suggests that the same interventions may not lead to the same result for Blacks and Whites.

For instance, Slavin and Madden (1979) found that different practices in schools improved the two groups' racial attitudes and behaviors in desegrated schools. Teacher participation in workshops dealing with intergroup relations, class discussions about race, minority group history or culture courses, and especially being assigned to work on a project with a student of another race improved White students' cross-racial affiliative attitudes and behaviors. Only teachers' participation in workshops and being assigned to work on a project improved any of the Black students' cross-racial attitudes and behaviors, and the one that was affected required the least intimacy (i.e., phoning another student). However, this difference was due, at least in part, to Blacks' more positive attitudes toward Whites than Whites expressed toward Blacks.

In his study of cooperative assignments in multi-racial/ethnic classrooms, S. W. Cook (1978) found a similar own-group bias for Whites such that they evaluated their White (and Mexican-American) peers positively and their Black classmates negatively. Blacks, on the other hand, rated White classmates as favorably as they rated their Black classmates. With regard to his interventions, S. W. Cook (1978) noted that "among the White Anglo students greater (positive) change occurred toward the less visibly different minority (Mexican-American) than toward the minority group that was more visibly different (Blacks)" (p. 107).

The Slavin and Madden (1979) and S. W. Cook (1978) studies suggest that different attitudinal structures may underlie Black and White students' cross-racial attitudes and interactions. One can also infer from the studies that racially tolerant role models (e.g., teachers), information (e.g., minority history), and structured interactions involving race (e.g., classroom discussions) may be more beneficial to Whites than Blacks. The racial identity theories offer one means of comprehending the underlying racial attitudinal structure and discovering when and why certain interventions work for some groups but not others. Whether or not they are the best alternative remains to be determined.

TRAINING AND COUNSELING IMPLICATIONS

Perhaps it is evident, but nevertheless will be reiterated here, effective racial identity training requires a trainer who has addressed her or his own racial identity conflicts. Bennett (1986) even implies that it might be more harmful to trainees to be "trained" by a group leader who minimizes or denies racial issues than it would be to remain untrained. It also seems likely that the same kinds of interactions that Helms (1984b; (see chapter 9) anticipated for counseling relationships could also occur in training situations. Thus, to the extent that a training experience is characterized by crossed (trainer and trainees have opposite racial identity attitudes) or regressive (trainee is more developmentally advanced than the trainer) relationships, the more likely it is to result in trainees' fixation, lack of receptivity, or dropping out of the activity. Moreover, the environmental congruence models suggest that mismatches with respect to interventions and the trainees' level of development may discourage further development.

Since there are few existing procedures for assessing either the trainer's or trainee's level of identity, it appears to be easier to make a crucial mistake than not. When one adds the relative absence of empirically verified interventions, the person who wishes to intervene to promote healthier identity development is left in somewhat of a quandary. Is the trainer ready to offer racially sensitive interventions? Is it better to leave the trainee as is or should one attempt to generate some change?

For now, the best answers to these kinds of questions seem to be that the successful intervener will have to use a combination of self-education to ensure the adequacy of her or his own identity development and clinical intuition to assess the trainee's level. Self-education should involve exposure to increasingly sophisticated materials and activities that correspond to the various stages of the models described heretofore. Additionally, both Black and White potential interveners could conceivably benefit from historical and cultural information written from a Black (and other visible racial group) perspective, since this is not a viewpoint that is inherent in American socialization experiences. Nevertheless, according to virtually all of the identity models, assimilation of accurate factual information is only the beginning of the self-exploration process. The intervener, who intends to lead others into the jungle of racial conflict, will first have to take the journey herself or himself.

References

Acosta, F. X., Yamamoto, J., & Evans, L. A. (1982). *Effective psychotherapy for low-income and minority patients.* New York: Plenum Press.

Adams, P. L. (1970). Dealing with racism in biracial psychiatry. *Journal of the American Academy of Child Psychiatry, 9*(1), 33–34.

Akbar, N. (1979). African roots of Black personality. In W. Smith, K. Burlew, M. Mosley, and W. Whiteney (Eds.), *Reflections on Black Psychology (79–87).* Washington, D.C.: University Press of America.

Akbar, N. L. (1974). Awareness: The key to Black mental health. *Journal of Black Psychology, 30,* 38–39.

Amir, Y. (1976). The role of intergroup contact in charge of prejudice and ethnic relations. In P. A. Katz (Ed.), *Toward the elimination of racism.* New York: Pergamon Press.

Anastasi, A. (1982). *Psychological testing: fifth edition.* New York: MacMillan.

Anderson, C., & Cromwell, R. L. (1977). "Black is beautiful" and the color preference of Afro-American youth. *Journal of Negro Education, 46,* 76–88.

Anson, R. S. (1987, May 11). Best intentions. *New York,* pp. 30–45.

Arredondo-Dowd, P., & Gonsalves, J. (1980). Preparing culturally effective counselors. *Personnel and Guidance Journal, 58,* 657–660.

Atkinson, D. R. (1983). Ethnic similarity in counseling psychology: A review of research. *The Counseling Psychologist, 11*(3), 79–92.

Atkinson, D. R., Furlong, M. J., & Poston, W. C. (1986). Afro-American preferences for counselor characteristics. *Journal of Counseling Psychology, 33*(3), 326–330.

Baldwin, J. (1963). *The fire next time.* New York: Dell.

Baldwin, J. A. (1979). Theory and research concerning the notion of Black self-hatred: A review and reinterpretation. *Journal of Black Psychology, 5*(2), 51–77.

Banks, J. A. (1981). The stages of ethnicity: Implications for curriculum reform. In J. A. Banks (Ed.), *Multi-ethnic education: Theory and practice* (pp. 129–139). Boston: Allyn & Bacon.

Banks, J. A. (1984). Black youths in predominantly White suburbs: An exploratory study of their attitudes and self-concepts. *Journal of Negro Education, 53*(1), 3–17.

Banks, W. (1972). The Black client and the helping professional. In R. Jones (Ed.), *Black Psychology*. New York: Harper & Row.

Banks, W. C. (1976). White preference in Blacks: A paradigm in search of a phenomenon. *Psychological Bulletin, 83,* 1179–1186.

Banks, W. C., McQuater, G. V., & Ross, J. A. (1979). On the importance of White preference and the comparative difference of Blacks and others: Reply to Williams and Morland. *Psychological Bulletin, 86,* 33–36.

Banks, W. M. (1972). The different effects of race and social class. *Journal of Clinical Psychology, 28,* 90–92.

Banks, W. M. (1980). The social context and empirical foundation of research on Black clients. In R. L. Jones (Ed.), *Black Psychology* (pp. 283–293). New York: Harper & Row.

Barnes, E. J. (1980). The Black community as the source of positive self-concept for Black children: A theoretical perspective. In R. L. Jones (Ed.), *Black Psychology: Second Edition* (pp. 106–130). New York: Harper & Row.

Bem, S. L. (1974). The measurement of psychological androgyny. *Journal of Counseling and Clinical Psychology, 42,* 155–162.

Bennett, M. J. (1986). A developmental approach to training for intercultural sensitivity. *International Journal of Intercultural Relations, 10,* 179–196.

Bierly, M. M. (1985). Prejudice toward contemporary outgroups as a generalized attitude. *Journal of Applied Social Psychology, 15*(2), 185–199.

Bowser, B. P., & Hunt, R. G. (1981). *Impacts of racism on White Americans.* Beverly Hills, CA.: Sage Publications.

Boyd-Franklin, N. (1987). Group therapy for Black women: a therapeutic support model. *American Journal of Orthopsychiatry, 57*(3), 394–401.

Boyle, S. P. (1962). *The desegregated heart.* New York: William Morrow.

Bradley, L. R. & Stewart, M. A. (1982). The relationship between self-concept and personality development in Black college students: A developmental approach. *Journal of Non-White Concerns in Personnel and Guidance, 10*(4), 114–125.

Branch, C., & Newcombe, N. (1980). Racial attitudes of preschoolers as related to parental civil rights activism. *Merrill-Palmer Quarterly, 26,* 425–428.

Branch, C. W., & Newcombe, N. (1986). Racial attitude development among young Black children as a function of parental attitudes: A longitudinal and cross-sectional study. *Child Development, 57,* 712–721.

Brand, E. S., Ruiz, R. A., & Padilla, A. (1974). Ethnic identification and preference: A review. *Psychological Bulletin, 81*(11), 860–890.

Brayboy, T. (1971). The Black patient in group therapy. *International Journal of Group Psychotherapy, 2*(3), 288–293.

Brink, W., & Harris, L. (1966). *Black and White*. New York: Simon & Schuster.

Brown, L. B. (1950). Race as a factor in establishing a casework relationship. *Social Casework, 31*, 91–97.

Burke, A. W. (1984). The outcome of the multi-racial small group experience. *International Journal of Social Psychiatry, 30*(1), 96–101.

Butler, R. O. (1975). Psychotherapy: Implications of a Black-consciousness process model. *Psychotherapy: Theory, Research, and Practice, 12*, 407–411.

Campbell, A. (1971). *White attitudes toward Black people*. Ann Arbor: Institute for Social Research.

Campbell, A., & Schuman, H. (1968). Racial attitudes in fifteen American cities. Supplemental Studies for the National Advisory Commission on Civil Disorders, Government Printing Office.

Caplan, N. (1970). The new ghetto man: A review of recent empirical studies. *Journal of Social Issues, 26*, 57–73.

Caplan, N. S., & Paige, J. M. (1968). A study of ghetto rioters. *Scientific American, 219*(2), 15–21.

Carlson, J. M., & Iovini, V. (1985). The transmission of racial attitudes from fathers to sons: A study of Blacks and Whites. *Adolescence, 20*(77), 233–237.

Carney, C. G., & Kahn, K. B. (1984). Building competencies for effective cross-cultural counseling: A developmental view. *The Counseling Psychologist, 12*(1), 111–119.

Carter, R. T. (1984). *The relationship between Black students' value orientations and their racial identity attitudes*. Unpublished manuscript, University of Maryland, College Park, MD.

Carter, R. T. (1987). *An empirical test of a theory on the influence of racial identity attitudes on the counseling process within a workshop*. Unpublished doctoral dissertation, University of Maryland, College Park, MD.

Carter, R. T., & Helms, J. E. (1988). The relationship between racial identity attitudes and social class. *The Journal of Negro Education, 57*(1), 22–30.

Carter, R. T., Fretz, B. R., & Mahalik, J. R. (August, 1986). An exploratory investigation into the relationship between career maturity, work role salience, value orientations and racial identity attitudes. Paper presented at the 94th Annual American Psychological Association Convention, Washington, DC.

Carter, R. T., & Helms, J. E. (1987). The relationship between Black value-orientations and racial identity attitudes. *Measurement and Evaluation in Counseling and Development, 19*(4), 185–195.

Casas, J. M. (1984). Policy, training, and research in counseling psychology: The racial/ethnic minority perspective. In S. D. Brown and R. W. Lent (Eds.), *Handbook of Counseling Psychology* (pp. 785–831). New York: John Wiley & Sons.

Chaiken, S., & Stangor, C. (1987). Attitudes and attitude change. *Annual Review of Psychology, 38*, 575–630.

Chandler, C. R. (1971). Value orientations among Mexican Americans in a southwestern city. *Sociology and Social Research, 58*(3), 262–271.

Cheek, D. (1976). *Assertive Black...puzzled White*. San Luis Obispo, CA: Impact Publishers.

Chesler, M. A. (1976). Contemporary sociological theories of racism. In P. A. Katz (Ed.), *Towards the elimination of racism* (pp. 21–71). New York: Pergamon Press.

Clanek, M. (1970). Racial factors in the countertransference: The Black therapist and the Black client. *American Journal of Orthopsychiatry, 40,* 39–46.

Clark, A., Hocevar, D., & Dembo, M. H. (1980). The role of cognitive development in children's explanations and preferences for skin color. *Developmental Psychology, 16*(4), 332–339.

Clark, K. B., & Clark, M. P. (1939). The development of self and the emergence of racial identifications in Negro pre-school children. *Journal of Social Psychology, 10,* 591–599.

Clark, M. L. (1982) Racial group concept and self-esteem in Black children. *Journal of Black Psychology, 8*(2), 75–88.

Cohen, E. G., & Roper, S. S. (1972). Modification of interracial interaction disability: An application of status theory. *American Sociological Review, 37,* 643–657.

Cohen, R. (1969). Conceptual styles, culture conflict, and nonverbal tests of intelligence. *American Anthropologist, 71,* 828–856.

Comer, J. P. (1980). White racism: its root, form, and function. In R. L. Jones (Ed.), *Black Psychology,* (2nd ed.) (pp. 361–366). New York: Harper & Row.

Cook, D. A. (1979). *The influence of career decision-making style on career indecision.* Unpublished master's thesis, Southern Illinois University, Carbondale.

Cook, S. W. (1978). Interpersonal and attitudinal outcomes in cooperating interracial groups. *Journal of Research and Development in Education, 12*(1), 97–113.

Cross, W. E., Jr. (1971). The Negro-to-Black conversion experience: Toward a psychology of Black liberation. *Black World, 20*(9), 13–27.

Cross, W. E., Jr. (1978). Models of psychological nigrescence: A literature review. *Journal of Black Psychology, 5*(1), 13–31.

Cross, W. E., Jr. (1985). Black identity: Rediscovering the distinction between personal identity and reference group orientation. In M. Spencer, G. Brookins, & W. Allen (Eds.), *Beginnings: The social and affective development of Black children* (pp. 155–171). Hillsdale, NJ: Erlbaum.

Cross, W. E., Jr. (1987). Two factor theory of Black identity: Implications for the study of identity development in minority children. In J. S. Phinney and M. J. Rotheram (Eds.), *Children's ethnic socialization* (pp. 117–133). Beverly Hills, CA: Sage Publications.

Cross, W. E., Jr., Parham, T. A., & Helms, J. E. (in press). Nigrescence revisited: Theory and research. In R. L. Jones(Ed.), *Advances in Black Psychology: Vol. 1.* Berkeley, CA: Cobb & Henry.

Crowne, D. P., & Marlowe, D. (1964). *The Approval motive: Studies in evaluative dependence.* New York: Wiley.

Davidson, J. P. (1974). *Empirical development of a measure of Black student identity.* Unpublished doctoral dissertation, University of Maryland, College Park.

Davis, L. (1979). Racial composition of groups. *Social work, 24*(3), 208–213.

Davis, L. E. (1980). When the majority is the psychological minority. *Journal of Group Psychotherapy, Psychodrama, and Sociometry, 33,* 179–184.

Davis, M., Sharfstein, S., & Owens, M. (1974). Separate and together: All Black therapy group in the White hospital. *American Journal of Orthopsychiatry,* *44*(1), 19–25.

Dawis, R. V. (1987). Scale construction. *Journal of Counseling Psychology,* 34, 481–489.

Dennis, R. M. (1981). Socialization and racism: The White experience. In B. P. Bowser and R. G. Hunt (Eds.), *Impacts of racism on White Americans* (pp. 71–85). Beverly Hills, CA.: Sage Publications.

Denton, S. E. (1986). *A methodological refinement and validation analysis of the developmental inventory of Black consciousness.* Unpublished doctoral dissertation, University of Pittsburgh, PA.

Dizard, J. E. (1970). Black identity, social class, and Black power. *Journal of Social Issues, 26*(1), 195–207.

Ehrlich, H. J. (1973). *The social psychology of prejudice: A systematic theoretical review and propositional inventory of the American social psychological study of prejudice.* New York: Wiley.

Engelman, L., & Hartigan, J. A. (1981). K-means clustering. In W. J. Dixon, M. B. Brown, L. Engelman, J. W. Frane, M. A. Hill, R. I. Jennrich, and J. D. Toporek (Eds.), *BMDP statistical software 1981* (pp. 464–473). Berkeley: University of California Press.

Erikson, E. H. (1963). *Youth: Change and challenge.* New York: Basic Books.

Erikson, E. H. (1968). *Identity: Youth and crisis.* New York: Norton.

Farley, R., Schuman, H., Bianchi, S., Colasanto, D., & Hatchett, S. (1978). Chocolate city, vanilla suburbs: Will the trend toward racially separate communities continue? *Social Science Research, 7*(4), 319–344.

Faulkner, J. (1983). Women in interracial relationships. [Special Issue: Women changing therapy: New assessments, values and strategies in feminist therapy]. *Women and Therapy, 2*(2–3), 191–203.

Festinger, L. (1957). *A theory of cognitive dissonance.* Stanford: Stanford University Press.

Floyd, I. (1969). *Self-concept development in Black children.* Unpublished senior thesis. Cited in C. W. Branch and N. Newcomb (1986), Racial attitude development among young Black children as a function of parental attitudes: A longitudinal and cross-sectional study. *Child Development, 57,* 712–721.

Freedman, A. M. & Perlmitter, J. (1976). Rebirth fantasy: Discovering racist attitudes and stereotypes. In H. L. Fromkin and J. J. Sherwood (Eds.), *Intergroup and minority relations: An experiential handbook* (pp. 90–93). La Jolla, CA: University Associates.

Frontline: Racism on College Campuses. Public Broadcasting Stations, (WETA), May 10, 1988.

Gaertner, S. L. (1976). Nonreactive measures in racial attitude research: A focus on "liberals." In P. A. Katz, (Ed.), *Towards the Elimination of Racism* (pp. 183–211). New York: Pergamon Press.

Ganter, G. (1977). The socio-conditions of the White practitioner: New perspectives. *Journal of Contemporary Psychotherapy, 9*(1), 26–32.

Gardiner, G. S. (1972). Complexity training and prejudice reduction. *Journal of Applied Social Psychology, 2,* 326–342.

Gardner, L. H. (1971). The therapeutic relationship under varying conditions of race. *Psychotherapy: Theory, Research, and Practice, 8*(1), 78–87.

Garza, R. T., & Lipton, J. P. (1982). Theoretical perspectives on Chicano personality development. *Hispanic Journal of Behavioral Sciences, 4*(4), 407–432.

Gay, G. (1984). Implications of selected models of ethnic identity development for educators. *The Journal of Negro Education, 54*(1), 43–52.

Gibbs, J. T. (1974). Patterns of adaptation among Black students at a predominantly White university: Selected case studies. *American Journal of Orthopsychiatry, 44*(5), 728–740.

Gibbs, J. T. (1987). Identity and marginality: Issues in the treatment of biracial adolescents. *American Journal of Orthopsychiatry, 57*(2), 265–278.

Giddings, P. (1984). *When and where I enter: The impact of Black women or race and sex in America.* New York: Bantam Books.

Giles, M., Cataldo, E., & Gatlin, D. (1975). White flight and percent Black: the tipping point reexamined. *Social Science Quarterly, 56,* 85–92.

Gill, N. T., Herdtner, T., & Lough, L. (1968). Perceptual and socioeconomic variables, instruction in body orientation, and predicted academic success in young children. *Perceptual and Motor Skills, 26,* 1175–1184.

Gilligan, C. (1982). *In a Different Voice.* Cambridge, MA: Harvard University Press.

Giordano, J., & Giordano, G. P. (1977). *The Ethno-cultural factor in mental health: A literature review and bibliography.* New York: Institute on Pluralism and Group Identity.

Gordon, M., & Grantham, R. J. (1979). Helper preference in disadvantaged students. *Journal of Counseling Psychology, 26,* 337–343.

Grace, C. A. (1984). *The relationship between racial identity attitudes and choice of typical and atypical occupations among Black college students.* Unpublished doctoral dissertation, Columbia University Teachers College, New York.

Graves, D. T. (1967). Psychological acculturation in a tri-ethnic community. *Southwestern Journal of Anthropology, 23*(4), 337–351.

Grier, W. H. & Cobbs, P. M. (1968). *Black rage.* New York: Bantam Books.

Griffin, J. (1961). *Black like me.* Boston: Houghton Mifflin.

Griffith, M. S. (1977). The influence of race on the psychotherapeutic relationship. *Psychiatry, 40*(1), 27–40.

Gruen, W. (1966). Composition and some correlates of the American core culture. *Psychological Reports, 18*(2), 483–486.

Gunnings, T., & Simpkins, G. A. (1972). A systemic approach to counseling disadvantaged youth. *Journal of Non-White Concerns, 1,* 4–8.

Haimowitz, M. L., & Haimowitz, N. R. (1950). Reducing ethnic hostility through psychotherapy. *Journal of Social Psychology, 31,* 231–241.

Hale, J. E. (1980). De-mythicizing the education of Black children. In R. L. Jones (Ed.), *Black Psychology* (pp. 221–229). New York: Harper & Row.

Hall, W. S., Cross, W. E., Jr., & Freedle, R. (1972). Stages in the development of Black awareness: An exploratory investigation. In R. Jones (Ed.), *Black Psychology* (pp. 156–165). New York: Harper & Row.

Halpern, F. (1973). *Survival Black/White.* New York: Pergamon Press.

Hardiman, R. (1979). *White identity development theory.* Unpublished manuscript.

Harrell, J. P. (1979). Analyzing Black coping styles: A supplemental diagnostic system. *The Journal of Black Psychology, 5,* 99–105.

Harren, V. A. (1979a). A model of career decision-making for college students. *Journal of Vocational Behavior, 14,* 113–119.

Harren, V. A. (1979b). *Assessment of career decision making.* Unpublished National Institute of Education progress report. Carbondale: Southern Illinois University, Psychology Department.

Harren, V. A., Kass, R., Tinsley, H. E. A., & Moreland, J. R. (1978). Influence of sex role attitudes and cognitive styles on career decision making. *Journal of Counseling Psychology, 25,* 380–398.

Harris, M. (1977). Tokenism or reality: Recommendations for the education of mental health workers against continued racist practices. *Journal of Contemporary Psychotherapy, 9*(1), 33–36.

Harrison, A., & Nadelman, L. (1972). Conceptual tempo and inhibition of movement in Black preschool children. *Child Development, 43,* 657–668.

Harvey, O. J., Hunt, D. E., & Schroeder, H. M. (1961). *Conceptual systems and personality organization.* New York: Wiley.

Hayes, W. A., & Banks, W. M. (1972). The nigger box or a redefinition of the counselor's role. In R. L. Jones (Ed.), *Black Psychology* (pp. 225–232). New York: Harper & Row.

Helms, J. E. (1984a). Racial identity attitudes and sex-role attitudes among Black women. Unpublished paper.

Helms, J. E. (1984b). Toward a theoretical explanation of the effects of race on counseling: A Black and White model. *The Counseling Psychologist, 12*(4), 153–165.

Helms, J. E. (1986). Expanding racial identity theory to cover counseling process. *Journal of Counseling Psychology, 33*(1), 62–64.

Helms, J. E. (1987). Cultural identity in the treatment process. In P. B. Pedersen (Ed.), *Handbook of cross-cultural counseling and psychotherapy* (pp. 239–245). Westport, CT: Greenwood Press.

Helms, J. E., (1989). Considering some methodological issues in racial identity counseling research. *The Counseling Psychologist, 17*(2), 227–252.

Helms, J. E., & Carter, R. T. (1987). The effects of racial identity attitudes and demographic similarity on counselor preferences. Manuscript submitted for publication.

Helms, J. E., & Parham, T. A. (in press). The development of the racial identity attitude scale. In R. L. Jones (Ed.), *Handbook of tests and measurements for Black populations,* (Vols. 1–2). Berkeley, CA: Cobb & Henry.

Hill, C. E., Helms, J. E., Spiegel, S. B., & Tichenor, V. (1988). Development of a system for assessing client reactions to therapist interventions. *Journal of Counseling Psychology, 35,* 27–36.

Hill, C. E. & O'Grady, K. (1985). List of therapist intentions illustrated in a case study and with therapists of varying theoretical orientations. *Journal of Counseling Psychology, 32,* 3–22.

Hilliard, A. (1976). *Alternatives to IQ testing: An approach to the identification of gifted minority children.* Sacramento: California State Department of Education.

Hopkins, E. (1987, January 19). Blacks at the top. *New York,* pp. 21–31.

Horowitz, E. L. (1936). The development of attitudes towards the Negro. *Archives of Psychology*, No. 194, 1–47.

Jackson, B. (1975). Black identity development. In L. Golubschick and B. Persky (Eds.), *Urban social and educational issues* (pp. 158–164). Dubuque, IA: Kendall-Hall.

Jackson, G. G. (1977). The emergence of a Black perspective in counseling. *Journal of Negro Education, 46* (Summer), 230–253.

Jackson, G. G. & Kirschner, S. (1973). Racial self-designation and preference for a counselor. *Journal of Counseling Psychology, 20,* 560–564.

Jahoda, M. (1958). *Current concepts of positive mental health.* New York: Basic Books.

Johnson, F. L., & Buttny, R. (1982). White listeners' responses to "sounding Black" and "sounding White": The effects of message content on judgements about language. *Communications Monographs, 49*(1), 33–49.

Jones, A. & Seagull, A. A. (1977). Dimensions of the relationship between the Black client and White therapist. *American Psychologist, 32,* 850–855.

Jones, E. E. (1978a). Black-White personality differences: Another look. *Journal of Personality Assessment, 42,* 244–252.

Jones, E. E. (1978b). Effects of race on psychotherapy process and outcome: An exploratory investigation. *Psychotherapy: Theory, Research, and Practice, 15,* 226–236.

Jones, E. E. (1982). Psychotherapists' impressions of treatment outcome as a function of race. *Journal of Clinical Psychology, 38*(4), 722–731.

Jones, E. E., & Davis, K. E. (1965). From acts to dispositions: The attribution process in person perception. In L. Berkowitz (Ed.), *Advances in experimental social psychology: Volume 2* (pp. 219–266). New York: Academic Press.

Jones, J. M. (1972). *Prejudice and racism.* Reading, MA.: Addison-Wesley Publishers.

Jones, J. M. (1981). The concept of racism and its changing reality. In B. P. Bowser and R. G. Hunt (Eds.), *Impacts of racism on White Americans* (pp. 27–49). Beverly Hills, CA.: Sage Publications.

Karp, J. B. (1981). The emotional impact and a model for changing racist attitudes. In B. P. Bowser and R. G. Hunt (Eds.), *Impacts of racism on White Americans* (pp. 87–96). Beverly Hills, CA: Sage.

Katz, J. H. (1977). The effects of a systematic training program on the attitudes and behavior of White people. *International Journal of Intercultural Relations, 1*(1), 77–89.

Katz, J. H., & Ivey, A. E. (1977). White awareness: The frontier of racism awareness training. *Personnel and Guidance Journal, 55*(8), 485–488.

Katz, P. A. (1976). The acquisition of racial attitudes in children. In P. A. Katz (Ed.), *Toward the elimination of racism* (pp. 125–150). New York: Pergamon Press.

Katz, P. A., & Zalk, S. R. (1974). Doll preferences: An index of racial attitudes? *Journal of Educational Psychology, 66*(5), 663–668.

Khoury, R. M., & Thurmond, G. T. (1978). Ethnic differences in time perception: A comparison of Anglo and Mexican Americans. *Perceptual and Motor Skills, 47*(3), 1183–1188.

Kibel, H. E. (1972). Interracial conflicts as resistance in group psychotherapy. *American Journal of Psychotherapy, 26,* 555–562.

Kleiner, R., Tuckman, J., & Lovell, M. (1960). Mental disorder and status based on race. *Psychiatry, 23,* 271–274.

Kluckhohn, C. (1951). Values and value-orientations in the theory of action. In T. Parsons & E. A. Shils (Eds.), *Toward a general theory of action* (pp. 388–433). Cambridge, MA: Harvard University Press.

Kluckhohn, F. R., & Strodtbeck, F. L. (1961). *Variations in value orientations.* Evanston, IL: Row Paterson.

Kohls, R., Carter, R. T., & Helms, J. E. (1984). Intercultural values inventory. Cited in R. T. Carter, *The relationship between Black American college students' value orientation and their racial identity attitudes.* Unpublished manuscript, University of Maryland, College Park.

Kovel, J. (1970). *White racism: A psychohistory.* New York: Pantheon.

Krogman, W. M. (1945). The concept of race. In R. Linton (Ed.), *The Science of man in world crisis* (38–61). New York: Columbia University Press.

Ladner, J. (1977). *Mixed families.* New York: Anchor Press/Doubleday.

Latimer, L. Y. (1986, April 20). Will integration hurt my Black son's education? *Washington Post,* C1, C4.

Linden, J. D., Stone, S. C., & Shertzer, B. (1965). Development and evaluation of an inventory for rating counseling. *Personnel and Guidance Journal, 44* (November), 267–276.

Lipsky, S. (1978). Internalized oppression. *Black Reemergence,* 5–10.

Livingston, L. B. (1971). Self-concept change of Black college males as a result of a weekend Black experience workshop. *Dissertation Abstracts International, 32,* 2423B. (University Microfilms No. AAC7124923).

Lunceford, R. D. (1973). Self-concept change of Black college females as a result of a weekend Black experience encounter workshop. *Dissertation Abstracts International, 34,* 1728A–1729A. (University Microfilms No. DCJ73–22678).

Maass, A., & Clark, R. D., III (1984). Hidden impact of minorities: Fifteen years of minority influence research. *Psychological Bulletin, 95,* 428–450.

Maass, A., Clark, R. D., III, & Haberkorn, G. (1982). The effects of differential ascribed category membership and norms on minority influence. *European Journal of Social Psychology, 12,* 89–104.

Marcia, J. E. (1966). Development and validation of ego identity status. *Journal of Personality and Social Psychology, 3,* 551–558.

Marwit, S. J. (1982). Students' race, physical attractiveness, and teachers' judgments of transgressions: Follow up and clarification. *Psychological Reports, 60*(1), 242.

Marx, G. T. (1967). *Protest and prejudice: A study of the Black community.* New York: Harper & Row.

Maslow, A. H. (1970). *Motivation and personality* (2nd ed.). New York: Harper & Row.

McAdoo, H. P. (1981). *Black families.* Beverly Hills, CA: Sage Publications.

McCaine, J. (1986). *The relationship of conceptual systems to racial and gender identity, and the impact of reference group identity development on interpersonal styles of behavior and levels of anxiety.* Unpublished doctoral dissertation, University of Maryland, College Park.

McCargo, J. P. (1987). *Perceived parental and peer influence on Black adolescents' racial identity development.* Unpublished master's thesis, University of Maryland, College Park.

McClain, L. (1983, July 24). How Chicago taught me to hate Whites. *Washington Post,* C1, C4.

McConaghy, J. B., & Hough, J. C., Jr. (1976). Symbolic racism. *Journal of Social Issues, 32,* 23–45.

McGoldrick, M., Pearce, J. K., & Giordano, J. (Eds.), (1982). *Ethnicity and family Therapy.* New York: Guilford Press.

McLaurin, M. A. C. (1987). *Separate pasts.* Athens, GA: University of Georgia Press.

McRoy, R. G., & Zurcher, L. A. (1983). *Transracial and inracial adoptees: The adolescent years.* Illinois: Charles Thomas.

McRoy, R. G., Zurcher, L. A., Lauderdale, M. L., & Anderson, R. E. (1984). The identity of transracial adoptees. *Social Casework, 65*(1), 34–39.

Milliones, J. (1980). Construction of a Black consciousness measure: Psychotherapeutic implications. *Psychotherapy: Theory, Research, and Practice, 17*(2), 175–182.

Mitchell, H. (1974). Psychological openness and sensitivity to the Black experience as predictors of the effectiveness of White counselors in simulated counseling relationships with Black clients. *Dissertation Abstracts International, 35,* 1984A. (University Microfilms No. DDJ74–22537).

Moore, J., Hauck, W. E., & Denne, T. C. (1984). Racial prejudice, interracial contact, and personality variables. *Journal of Experimental Education, 52*(3), 168–173.

Moore, P., Jr. (1982). Time to hang together. *The Washington Post Magazine,* pp. 14–15.

Morin, R. J. (1977). Black child, White parents: A beginning biography. *Child Welfare, 66*(9), 576–583.

Morten, G. H. (1984). Racial self-labeling and preference for counselor race. *Journal of Non-white Concerns in Personnel and Guidance, April,* 105–109.

Mullen, C. (1972). Cited in D. Bradby (1986), *Bi-racial counseling effects of White counselors' knowledge of the Black cultural experience and Black clients' racial identity attitudes on clients' satisfaction with counseling.* Unpublished Master's thesis, University of Maryland, College Park.

Nobles, W. W. (1976). African science: The consciousness of self. In L. King, V. J. Dixon, & W. W. Nobles (Eds.), *African philosophy: Assumption and paradigms for research on Black persons* (pp. 163–174). Los Angeles: Fanon Research Center.

Nobles, W. W. (1980). Extended self: Rethinking the so-called Negro self-concept. In R. L. Jones (Ed.), *Black psychology* (pp. 99–105). New York: Harper.

Norman, D., & Atlas, J. W. (1978). Decision-making skills: Minority group preparation for the future. *Journal of Non-white Concerns in Personnel and Guidance, 6*(2), 78–86.

Orlinsky, D. E., & Howard, K. I. (1978). The relationship of process to outcome in psychotherapy. In S. L. Garfields & A. E. Bergin (Eds.), *Handbook of psychotherapy and behavior change* (2nd ed.), (pp. 283–330). New York: Wiley.

Paicheler, G. (1977). Norms and attitude change, II: The phenomenon of bi-polarization. *European Journal of Social Psychology, 7,* 5–14.

Palmer, F. H. (1970). Socioeconomic status and intellectual performance among Negro preschool boys. *Developmental Psychology, 3,* 1–9.

Papajohn, J. C., & Spiegel, J. P. (1971). The relationship of culture value orientation change and Rorschach indices of psychological development. *Journal of Cross-Cultural Psychology, 2*(3), 257–272.

Papajohn, J., & Spiegel, J. P. (1975). *Transactions in families.* San Francisco: Jossey-Bass.

Parham, T. A. (1982). *The relationship of Black students' racial identity attitudes to self-esteem, affective states, social class, and mental health.* Unpublished doctoral dissertation, Southern Illinois University, Carbondale.

Parham, T. A. (1989). Cycles of psychological Nigrescence. *The Counseling Psychologist, 17,* 187–226.

Parham, T. A., & Helms, J. E. (1981). The influence of Black students' racial identity attitudes on preference for counselor's race. *Journal of Counseling Psychology, 28,* 250–257.

Parham, T. A., & Helms, J. E. (1985a). Attitudes of racial identity and self-esteem in Black students: An exploratory investigation. *Journal of College Student Personnel, 26*(2), 143–147.

Parham, T. A., & Helms, J. E. (1985b). The relationship of racial identity attitudes to self-actualization of Black students and affective states. *Journal of Counseling Psychology, 32,* 431–440.

Patterson, A. M. (1981). *Counseling effectiveness of White counselors trained in racial awareness.* Unpublished doctoral dissertation, University of Maryland, College Park.

Pearl, D. (1954). Ethnocentricism and the self-concept. *Journal of Social Psychology, 40,* 137–147.

Pearl, D. (1955). Psychotherapy and ethnocentricism. *Journal of Abnormal and Social Psychology, 50,* 227–230.

Perney, V. H. (1976). Effects of race and sex on field dependence-independence of children. *Perceptual and Motor Skills, 42,* 975–980.

Peterson, S., & Magaro, P. (1969). Reading and field dependence: A pilot study. *Journal of Reading, 12,* 287–294.

Pettigrew, T. F. (1981). The mental health impact. In B. P. Bowser & R. G. Hunt (Eds.), *Impact of racism on White Americans* (pp. 97–118). Beverly Hills, CA: Sage Publications.

Pinderhughes, C. A. (1973). Racism and psychotherapy. In C. Willie, B. M. Kramer, & B. S. Brown (Eds.), *Racism and mental health* (pp. 61–121). Pittsburgh: University of Pennsylvania Press.

Pomales, J., Claiborn, C. D., & LaFromboise, T. D. (1986). Effects of Black students' racial identity on perceptions of White counselors varying in cultural sensitivity. *Journal of Counseling Psychology, 33,* 57–61.

Ponterotto, J. G., & Wise, S. C. (1987). A construct validity study of the racial identity attitude scale. *Journal of Counseling Psychology, 34,* 218–223.

Pope, B. R. (1978). *The relationship of race, racial attitudes, and need for approval to interracial intimacy.* Unpublished doctoral dissertation, Southern Illinois University, Carbondale.

Price-Williams, D. R., & Ramirez, M. (1974). Ethnic differences in delay of gratification. *Journal of Social Psychology*, 93(1), 23–30.

Pushkin, I., & Norburn, V. (1983). Ethnic preferences in young children and in their adolescence in three London districts. *Human Relations*, 36(4), 309–344.

Quaytman, W. (1977). Concluding remarks: The White professional's dilemma. *Journal of Contemporary Psychotherapy*, 9(1), 47–48.

Reid, P. T. (1979). Racial stereotyping on television: A comparison of the behavior of both Black and White television characters. *Journal of Applied Psychology*, 64, 465–471.

Richardson, T. (1987). *The relationship of Black males' racial identity attitudes to perceptions of parallel counseling dyads.* Unpublished master's thesis, University of Maryland, College Park.

Riley, R. T., & Denmark, F. (1974). Field independence and measures of intelligence: Some reconsiderations. *Social Behavior and Personality*, 2, 25–29.

Riordan, C. (1978). Equal-status interracial contact: A review and revision of the concept. *International Journal of Intercultural Relations*, 2(2), 161–185.

Roebuck, J. R., & Neff, R. L. (1980). The multiple reality of the "redneck:" Toward a grounded theory of the Southern class structure. *Studies in Symbolic Interaction*, 3, 233–262.

Rogers, C. R. (1951). *Client-centered therapy.* Boston: Houghton Mifflin.

Rokeach, M. (1973). *The nature of human values.* New York: Free Press.

Rubin, I. (1967). The reduction of prejudice through laboratory training. *Journal of Applied Behavioral Science*, 3, 29–50.

Sattler, J. M. (1977). The effects of therapist-client similarity. In A. S. Gurman & A. M. Razin (Eds.), *Effective psychotherapy: A handbook of research* (pp. 252–290). New York: Pergamon Press.

Schultz, C. (1958). *FIRO.* New York: Rinehart.

Sciara, F. J. (1983). Skin color and college student prejudice. *College Student Journal*, 17(4), 390–394.

Scott, R. R., & McPartland, J. M. (1982). Desegregation as national policy: Correlates of racial attitudes. *American Educational Research Journal*, 19(3), 397–414.

Shade, B. J. (1982). Afro-American cognitive style: A variable in school success? *Review of Educational Research*, 52, 219–244.

Shipp, P. L. (1983). Counseling Blacks: A group approach. *The Personnel and Guidance Journal*, 62(2), 108–111.

Siegel, B. (1970). Counseling the color-conscious. *School Counselor*, 17, 168–170.

Slavin, R. E., & Madden, N. A. (1979). School practices that improve race relations. *American Educational Research Journal*, 16(2), 169–180.

Smith, E. J. (1980). Profile of the Black individual in vocational literature. In R. L. Jones (Ed.), *Black psychology* (pp. 324–357). New York: Harper & Row.

Smith, L. (1961). *Killers of the dream.* New York: Norton.

Smith, O. S., & Gundlach, R. H. (1974). Group therapy for Blacks in a therapeutic community. *American Journal of Orthopsychiatry*, 44(1), 26–36.

Sorce, J. (1979). The role of physiognomy in the development of racial awareness. *Journal of Genetic Psychology*, 134(1), 33–41.

Spaights, E., & Dixon, H. E. (1984). Socio-psychological dynamics in pathological Black-White romantic alliances. *Journal of Instructional Psychology, 11*(3), 132–138.

Steele, R. E., & Davis, S. E. (1984). An empirical and theoretical review of articles in *the Journal of Black psychology*: 1974–1980. *Journal of Black Psychology, 10*, 29–42.

Stinchcombe, A. L., McDill, M. S., & Walker, D. (1969). Is there a racial tipping point in changing schools? *Journal of Social Issues, 25*, 127–136.

Stuart, I. R. (1967). Perceptual style and reading ability: Implications for an instructional approach. *Perceptual and Motor Skills, 24*, 135–138.

Sue, D. W. (1980). *Counseling the culturally different: Theory and practice.* New York: John Wiley & Sons.

Sue, S., McKinney, H., Allen, D., & Hall, H. (1974). Delivery of community mental health services to Black and White clients. *Journal of Consulting and Clinical Psychology, 42*(6), 794–801.

Suggs, R. C. (1975). An identity group experience: Changing priorities. *Journal of Non-White Concerns, 3*(2), 75–81.

Szapocznik, J., Scopetta, M. A., Aranalde, M. A., & Kurtines, H. (1978). Cuban value structure: Treatment implications. *Journal of Consulting and Clinical Psychology, 46*, 961–970.

Szapocznik, J., Scopetta, M. A., & King, O. E. (1978). Theory and practice in matching treatment to the special characteristics and problems of Cuban immigrants. *Journal of Community Psychology, 6*, 112–122.

Tabachnick, B. R. (1962). Some correlates of prejudice toward Negroes in elementary age children. *Journal of Genetic Psychology, 100*, 193–203.

Tanford, S., & Penrod, S. (1984). Social influence model: A formal integration of research on majority and minority influence processes. *Psychological Bulletin, 95*, 189–225.

Taylor, D. M. (1980). Ethnicity and language: A social psychological perspective. In H. Giles, W. P. Robinson, & P. M. Smith (Eds.), *Language: Social psychological perspectives* (pp. 133–139). New York: Pergamon Press.

Taylor, D. M., & McKirnan, D. J. (1978). Four stages in the dynamics of intergroup relations. Cited in H. Giles, W. P. Robinson, & P. M. Smith (Eds.), *Language: Social psychological perspectives* (pp. 135–137). New York: Pergamon Press.

Taylor, J. (1986). Cultural conversion experiences: Implications for mental health research and treatment. Cited in W. E. Cross, Jr., T. A. Parham, & J. E. Helms, *Nigrescence revisited: Theory and research.* In R. Jones (Ed.), *Advances in Black Psychology: Volume 1.* Berkeley, CA: Cobb & Henry.

Terrell, F., & Terrell, S. (1984). Race of counselor, client sex, cultural mistrust level, and premature termination from counseling among Black clients. *Journal of Counseling Psychology, 31*, 371–375.

Terry, R. W. (1977). *For Whites only.* Grand Rapids, MI: William B. Eerdmans.

Terry, R. W. (1981). The negative impact on White values. In B. P. Bowser & R. G. Hunt (Eds.), *Impacts of racism on White Americans* (pp. 119–151). Beverly Hills, CA: Sage Publications.

Thomas, C. (1971). *Boys no more.* Beverly Hills, CA: Glencoe Press.

Tobin, J. (1965). On improving the economic status of the Negro. *Daedalus, Fall,* 878–898.

Toldson, I. & Pasteur, A. (1975). Developmental stages of Black self-discovery: Implications for using Black art forms in group interaction. *Journal of Negro Education, 44,* 130–138.

Tomlinson, T. M. (1970). Militance, violence, and poverty: Ideology and foundation for action. In N. E. Cohen (Ed.), *The Los Angeles riots: A sociopsychological study* (326–379). New York: Praeger.

Tounsel, P. L., & Jones, A. C. (1980). Theoretical consideration for psychotherapy with Black clients. In R. L. Jones (Ed.), *Black psychology* (pp. 429–438). New York: Harper & Row.

Triandis, H. (1977). The future of pluralism. *Journal of Social Issues, 32*(4), 179–208.

Trimble, J. E. (1976). Value differences among American Indians: Concerns for the concerned counselor. In P. Pederson, W. J. Lonner, & J. G. Draguns (Eds.), *Counseling across cultures* (pp. 65–81). Honolulu: The University Press of Hawaii.

Turner, S., & Armstrong, S. (1981). Cross-racial psychotherapy: What the therapists say. *Psychotherapy: Theory, Research, and Practice, 18,* 375–378.

Vinson, A. (1974). An investigation concerning personality characteristics, classroom climate, and academic achievement. *Journal of Negro Education, 43,* 334–338.

Vontress, C. E. (1970). Counseling Blacks. *Personnel and Guidance Journal, 48,* 713–719.

Vontress, C. E. (1971a). *Counseling Negroes.* Boston: Houghton Mifflin.

Vontress, C. E. (1971b). Racial differences: Impediments to rapport. *Journal of Counseling Psychology, 18,* 7–13.

Ward, D. (1985). Generations and the expression of symbolic racism. *Political Psychology, 6*(1), 1–18.

Webster, D. W., Sedlacek, W. E., & Miyares, J. (1979). A comparison of problems perceived by minority and White university students, *Journal of College Student Personnel, 20,* 165–170.

Welsing, F. C. (1974). The Cress theory of color-confrontation. *The Black Scholar, 5*(4) 32–40.

Wilkins, R. W. (1982). *A man's life: An autobiography.* New York: Simon & Schuster.

Willhelm, S. M. (1971). *Who needs the Negro?* Cambridge, MA: Schenkman.

Williams, J. (1987). *Eyes on the prize: America's civil rights years, 1954–1965.* New York: Penguin.

Williams, J. E., & Morland, J. K. (1979). Comment on Banks' "White preference in Blacks: A paradigm in search of a phenomena." *Psychological Bulletin, 86,* 28–32.

Williams, K. H., Williams, J. E., & Beck, R. C. (1973). Assessing children's racial attitudes via a signal detection model. *Perceptual and Motor Skills, 36*(2), 587–598.

Williams, R. L. (1972). *The Black Intelligence Test for Cultural Homogeneity.* Washington University, St. Louis, MO.

Williams, R. L. (1974). Scientific racism and IQ—The silent mugging of the Black community. *Psychology Today, 32,* 34, 37–38, 41, 101.

Winfrey, O. (1987). "The Oprah Winfrey Show: Transracial Adoption." New York: Journal Graphics Inc.

Witken, H. A., & Goodenough, D. R. (1979). Psychological differentiation: Current status. *Journal of Personality and Social Psychology, 37,* 1127–1145.

Wittmer, J., Lanier, J. E., & Parker, M. (1976). Race relations training with correctional officers. *Personnel and Guidance Journal, 54*(6), 302–306.

Wright, B. H. (1985). The effects of racial self-esteem on the personal self-esteem of Black youth. *International Journal of Intercultural Relations, 9,* 19–30.

X, Malcolm (1973). *The autobiography of Malcolm X.* New York: Ballantine Books.

Yalom, I. D. (1970). *The theory and practice of group psychotherapy.* New York: Basic Books.

APPENDICES

I

Counseling Racial Simulators

JANET E. HELMS

Instructions: Separate "roles" for counselors and clients are described. The roles have been designed to elicit feelings and attitudes associated with the stages of racial identity. These roles (excluding the information in parentheses) should be transferred to index cards. Both participants in the training activity (that is, "counselor" and "client") should be given a description of their own role, but not the other person's role. Participants are then instructed to act out their respective roles during a counseling simulation of about 15 minutes. Counselors are also advised to use their customary helping skills in working with the client while in the counselor role. Following the simulation, participants should be encouraged to share their reactions to the interaction and observers should be encouraged to share their perceptions. Feedback may be given either formally or informally (see chapter 14). Roles should be distributed without regard to the actual race/ethnicity of the participants. That is, for example, Whites may be assigned Black counselor or client roles. This type of cross-racial role-playing provides valuable information about how the racial groups' stereotypes of one another influence their communication processes.

CLIENT ROLES

Role 1. Although you grew up in a primarily Black environment, you have only recently discovered what it means to be a Black person. You're *excited* about acknowledging your Blackness. You have begun to change your lifestyle to reflect your new-found Blackness and you talk about Black, Black, Black whenever you can. If asked to state your racial philosophy, you might say, "I intend to be Black and proud." Your presenting problem is that you no longer feel comfortable around your White friends and you do not have any Black friends. (Encounter)

Role 2. You are a White female who has always been curious about other cultures. You have traveled extensively; you have read about Black people and think it would be great to have a Black friend. Your general philosophy of life is that people are people and a person's race does not matter. Your presenting problem is that when you began dating a Black male, your friends and family began reacting to you in ways that you find troubling. Although you are attracted to the man, you do not want to antagonize your family and friends. (Contact)

Role 3. You are a White male college freshman. During high school, you had several Black friends, your social group was integrated, and, in fact, your best friend was a Black male teammate. However, now that the two of you are away from home, you find that your friend acts like he does not know you any more. He does not invite you to join him when he goes out with his Black friends and he does not seem to care about how you feel. Your presenting problem is that you feel lonely, confused, and helpless, and wonder why things have changed. (Disintegration)

Role 4. You are a Black male mechanical engineer employed in a prestigious company. Although all of the other employees (except a secretary) in your office are White, you did not anticipate that this would be a problem for you because as the child of an army officer, you usually found yourself in situations where you were the only Black. Your father taught you that race is an excuse that Black people use to excuse their failures and that whatever you want in life you can obtain if you work hard enough. This is the philosophy that you have followed so far in your life. However, in your office you have begun feeling increasingly isolated. Your office mates have parties, but do not invite you; business deals are made during golfing dates at "exclusive" clubs; and your immediate supervisor only communicates with you through the Black secretary. Your presenting problem is that you wonder what you have done wrong. (Preencounter)

Role 5. You are a Black woman who is on welfare. Although you have three children, you have never been married. You want to work, but every time you get a job in the Black community, the welfare department threatens to take away your aid to dependent children payments. You can't make ends meet on the welfare payments and you can't make them meet if you work. You are angry and hostile and believe that Whites are responsible for keeping you down. The reason that you want counseling is because you feel helpless and worthless. (Immersion/Emersion)

Role 6. You are a Black high school dropout. You left your predominantly White high school two years ago because you felt like your teachers did not care about you. You are proud of your culture, you have read a lot about African history and know what your people have contributed to the world. Consequently, you believe that if you can obtain appropriate academic skills, you can "move mountains." You are not angry with White people in general; in fact, you believe that you understand most of them better than they understand you. Still, you are unwilling to give up your values in order to get an education. You want help finding and getting into an educational program that will help you meet your goals. (Internalization)

Role 7. You are a White male senior majoring in pre-medicine. You want to apply to medical school, but you are afraid that you will not get in, even though your grades are high, because schools are holding so many slots open for minorities. You feel very angry at Blacks especially because they are always getting special privileges that they don't deserve. Sure slavery existed once, but that has nothing to do with you. Your presenting problem is that you want help making a career choice. (Reintegration)

Role 8. You are a White female public defender employed in an office in which most of the other lawyers are White males and most of the clients are Black males. Even though you grew up in a White environment, you learned that Black people are the way they are because they have not had the cultural experiences that would allow them to better themselves. Your office mates do not seem to understand this principle and they are always calling you names like "White liberal" and "patsy." Your Black clients also do not seem to appreciate your efforts to help them and often take advantage of you. Although you do not want to, you are beginning to feel anger toward your clients and you think these feelings may interfere with your capacity to help them. (Pseudo-Independent)

Role 9. You are a White male psychology professor. You have worked hard to overcome the racist socialization that you received as a child and feel that you have begun to notice that a lot of subtle and not-so-subtle racism occurs in your predominantly White university. When you point this out to your colleagues and try to help them see why racism is *their* problem, they ostracize you. You think your viewpoint is going to hurt your chances for promotion. Although you believe that you should be able to solve this problem yourself, you are beginning to feel lonely, depressed, and afraid. Your presenting problem is that you just want someone to talk to. (Immersion/Emersion)

Role 10. You are a White female who grew up in a multicultural farming community. You were always very active socially and particularly value your social experiences in the 4-H club. In the club, many of your friends were Blacks, and you felt as comfortable and accepted in their homes as they did in yours. As a result of these kinds of experiences, you learned that people are similar in some ways and different in some ways, but it doesn't matter if you try to understand each other's viewpoint. When you moved to the city, you were surprised to find that Blacks and Whites live in different parts of the city and you rarely even see a Black person. There is much racial conflict in the city and you feel you should do something about it, but you don't know what. You hope a counselor can help you decide what to do. (Autonomy)

COUNSELOR ROLES

Role 1. You do not respect and/or like Black people even though you do have some African ancestry. You prefer to identify with Whites and you believe you have accomplished what you have by being like Whites and living in their world. If asked to state your racial philosophy, you might say something like, "I think Blacks make too much of race as an issue." Try to help your client with this philosophy in mind. (Preencounter)

Role 2. You are a White counselor of whatever sex you are. You came from an environment in which racial issues were never discussed. So you have had to develop your own philosophy about racial issues. If asked to state your philosophy, you would probably say, "People are people regardless of race. Blacks are just Whites with darker faces." With this philosophy in mind, try to help your client. (Contact)

   Role 3. You are a Black counselor who was raised in a primarily Black environment. Your perception is that Blacks always get the short end of the stick in American society and you're "damn mad" about it. If asked to state your racial philosophy, you might say, "Blacks have taken enough in this world and I won't take anymore crap." Try to help your client with this philosophy in mind. (Immersion/Emersion)

   Role 4. You grew up in a well-to-do White community and never interacted with Blacks until you joined a "radical group" in college. Since then you have tried to be accepted by Black people as one of them, but find that you are often rejected by them. If asked to state your racial philosophy, you would say, "Blacks seem to blame Whites for their problems no matter what we do. I don't know why they won't accept me." Try to help your client with this philosophy in mind. (Disintegration)

   Role 5. You have always lived in integrated neighborhoods either by your parents' or your choice. You feel as comfortable around Blacks as you do around Whites although you are White. You challenge racism on an individual and system level whenever you can. With this philosophy in mind, try to help your client. (Autonomy)

   Role 6. You are the sort of person that people would say has "pulled himself or herself up by the boot straps." Even though you had no financial support from your family and teachers didn't think that a poor Black kid was worth their time, you managed to obtain a professional degree in a mental health program. Not only were you the first person in your family to attend college, but you were an honor student in a predominantly White ivy league school. You were hired by a mental health agency to increase its minority personnel. Lately you have begun to feel that no matter what you accomplish, your White employers will always treat you like an "unqualified Black person." You are confused. Will you ever be good enough for them? With this philosophy in mind, try to help your client. (Encounter)

   Role 7. For as long as you can remember, you have wanted to be a mental health professional. So you entered graduate school to obtain the necessary training. Lately, you have begun to wonder if you made the right career choice. All of your professors seem to be "White liberals" bent on brainwashing you into believing positive things about Blacks. You know they are inferior to Whites—the *Bible* says so. You do not want to be their therapist and you are getting tired of pretending that you do just to get a degree. With this philosophy in mind, try to help your client. (Reintegration)

   Role 8. You have attempted to learn as much as you can about Black culture and feel comfortable with your African roots. Although you know that racism exists, you do not blame all White people for it. Nevertheless, you fight racism and other forms of oppression when you can, even when it might cost you a friendship. (Internalization)

   Role 9. Although you are a White person who has lived in predominantly White environments all of your life, attended a White school, and have mostly White colleagues, you do not believe that you are a racist. In fact, you do all you can to help Blacks become more like Whites. You explain racism to them;

you study how racism causes problems for them, and you sympathize with them when they tell you how they have been hurt by racism. With this philosophy in mind, try to help your client. (Pseudo-Independent)

Role 10. Although your formal education included nothing about culture and racism, you have managed to educate yourself about these things by reading, attending workshops, and consulting with racially and culturally diverse colleagues, consultants, students, and clients. As a result of your self-education, you have come to realize that racism is a White problem and, consequently, is something that only you and other Whites can abolish. Therefore, you have begun trying to help your White friends and family see their responsibility for racism, and how it harms them. With this philosophy in mind, try to help your client. (Immersion/Emersion)

II

Black Racial Identity Attitude Scale[1] (Form RIAS-B)

JANET E. HELMS AND THOMAS A. PARHAM

This questionnaire is designed to measure people's social and political attitudes. There are no right or wrong answers. Use the scale below to respond to each statement. On your answer sheet, blacken the number of the box that describes how you feel.

1 Strongly Disagree	2 Disagree	3 Uncertain	4 Agree	5 Strongly Agree

1.   I believe that being Black is a positive experience.

2.   I know through experience what being Black in America means.

3.   I feel unable to involve myself in white experiences and am increasing my involvement in Black experiences.

4.   I believe that large numbers of Blacks are untrustworthy.

5.   I feel an overwhelming attachment to Black people.

6.   I involve myself in causes that will help all oppressed people.

7.   I feel comfortable wherever I am.

[1]To avoid respondent reactivity, the title "Social Attitude Scales" should replace this title when the measure is administered.

1	2	3	4	5
Strongly Disagree	Disagree	Uncertain	Agree	Strongly Agree

8. I believe that White people look and express themselves better than Blacks.

9. I feel very uncomfortable around Black people.

10. I feel good about being Black, but do not limit myself to Black activities.

11. I often find myself referring to White people as honkies, devils, pigs, etc.

12. I believe that to be Black is not necessarily good.

13. I believe that certain aspects of the Black experience apply to me, and others do not.

14. I frequently confront the system and the man.

15. I constantly involve myself if Black political and social activities (art shows, political meetings, Black theater, etc.)

16. I involve myself in social action and political groups even if there are no other Blacks involved.

17. I believe that Black people should learn to think and experience life in ways which are similar to White people.

18. I believe that the world should be interpreted from a Black perspective.

19. I have changed my style of life to fit my beliefs about Black people.

20. I feel excitement and joy in Black surroundings.

21. I believe that Black people came from a strange, dark, and uncivilized continent.

22. People, regardless of their race, have strengths and limitations.

23. I find myself reading a lot of Black literature and thinking about being Black.

24. I feel guilty and/or anxious about some of the things I believe about Black people.

25. I believe that a Black person's most effective weapon for solving problems is to become part of the White person's world.

26. I speak my mind regardless of the consequences (e.g., being kicked out of school, being imprisoned, being exposed to danger).

27. I believe that everything Black is good, and consequently, I limit myself to Black activities.

28. I am determined to find my Black identity.

29. I believe that White people are intellectually superior to Blacks.

30. I believe that because I am Black, I have many strengths.

31. I feel that Black people do not have as much to be proud of as White people do.

1	2	3	4	5
Strongly Disagree	Disagree	Uncertain	Agree	Strongly Agree

32. Most Blacks I know are failures.

33. I believe that White people should feel guilty about the way they have treated Blacks in the past.

34. White people can't be trusted.

35. In today's society if Black people don't achieve, they have only themselves to blame.

36. The most important thing about me is that I am Black.

37. Being Black just feels natural to me.

38. Other Black people have trouble accepting me because my life experiences have been so different from their experiences.

39. Black people who have any White people's blood should feel ashamed of it.

40. Sometimes, I wish I belonged to the White race.

41. The people I respect most are White.

42. A person's race usually is not important to me.

43. I feel anxious when white people compare me to other members of my race.

44. I can't feel comfortable with either Black people or White people.

45. A person's race has little to do with whether or not he/she is a good person.

46. When I am with Black people, I pretend to enjoy the things they enjoy.

47. When a stranger who is Black does something embarrassing in public, I get embarrassed.

48. I believe that a Black person can be close friends with a White person.

49. I am satisfied with myself.

50. I have a positive attitude about myself because I am Black.

III

White Racial Identity Attitude Scale[1] (Form WRIAS)

JANET E. HELMS AND ROBERT T. CARTER

This questionnaire is designed to measure people's social and political attitudes. There are no right or wrong answers. Use the scale below to respond to each statement. On your answer sheet beside each item number, write the number that best describes how you feel.

1	2	3	4	5
Strongly Disagree	Disagree	Uncertain	Agree	Strongly Agree

1. I hardly think about what race I am.

2. I do not understand what Blacks want from Whites.

3. I get angry when I think about how Whites have been treated by Blacks.

4. I feel as comfortable around Blacks as I do around Whites.

5. I involve myself in causes regardless of the race of the people involved in them.

6. I find myself watching Black people to see what they are like.

7. I feel depressed after I have been around Black people.

8. There is nothing that I want to learn from Blacks.

9. I seek out new experiences even if I know a large number of Blacks will be involved in them.

[1]To avoid respondent reactivity, the title "Social Attitude Scales" should replace this title when the measure is administered.

1	2	3	4	5
Strongly Disagree	Disagree	Uncertain	Agree	Strongly Agree

---

10. I enjoy watching the different ways that Blacks and Whites approach life.

11. I wish I had a Black friend.

12. I do not feel that I have the social skills to interact with Black people effectively.

13. A Black person who tries to get close to you is usually after something.

14. When a Black person holds an opinion with which I disagree, I am not afraid to express my viewpoint.

15. Sometimes jokes based on Black people's experiences are funny.

16. I think it is exciting to discover the little ways in which Black people and White people are different.

17. I used to believe in racial integration, but now I have my doubts.

18. I'd rather socialize with Whites only.

19. In many ways Blacks and Whites are similar, but they are also different in some important ways.

20. Blacks and Whites have much to learn from each other.

21. For most of my life, I did not think about racial issues.

22. I have come to believe that Black people and White people are very different.

23. White people have bent over backwards trying to make up for their ancestors' mistreatment of Blacks, now it is time to stop.

24. It is possible for Blacks and Whites to have meaningful social relationships with each other.

25. There are some valuable things that White people can learn from Blacks that they can't learn from other Whites.

26. I am curious to learn in what ways Black people and White people differ from each other.

27. I limit myself to White activities.

28. Society may have been unjust to Blacks, but it has also been unjust to Whites.

29. I am knowledgeable about which values Blacks and Whites share.

30. I am comfortable wherever I am.

31. In my family, we never talked about racial issues.

32. When I must interact with a Black person, I usually let him or her make the first move.

1	2	3	4	5
Strongly Disagree	Disagree	Uncertain	Agree	Strongly Agree

33. I feel hostile when I am around Blacks.

34. I think I understand Black people's values.

35. Blacks and Whites can have successful intimate relationships.

36. I was raised to believe that people are people regardless of their race.

37. Nowadays, I go out of my way to avoid associating with Blacks.

38. I believe that Blacks are inferior to Whites.

39. I believe I know a lot about Black people's customs.

40. There are some valuable things that White people can learn from Blacks that they can't learn from other Whites.

41. I think that it's okay for Black people and White people to date each other as long as they don't marry each other.

42. Sometimes I'm not sure what I think or feel about Black people.

43. When I am the only White in a group of Blacks, I feel anxious.

44. Blacks and Whites differ from each other in some ways, but neither race is superior.

45. I am not embarrassed to admit that I am White.

46. I think White people should become more involved in socializing with Blacks.

47. I don't understand why Black people blame all White people for their social misfortunes.

48. I believe that White people look and express themselves better than Blacks.

49. I feel comfortable talking to Blacks.

50. I value the relationships that I have with my Black friends.

(Not for reproduction or modification without the author's permission.)

Author Index

Subject Index

137–38, 150, 156, 157, 163, 166,
169, 171, 172, 174, 175, 194, 198,
200, 201, 212; modes, 19–20, 29,
35–36, 40. *See also* Racial identity

Measures, 34, 35, 41, 44, 45, 80, 90,
102, 103, 130, 146, 175; of client
reactions, 74, 146, 147, 148, 149–
52, 153, 156, 157, 158, 159, 160,
162–63, 171, 173, 174; of counselor intentions, 146, 147, 148, 149–
52, 153, 156, 157, 159, 160, 162–
63; Doll test, 95, 96; of interviews,
35, 45, 46, 47, 212; Q-sort, 35; of
social desirability, 69
Melting pot norm, 6, 17
Mental Health, 4, 10, 17, 18, 25, 49,
53, 68, 83, 88, 90, 100, 130, 141,
146, 165, 197, 205, 214, 219
Minority Status: defined, 191–92,
194, 195, 196, 198; and racial
identity, 192; and social influence,
193, 195, 196, 197, 198, 200, 201

Native Americans, 34, 107
Negro-to-Black conversion. *See* Nigrescence
Nigrescence (NRID), 9, 17–31, 33,
102, 165, 167; defined, 17; as developmental process, 17; theory,
11–19, 21, 33, 101, 121, 130, 135,
169, 173, 192

"Oprah Winfrey Show," 29–31

Parallel relationships, 174, 177, 180,
184, 189, 200–201, 202, 203. *See
also* Interaction model
Personal identity, 5–6, 17, 20, 21, 22,
25, 26, 27, 28, 31, 34, 46, 66, 85,
88, 90, 100, 101, 102, 103
Preencounter stage, 19, 20–24, 34,
35, 36, 37, 38, 39, 41, 44, 46, 84,
93, 98, 102, 121, 122, 123, 127,
128, 130, 136, 141, 150, 156, 157,
166, 169, 171, 173, 174, 175, 180,
181, 184, 190, 193, 194, 197, 198,
200, 201, 210, 212; modes, 21–24,
25, 27, 102. *See also* Racial identity

Progressive relationships, 177, 181,
189, 200, 203. *See also* Interaction
model
Pseudo-Independent stage, 61–62,
68, 69, 72, 75, 79, 80, 97, 100, 112,
115, 140, 149, 150, 151, 155, 156,
157, 161, 162, 194, 197, 214. *See
also* Racial identity

Race, 3, 4, 5, 7, 10, 23, 26, 53, 57,
59, 66, 68, 79, 83, 84, 86, 87, 88,
94, 96, 98, 99, 101, 102, 103, 109,
112, 135, 137, 139, 140, 141, 147,
159, 165, 167, 180, 184, 185, 189,
197, 210, 212, 213, 214, 218
Race perspective, 57, 145, 148–49,
152
Racial consciousness, 7, 49, 50, 53,
61, 193, 216
Racial designation, 3, 7, 10, 33, 34,
123, 124, 167–68
Racial discrimination, 10, 17, 27, 57–
58, 89
Racial group membership, 3, 4, 5, 6,
7, 20, 21, 22, 33, 62, 88, 89, 94,
101, 105, 107, 117, 145, 152, 153,
196
Racial identity, 3, 4, 5, 6, 7, 8, 9, 10,
22, 31, 33, 45, 49, 94, 100, 140,
173, 175, 189; Black theories of, 4,
5, 8, 9–17, 35, 86, 87, 97, 121, 190,
192, 200, 210; components of, 5–6,
31, 46, 85, 206; defined, 3, 4, 5; as
a developmental process, 3, 4, 6, 7,
8, 18, 19–31, 32, 35, 36–38, 40, 41,
45, 46, 47, 49, 50, 53, 54, 66, 67,
68, 79–80, 83, 87, 91, 92, 95, 98,
100, 102, 105, 117, 118, 152, 153,
159, 165, 174, 181, 185, 190, 191,
192, 193, 197, 199, 204, 207, 210,
213, 214, 217; measurement of, 8,
33, 34, 35–45, 71, 121, 131; perspective, 9, 145, 166, 167, 175,
206; resolutions of, 6, 7, 17, 21, 22,
23, 173, 210; stages, 18, 19 32, 36,
37, 38, 41, 45, 54, 55, 58–66, 83,
84, 90, 91, 102, 103, 141, 180, 188,
190, 196, 198, 201, 206, 217; stage
theories, 6–7, 19–31, 35, 38, 67–

Contributors

DEEJON BRADBY is a therapist on the staffs of the Washington Assessment and Therapy Services and Community Connections, Inc. in Washington, D.C.

ROBERT T. CARTER is Assistant Professor of Psychology and Education in the Counseling Psychology Program, Teachers College, Columbia University. He is a member of the Editorial Board of *The Journal of Counseling Development*.

JANET E. HELMS is an Associate Professor of Psychology at the University of Maryland and Fellow in Divisions 17 (Counseling Psychology) and 45 (Ethnic Diversity) of the American Psychological Society. She is an affiliate of the Counseling Center at the University of Maryland and is a licensed psychologist and private practitioner in Maryland and Washington, D.C. She has authored many empirical and theoretical articles and book chapters on the topics of personality assessment and racial identity in the therapy process.

THOMAS A. PARHAM is Director of the Career Planning and Placement Center and an adjunct faculty member of the University of California, Irvine. He is currently coauthoring a book entitled *Black Psychology*.